Legalizing Cannabis Extracts
Edibles in the Supreme Court of Canada

By Owen Smith

In homage to Jack Herer and the legacy of cannabis books that provide extensive references to news media articles, this book is accompanied by a Digital Timeline that features all of the events, media articles, video coverage and our own writing from the *Cannabis Digest* on the subject over the course of the trial. It can be found at the following website.

R. v. Smith Digital Timeline Reference

QR Code
Scan with your camera.
Best results in landscape view.

Web Link
www.tiki-toki.com/timeline/entry/196941/R.-v.-Smith-Timeline

Dedicated to my Sister, Ceri Smith

CONTENTS

Part 1 – Before the Trial

Owen Edward Smith	15
Leon Edward (Ted) Smith	22
Chris Bennett	27
R. v. Smith and Budda	30
Mushrooms	32
Spirituality	36
Travel	38
Festivals	40
Dana Larsen	43
A Dream	46
My Sister, Ceri	48
Making Medicine	53
Analytical Testing	59
Arrested	62
Charges?	72
Charges	78
Kirk Tousaw	82
Other Medical Cannabis Rulings	84
The Harper Conservative Government	87
Fundraising	90

Part 2 - The Trial

The Courthouse	93
Voir Dire	95
Constable Colin Brewster	98
Ted Smith	100
Gayle Quin, Medicine Woman	116
Sandra Large	125
Gina Herman	133
Ruth Arthurs	141
Dr. David Pate	144
The EndoCannabinoid System	146
History of Use	148
Botanical Details	149
Accidental Hash Making	154
Cannabinoid Ratios	155
Terpenes	157
Side Effects	159
Tachycardia	161
Cannabis Affects People Differently	162
Concentrating Cannabis	163
Natural Contaminants	166
Decarboxylation	168

Localization	169
Skin	170
Methods of Ingestion	172
Sniper Vs. Shotgun	176
Relatively Safe	178
Start Low and Go Slow	180
Synergy with Opiates	181
Clinical Trials	183
Blocking Research	185
Other Cannabinoids	189
Smoking Cannabis	191
Potency and Tolerance	193
Rates of Onset	195
Clinical Trials	197
Research	199
The Placebo Effect	201
Driving Ability	202
Adverse Mood Reactions	203
Contraindications	205
Follow-up	206
Contaminants	207
Schizophrenia	208

Peter Eccles QC	211
Chief Science Officer for Health Canada	213
More Study Needed	215
Edible Cannabis is Ineffective	217
Adverse Effects	219
Entourage Theory	220
Risks of Petrochemical Extraction	221
Standardization	222
Limited Expertise	223
Information for Health Care Practitioners	224
Evidence	225
Employer Bias	227
Methods of Ingestion	232
Alternative Routes of Administration	234
Schizophrenia	236
Cannabinoids	238
Tolerance	240
Dosing	241
Contraindications	242
THC and CBD synergy	246
Adverse Effects	248
Eric Ormsby	251

Final Arguments	254
The Decision	256
Established Scientific Facts	261

Part 3 – After the Trial

Taxes	268
Jury Trial	269
Recorded History of Cannabis Extracts	274
Before Common Era	275
In the Common Era	265
In the Modern Era	279
Court of Appeal: Issue of Standing	282
Herb of Life	284
The Appeal Decision	288
Established Scientific Facts	290
Interveners	292
Supreme Court of Canada	294
Our Arguments	296
Government Arguments	298
Standing	300
A Letter to the Queen	302
Supreme Court of Canada Decision	305

Media Storm	309
Government Response	313
Industry Response	315
Hayley's Comet	318
Alex and Gwen Repetski	321
The Road to Legalization	324
Legalization	330
First Nations	336
Precedents	340
Psychedelics	344
Conclusion	347

Foreword by Ted Smith

Turning potentially bad situations around into monumental victories is the hallmark of heroism.

Challenging massive institutions in small, concerted efforts, cannabis activists around the world have fought for decades to cast off the shackles of prohibition. Many attempts to challenge the laws have ended in disappointment, with advocates and growers losing freedom, assets, jobs, friends, and occasionally their lives. However, collectively these efforts have successfully changed laws and attitudes, spreading the call for legalization like wildfire around the globe.

If there is a fairy tale to be told about how cannabis became legal in Canada, this is it.

When Owen was arrested, it was immediately clear to us that this was a perfect opportunity to fundamentally change the way cannabis was viewed as a medicine, both in law and in practice. Watching the case progress and ultimately smash Health Canada's inadequate medical cannabis program has been nothing short of magical.

Ironically, while I witnessed this trial and its aftermath dramatically affect the medical cannabis scene and act as the final straw in prohibition itself, I was increasingly drawn away from the action to care for my love, Gayle Quin. This may appear to be Owen's story, but if it is a story about anyone, it is a story about her.

Gayle helped write and publish the cookbook online. Gayle rented the apartment Owen was arrested in and was his boss. Gayle taught the free lectures at the University of Victoria about how to make cannabis products. Gayle testified in the trial in Victoria.

Gayle stayed alive for two more years than anyone ever thought possible by using cannabis suppositories. Gayle watched the Supreme Court of Canada hearing from the hospital bed we had set up at home for her. Gayle was everything to me. Gayle died of cancer, peacefully at home.

Gayle inspired everyone to be a better person.

This story would never have been told without her.

The only thing that brought me from the depths of despair after losing her was the thought of losing the club to legalization. It has been close. Thankfully, soon after Gayle's death, I somehow met another amazing woman, Clea Maclean, who has helped me get back on my feet and fight. Both internal and external problems have threatened the group since I returned in 2017, yet the VCBC has continued to thrive in the face of adversity.

That is another story that is yet to be complete. Indeed, this tale is akin to *The Hobbit* compared to my unfinished *Lord of the Rings* story.

For those interested in Canadian history, the story being told here provides intricate details of why and how we were able to strike the fatal blow to cannabis prohibition. For those interested in cannabis history, this tale documents the fascinating time period during which thousands of Canadians resisted the law until the government caved and legalized it. For those simply looking for a good, real-life story to read, we have heartache and humor, suspense and drama, politics and science, all wrapped into an epic tale comparable to David and Goliath.

Regardless of why you are reading this book, you will be left with a sense of hope for a better future, a sense of security that, in fact, the world sometimes does reward people for doing the right thing, and a sense of justice in a world that seems systematically unfair.

The events and individuals depicted in this book are based on transcripts from a legal trial, which are part of the public record. The information has been presented as accurately as possible according to these documents. Any opinions or interpretations are solely those of the author, and his boss.

Part 1
Before the Trial

OWEN EDWARD SMITH

I was born in St. Mary's Hospital in Hampshire, England. The name Hamp-shire combines the German word Hampf, which means Hemp, with the old English word Shire, which means 'care, official charge', or 'place where hobbits come from'. I was born in 1982, the same year Queen Elizabeth signed the Canadian Charter of Rights and Freedoms, the document I would use 30 years later as my legal defence.

I was blessed with an older brother, Dave, who despite the necessary brotherly torments, also sang in the Methodist church choir with me and my younger sister, Ceri. My parents were Welsh born and their parents, Irish and Scottish.

I emigrated to Victoria, British Columbia, Canada with my family when I was 11 years old, in 1994. Moving from the south of England, my parents could have had no idea of the hotbed of cannabis advocacy that they were planting me in. Only 1 year after we arrived, Canada's first west coast compassion clubs were opening. There was one in Vancouver called the British Columbia Compassion Club Society (BCCCS) and one in Victoria, previously known as the Cannabis Buyers Club of Canada, now the Victoria Cannabis Buyers Club (VCBC).

Nobody in my family brought any knowledge of cannabis or its properties to Canada. I mostly learned about it through the standard channels: teachers at school, PSA's, advertisements, stories on TV and film and the opinions of adults. As a teenager, I would turn down offers to try cannabis as prohibition had settled a number of ideas into my developing mind. People who consume cannabis are lazy, selfish, messy, stinky and or stupid: don't throw your life away, just say no.

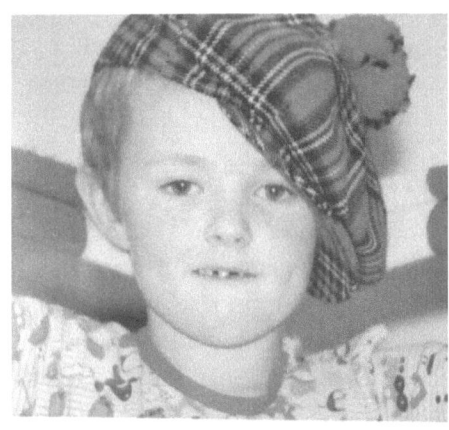

(Me as a child in England)

However, eventually, my older brother initiated me with a series of *Buckets*, a homemade device otherwise known as a Gravity Bong.

This device consists of a bucket full of water and a 2 liter pop bottle with the bottom cut out. A tin foil bowl is placed over the mouthpiece with pin holes poked through it. With the pop bottle submerged up to its neck in the bucket-water, cannabis is placed in the tin foil bowl. A lighter is then held over the bowl as the bottle is lifted out of the water. The vacuum created by the air rushing through the bowl causes the bottle to fill with clouds of smoke. I then remove the bowl, place my mouth *near* to the top, but not on it, and inhale while pushing the bottle back into the water. This forces 2 liters of smoke out of the top of the bottle and into my green lungs.

I recall hearing my heart rate pulse so loudly that I thought everybody else could hear it. They couldn't. I wasn't sure what to think of my experience, I had laughed a lot but I'd also felt guilty.

After I had tried cannabis a few times, I enjoyed it and began consuming it occasionally. I experienced pleasure and relaxation and found it helped me get into a state of flow when juggling a soccer ball. I slowly began to challenge the negative notions that I'd harbored from childhood. I attended an outdoor public screening of *Reefer Madness* in all of its ridiculous glory; but I would continue to struggle with guilt around the idea that cannabis might be limiting me from achieving my full potential.

In high school, my law class visited the Victoria courthouse to observe a random trial. The trial was about a man who had robbed the *McDonalds* in downtown Victoria. The defense lawyer was arguing that because the defendant had smoked cannabis before the robbery, he was out of his mind and could not be held responsible for the crime. He would plead insanity and request time in a rehabilitation centre instead of jail. Reefer madness was not just a wacky propaganda movie from the 1930's; it was a legal defense.

Later, in college, I came across a sociological book titled *The Outsiders: Studies in the Sociology of Deviance* by Howard Becker (1963). It explored how guidance significantly shapes the subjective psychoactive cannabis experience. Becker's work showed that individuals without someone to guide them, like a sibling or a knowledgeable friend, during their initial cannabis experiences often reported feeling little to no effect. This aligned with my own experience: it was my older brother who introduced me to cannabis as a fun thrill while society had outlined cannabis' various potential negative health consequences.

I began to understand that *how you perceive cannabis shapes your experience of its effects*. I began to consider how the media's use of popular actors, musicians and celebrities to frame cannabis negatively was actually making things worse for people.

Becker argued that deviance is not inherent in any particular act but is instead created by society's reaction to that act. In this sense, cannabis consumers were labeled as lazy, criminal, or morally corrupt not because of the plant itself, but because society had decided to cast them in that role.

(Me as a teenager in Canada)

An individual caught using cannabis might not see themselves as a "criminal." However, once labeled as a "drug user" by law enforcement and media, they may internalize this label. This could lead to changes in behavior, social interactions, and self-identity, potentially reinforcing their deviant status. Once labeled a deviant, a vicious cycle was initiated as that person would become more likely to commit further deviant acts.

This labeling process helped explain the problem with "Gateway Theory", a central argument in the war on drugs. Gateway theory claimed that cannabis use inevitably led to harder drugs like heroin and cocaine. However, research consistently disproved this theory, showing that most people who use cannabis do not transition to harder substances (Hall and Lynskey 2005). In fact, evidence suggests that criminalizing people who use cannabis, rather than cannabis itself, contributed to their exposure to more dangerous substances by forcing them into illicit markets.

I learned about *moral panic* (Cohen 1972), which helped explain *Reefer Madness* and the fear-driven rhetoric surrounding cannabis that I had been exposed to throughout my youth. Cohen described how societies create "folk devils", groups or behaviors that are portrayed as existential threats to social order. People who consume cannabis, much like those depicted in the 1930s film *Reefer Madness* (Gasnier 1936), were cast as these folk devils.

The media I grew up with framed cannabis as a gateway to moral and social decay. This "panic" created an atmosphere of fear and suspicion that reinforced social control and was used to justify harsh drug policies. By criminalizing cannabis, the state wasn't just controlling a plant, it was controlling people, especially those whose lifestyles or ideologies challenged mainstream values.

It was Woody Harrelson's 1999 documentary *Grass* (Mann 1999) that illustrated to me for the first time the racist and political motivations behind cannabis prohibition. The film chronicled the history of the drug war in the United States and its connections to racial oppression. The same arguments that were used to discredit cannabis and its imbiber, rooted in fear, misinformation, and moral panic, were tied to broader efforts to control marginalized populations, particularly Black communities. This mirrored the ways that laws around cannabis use in Canada disproportionately affected Indigenous populations.

But it wasn't just about subversion or counterculture; the state's response to cannabis revealed a deeper pattern of repression. Stories like that of Vladimir Bukovsky (1978), a Soviet dissident repeatedly incarcerated in psychiatric hospitals for opposing the regime, echoed the way people who supported cannabis were outcast and discredited. Bukovsky's diagnosis of "sluggish schizophrenia", a label used to justify his confinement, reminded me of the way *medicalization* was used to control deviant behavior in the West. Claims about cannabis causing A-motivational syndrome or schizophrenia were used to delegitimize those who challenged prohibition, much like how Bukovsky's dissidence was pathologized to suppress his activism. This wasn't just about public health; it was about controlling dissent and maintaining the status quo.

These medicalized characterizations of the cannabis community clashed with my love for the music of the 60s, as well as 90s hip hop that each held cannabis in high esteem against the injustices of war and economic oppression. Their music, and their public use of cannabis, was a challenge to the power structures that had framed cannabis as deviant. The way the counterculture embraced cannabis paralleled what *subcultural theory* describes: cannabis use became part of an alternative value system that rejected mainstream norms.

I learned that in 1961, a Single Convention on Narcotic Drugs (United Nations 1961) spearheaded by the United States had enshrined cannabis prohibition across much of the world, despite limited evidence of its harmfulness. However, in 1969, Timothy Leary, a psychologist and counterculture icon, successfully invalidated the cannabis law, called the Marihuana Tax Act of 1937, in U.S. courts (Leary v. United States 1969), creating a brief legal void for cannabis regulation in the United States. Leary's case was emblematic of the growing resistance to cannabis prohibition, particularly among youth and intellectuals who saw the drug laws as an unjust tool of control. Leary, who famously advocated for expanding consciousness through the use of cannabis and psychedelics, became a symbol of rebellion against the establishment. His legal victory signaled that the foundations of cannabis prohibition were shakier than they appeared.

In Canada, 1969 marked the beginning of the Le Dain Commission (Le Dain et al. 1972), a government-sponsored inquiry that sought to assess the social, medical, and legal implications of cannabis laws. This four-year study reflected a growing recognition that the punitive approach to cannabis might not align with the emerging scientific understanding of the plant's effects. The Commission heard from a range of experts, users, and policymakers, many of whom argued that cannabis was far less harmful than previously believed.

Meanwhile, in 1971, U.S. President Richard Nixon doubled down on cannabis prohibition by signing the Controlled Substances Act (United States 1971), placing cannabis in Schedule I alongside heroin and LSD. This classification designated cannabis as having no medicinal value and a high potential for abuse, despite growing evidence to the contrary. Nixon's decision was deeply political; according to his former domestic policy chief, John Ehrlichman, the war on drugs was a strategic tool to disrupt and criminalize two key groups: the anti-war left and Black Americans. By associating these groups with drugs like cannabis, the government could justify increased surveillance, policing, and imprisonment under the guise of public health and safety.

In 1973, the LeDain Commission recommended decriminalizing cannabis, acknowledging that the criminal justice approach was causing more harm than the drug itself. However, despite the evidence, the Canadian government chose not to act on the Commission's findings, a decision that speaks to the broader socio-political forces at play.

The Le Dain Commission's recommendations in 1973, like those of many other governmental studies worldwide, were ignored in favor of a continued prohibitionist approach.

This political demonization of cannabis threw the credibility of all other anti-drug education into question (Hari 2015). Generations of young people who enjoy cannabis have been led to wonder if other illegal drugs are not also relatively benign. Cannabis is not a gateway drug; cannabis prohibition is a gateway policy. (Mallea 2014)

As I researched these histories, I began to see how the continued presence of cannabis prohibition was a reflection of broader power dynamics. Governments around the world were not simply concerned with public safety; they were concerned with maintaining control over the populations who used cannabis, particularly when those populations were seen as rebellious or politically inconvenient.

(Graphic by Owen Smith)

Leon Edward (Ted) Smith

In the late nineties, cannabis was still sold in tiny 1 inch square baggies. When our guy didn't respond to his pager, the only place my friends knew to buy cannabis was in front of City Hall. We would sit across the street in a car and whoever lost the 'rock, paper, scissors' would take a crumpled handful of five notes and ask the grizzly looking people loitering on the front steps for a dime bag. Pinching open the bag, it was commonly wet and underweight. This worked until my friends asked an undercover cop.

My brother told me about a guy who held marijuana meetings every Wednesday at the University of Victoria and later in downtown Victoria. The first time I went to see Ted Smith speak, it was nighttime behind the British Columbia Provincial Parliament buildings. A circle had formed around a large fountain and Ted was wearing a full dinosaur costume and wielding a megaphone. He spoke about the environmental damage caused by big oil and the embarrassing pollution that harms our incredibly beautiful marine ecosystems. We scored an eighth from someone in the crowd. It was better quality than the weed we had bought at City Hall.

Shortly after I graduated from high school, I decided to attend the weekly Hempology101 meeting at the University of Victoria. My memories of these Wednesday meetings at UVIC are wrapped in sunshine, blue sky and green fields with laughing faces playing frisbee and kicking hackysacks and soccer balls. Every wednesday at 4:20, students would pour out of class to gather in the center of campus, claiming the fountain area in front of the library. It became the largest student club, surpassing the rowing team.

The group preferred to be situated where everyone could see them, visibility being part of the plan to bring this issue to the forefront among young intellectuals. As the meeting size grew, it moved out into the adjacent field, forming a circle of around 380 students at its largest. This weekly session was my introduction to cannabis advocacy. I circled up alongside a great diversity of young people all surrounding one man with a microphone, Ted Smith.

Ted was captivating. He whirled about the center of the group, ponytail bobbing, with a microphone cord whipping about his feet like an angry snake. He would tell us the latest in cannabis news from around the world: whether it was a new study published or a grow op busted; a person wrongly imprisoned for cannabis or new legislation tabled. Each week, Ted was the one stop media source

for all your cannabis interests. A font of rebellion, he preached an end to the drug war, charismatically stuffing our ears and blowing our minds in a time when we had falsely outlawed a plant with ancient, sacred ties to humanities' liberation. And of course, there were joints. After the updates and news, a few volunteers with squirrely beards and funky hats would shuffle around the circle, casually handing out dozens of pre-rolled roach joints.

All week, Ted and his friends would diligently smoke joints so that the roach recycling program was always well stocked with enough sticky, oily roaches to get hundreds of students high. Each week volunteers would break open the roaches and roll a hearty quiver of dank roach joints. The largest session that I attended was in the underground parking lot across from the Victoria courthouse where a quarter pound of roaches had been assembled into a squadron of phatty bombers. As tough as I used to puff, I wandered away from that circle long before it was over and returned some time later to see a group of diehard smokers re-rolling the roach joint roaches into second, third or fourth generation roach joints.

As the smoke billowed, Ted became impassioned, raging against the injustices of the drug war. In front of Ted was a blanket and laid out upon it were pamphlets, membership cards, CannaBonds and books. Local glass blowers from around the island would lay down a blanket beside him and display their wares for sale. Membership to Hempology101 was free, its mandate, "Legalization through Education". The Cannabonds, purchased for a meager $25, promised a ¼ ounce of cannabis once it became legal. The proceeds went toward the continued activism of Hempology 101.

These books were my first forays into cannabis specific literature. *The Emperor Wears No Clothes* by Jack Herer (1985) is a cannabis culture classic. It was the stark rebuttal to prohibition rhetoric. Jack saw himself as the boy in 'The Emperor's New Clothes,' the

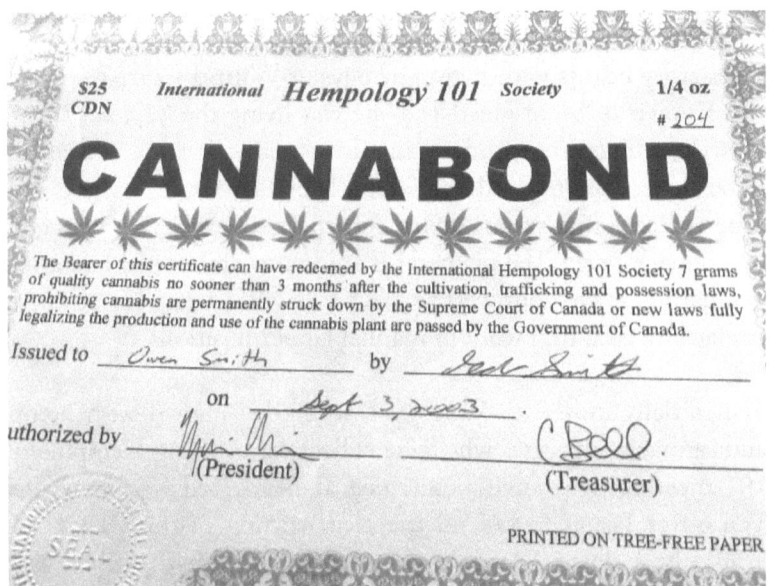

one who boldly points out the Emperor's nakedness while everyone else remains too ingratiated to speak the truth.

Other books included Ted's *Hempology 101 Textbook*, now in its fourth edition; which gives a well rounded view of the history and uses of cannabis. Also, Susan Boyds' *From Witches to Crack Moms: Women, Drug Law, and Policy* (Boyd 2004) that draws a parallel between the propagandizing, persecution and punishment of our modern drug war and that of witches in the Middle Ages.

Ted and I have similar names: Leon Edward Smith and Owen Edward Smith. At a Hempology 101 meeting I recall Ted explaining that he likes his nickname because *to ted* means to spread manure to prepare bedding for the next generation of plants (Oxford English Dictionary n.d.).

Ted Smith was born during the summer of Woodstock in 1969. He is deeply rooted in the culture and spirit of that era. He hails from Ontario, where his family has been farming for seven generations on both sides.

Ted's story begins with his rugby days at Wilfrid Laurier University. Known as "Acid Head Ted" he was living the *"Animal House"* lifestyle, selling drugs, and getting drunk daily. He was preparing to be an accountant until one fateful Metallica concert where Ted experienced a mushroom fueled spiritual revelation that changed his course forever. Ted pivoted his studies to philosophy and after graduating, moved out west to start a new life, using his physical strength to earn him work in manual labour positions.

Ted initially moved to Vancouver, where he aligned with hemp and cannabis advocates who were collectively hosting Hempology 101 meetings. An environmentalist at heart, Ted was drawn to Vancouver Island to defend the clear-cutting of the Clayoquot Sound by industrial logging companies. His friend, author, and historian Chris Bennett, was also adamant about protecting the old growth and promoting the use of hemp for pulp fiber processing. Ted and Chris became friends.

CHRIS BENNETT

From my perspective, the most compelling book available on Ted's blanket was the newly revealed history of cannabis. A book called "*Sex, Drugs, Violence and the Bible*" made me seriously reconsider reconsider what I thought about cannabis. In this book, author Chris Bennett (2001) paints a picture of our lost cannabis history. He presents the idea, backed by academic research and archaeological discoveries, that cannabis was well known to antiquity. It was also incredibly popular.

Chris writes of an ancient world with a prohibition that resembles our own time, where a wealthy section of society claimed exclusive rights to manufacture, process and distribute cannabis. Back then it was the priestly caste and royalty that kept cannabis away from the common people; while in our own time it is the pharmaceutical industry and government that claim exclusive right to distribute cannabis in the very few products that they manufacture.

In ancient times, those living in areas surrounding the populated centers saw the people's suffering and decided they would provide this medicinal plant to all who needed it and even teach people how to provide for themselves. Because of this, while being wildly popular and-having miraculous medicinal effects, these rebel medicine providers were seen as dissidents and persecuted.

Stories of demon possession in the ancient world that were treated with holy anointing oil sound strikingly similar to cases of epilepsy in our modern world. In his book, SDVB Chris quotes the book of Mark relating to a condition called "Capernaum Demoniac",

"There is the cry preceded by the unconsciousness, the sudden fall, the convulsive seizure, the gnashing of the teeth, the foaming at the mouth, the rolling on the ground; then the utter exhaustion so that in the graphic words of the father, the boy 'is shriveled up'" (Mark 9.18).

Mark 6:13, states: "And they cast out many devils, and anointed with oil many that were sick, and healed them."

Bennett (2001) discusses the etymological argument for cannabis as the holy anointing oil in the context of ancient Hebrew rituals. The Hebrews adopted the ancient kaneh-bosm anointing rite, which was used for the installation of all priests and kings. The recipe for this anointing oil, as recorded in Exodus 30:22-23, included over nine pounds of flowering cannabis tops (Hebrew Kaneh-bosm) extracted into about 6.5 liters of olive oil, along with large amounts of cinnamon, myrrh and cassia. This potent cannabis holy oil was used by the Levite priesthood and later by the Hebraic monarchs for spiritual revelations and inspirations provided by the "Spirit of the Lord".

Dr. Lester Grinspoon, a medical cannabis advocate, has provided testimonials from modern epilepsy sufferers noting the profound effects of cannabis in controlling their seizures. He cited studies such as the "Antiepileptic action of marihuana-active substances" (Davis and Ramsey 1949), "Anticonvulsant Nature of Marihuana smoking" (Consroe and Wood 1975), and "Chronic Administration of Cannabidiol to Healthy Volunteers and Epileptic Patients" (Cunha et al. 1980).

Interestingly, cannabis has been shown to be effective in the treatment not only of epilepsy but of many other ailments that Jesus and the disciples are told to have healed, such as skin diseases, eye problems and menstrual problems (Grinspoon and Bakalar 1993).

Chris proposes that "if cannabis was one of the main ingredients of the ancient Christian anointing oil, as history indicates, and receiving this oil is what made Jesus the Christ and his followers Christians, then persecuting those who use cannabis could be considered anti-Christ" (Bennett 2001, 213).

Meanwhile, In 1999-2000, a man named Terry Parker fought successfully in the Canadian courts to gain initial access (called a Section 56 exemption) for the use of cannabis oil for his epileptic condition (R. v. Parker 2000).

It was easy to start seeing the parallels. Ted and his friends are a group rebelling against the shortfalls of the medical establishment. Supported by growers in the surrounding region they provide this forbidden medicine to people in need, like those with epilepsy, cancer and HIV/AIDS. I could see how stigmatized cannabis currently is among the public and I hoped that their story wouldn't end in any way like the story I was told as a child, that of Jesus Christ.

Surely nobody would want to stop someone trying to help an epileptic child from seizing to death.

R. v. Smith and Budda

While studying at college, I sat in on the 2003 trial of R. v. Smith & Budda presided over by Justice Chaperon. Ted's cannabis store, the Victoria Cannabis Buyers Club, had been raided by police. Ted was facing charges along with his baker at the time, Colby Budda.

While scrawling notes for an English class report and giving the judge the occasional sturdy look, I ate a couple of peanut butter cannabis cookies. I knew nobody could tell by looking or smelling that a cookie had cannabis in it, you could barely even taste it over the peanut butter. As my lids moved closer together and my eyes began to glaze over, I listened intently to the arguments before the court. The prosecution was talking about a study that was performed on a group of rhesus monkeys. The study, which was part of Ronald Reagan's "Just Say No" campaign, concluded that "the active ingredient in marijuana [THC] impairs the brain's circuitry" (Heath et al. 1980).

To counter this claim, and others, Ted brought an expert witness to assess the scientific validity of the studies. The expert explained that the study employed questionable methods, including the shackling of monkeys in airtight gas masks without adequate oxygen, leading to hypoxia (Herer 1985). The monkeys were forced to inhale the equivalent of 63 high-potency "marijuana cigarettes" in five minutes. Not even Hempology could compete with that. The study was never replicated, and the expert pointed out prominent follow-up studies that directly repudiated its conclusions (National Academy of Sciences 1982; Institute of Medicine 1999).

This was the first time I saw a prosecutor, after extolling the arguments of cannabis prohibition, go red faced, slump back in his chair and give up hope. It wouldn't be the last.

Ted established a precedent that day for the distribution of medical cannabis through storefront dispensaries. It was a front page feature on the website of the most prominent cannabis lawyer in Canada, John Conroy. It became part of the expanding legal basis for the creation of more unregulated cannabis dispensaries across Canada.

Ted had built a sturdy camp in the capital city of Canada's most infamous cannabis province to launch a relentless siege on the dark fortress of cannabis prohibition. When considering the big picture perspective, Ted would use a Star Wars analogy with himself leading a band of outcasts from his rebel base on Vancouver Island against the impending doom of an Alberta built Death Star captained by Darth sweater-vest, the presiding Prime Minister of Canada, Steven Harper.

Mushrooms

I focused my studies on the humanities: enjoying philosophy, psychology, sociology and anthropology. Cannabis and the war on drugs bridged into all of these areas of interest and so I focused my research papers on cannabis and psychedelics. There is a lot more of human history entwined with psychoactive plants than those of us born at the end of the 20th century were taught in high school. If you follow society's strict direction, the options available to temporarily alter your own consciousness are few.

By the time I was 20, I had suffered several black-out experiences with alcohol that landed me a cold hard cot in a drunk tank overnight. I found myself, at one time, stumbling across a cold cell in my underwear, bruised and blinded by pepper spray with raw wrists and (temporarily) deaf in one ear. I had been fighting with police officers and I didn't remember any of it.

In contrast to my alcohol fueled urban mischief, my first experiences with Psilocybin mushrooms were with friends at the epically gorgeous beaches and mountains along Vancouver Island's south coast. The sheer majesty of the coastline brought me a feeling of unity with nature that was deeply enjoyable and felt therapeutic for my lost sense of home as an immigrant.

Many of my mushroom experiences are too personal to translate well. When closing my eyes I could watch and subtly manipulate an unfolding visual landscape. It was as if I were flying through worlds of color and shape that reacted to the gentlest pressure of my mind.

Mushrooms evoked a focus on ritual and preparedness. Sometimes I would meet with my best friend, a student of Chinese Medicine, who made *scooby snacks*. He compounded different mushrooms and herbs to complement the psychoactive experience. We would throw I Ching coins and set intentions for our journey. We would each play copies of the same CD at the same time to synchronize our audio experience as we hiked to the top of a mountain to write poetry.

With psilocybin I experienced less stress and more focus on my life and studies. I began practicing Kundalini yoga and having visionary experiences during Savasana that continued to help me feel more connected to nature. When I eventually combined mushrooms and Kundalini Yoga on a beach in Ucluelet during a 3-day Full moon at *SoundWave music festival*, I experienced ego death. As I relaxed between each pose I felt a cool moist blissful sensation wrap around my body and as I finished the set it felt as if a gentle rain of blissful stimulation sprinkled down onto my head and shoulders. I felt intimately connected to the world around me as if the waves of the ocean crashed with the fulfilment of each thought.

In this timeless state, I explored a quality of the psilocybin mushroom that had been described by psychedelic luminary, Terence McKenna: its ability to respond and answer questions. The moment I finished formulating a question in my mind I would begin to comprehend the answer, which would arrive complete with the crashing of the seventh wave. I was only limited by my ability to ask good questions. It was as if I had a personal version of Google or Chat-GPT in my head (McKenna 1993).

I asked "What is going to happen to me?" and as my closed eye visualization began to shift, I realized that I didn't want to know the answer. It was going to be too good to spoil the surprise.

Another time, after eating psilocybin mushrooms, I covered myself entirely in red dusty earth and sat on the precipice of a cliff overlooking the pacific ocean. I was discussing philosophy with a friend and came to the conclusion that no matter how beautiful and wonderful my thoughts, imagining or visions could be, they would always be a shadow of the real world, never making an impact as much as the smallest acts in the world. I decided that I had to involve myself in society and try to make a real difference.

As it is with cannabis, the mindset of the individual consuming mushrooms is foundational to the individual's experience. If, on some level, you believe mushrooms are bad for you then you are more likely to have a bad experience with them. If, like me, you had been studying their sacred use, you may be primed for a different experience. The psychological condition of the individual (the mindset) and the environment (the setting) in which the experience occurs are both critical factors in shaping the experience (Leary, Metzner, and Alpert 1964).

Unknowingly I had become *California sober*, by limiting my consumption of psycho-actives to cannabis and psychedelics and avoiding alcohol and synthetics. The time tested plant based allies that have evolved over millenia alongside humankind seemed to me the safer route. The drug war had put everything in one basket but there was a general consensus among my friends that synthetics were the much more dangerous option.

At this time I was deciding what to do with my life. I could see two roads before me. My father had generously offered me the family company, and while electrician work is a vital and important service, I knew that I wanted to use my authentic perspective to do something that would make a lasting positive difference in the world.

One midsummer night I decided to eat 3.5 grams of dried psilocybin mushrooms and watch the 4-hour Woodstock documentary. At intermission, I went outside to smoke my color-changing sherlock glass pipe. It was past midnight as I sat cross legged in the center of a fairy ring of mushrooms that had formed in my backyard. I toked and I meditated until I felt the whole world was settled and calm. An eerie peace hovered over the suburban neighborhood as I gripped my pipe and cleared my thoughts.

"What should I do with my life?"

I heard the words, "Help Ted".

I made a plan and soon started to visit Ted at his apartment in downtown Victoria to offer my help as a graphic designer.

Spirituality

I considered myself a seeker of spiritual understanding. I had developed a love for Christianity as a child but began to question and ultimately reject much of it as a teenager. My studies and peer groups at college exposed me to a vast array of ideas that had superseded anything I learned as a youth. While Buddhism and Taoism were both appealing to me, I found my closest match with a Qi Gong discipline called Falun Gong.

I felt that their precepts of Zhen (truthfulness), Shan (compassion), and Ren (endurance) were a steady foundation from which to act confidently. I enjoyed the exercises and the teachings resonated with me deeply. I understood from the teachings that these precepts are a representation of the nature of the Universe and that cultivating alignment with them would bring me closer to union with the higher of life.

I learned that this group had been persecuted by their government while meditating, and that they continued to meditate despite the persecution (Ownby 2008). In 1999 they had become more popular than the communist party government, and despite having no political aims, and teaching very simple moral principles, they were deemed a threat (Tong 2009).

Practitioners were encouraged to help clarify the truth about their teachings and created a newspaper to counter government misinformation. The teachings and meditation circles were offered free and I often joined them before walking across the campus to circle up with Hempology 101. Both groups were facing the daunting task of countering well-funded state prohibitions for relatively benign activities.

However, my understanding of the spiritual practice was that it did not encourage anybody to break the law, and it was strictly against smoking. At the time, I enjoyed smoking cannabis and I knew that if I were to get a job with the compassion club, I would be breaking the law.

As I sought a job with the VCBC, I would stop practicing Falun Gong but the teachings stuck with me and meditating on the combined effect of the three core principles helped me on this journey. This was a difficult decision for me as I knew that the compassion club was helping people to stop smoking, and that it shouldn't be illegal at all. I knew that I would be giving people the option to eat cannabis or put it on their skin. I knew that in the future, I might be vindicated.

Travel

In my last year at college, I volunteered as the Hempology 101 student club president and, as a burgeoning graphic design artist, made the poster for their 6th annual convention and hosted as MC. By this time, Hempology had become the largest student club on campus. I kept making enquiries about helping the VCBC as a baker and product maker but there wasn't a job available at the time. After completing my college degree, I left Victoria to learn gardening skills by working on organic farms.

With my life in a backpack, I set out to explore what had been described to me as the Bermuda triangle of British Columbia: Salt Spring Island, near Victoria; Nelson in the Kootenay mountains; and Robert's Creek, north of Vancouver on the Sunshine Coast.

In the little mountain town of Nelson, BC, while eating from soup kitchens and food banks, I always managed to find a little cannabis. I became acquainted with members of the local cannabis network, spending time with street level dealers, middle men and growers. *The Holy Smoke* was a legendary art and glass shop as well as a dispensary. It had a giant picture of Peter Tosh painted on the side that overlooked the town. If you were old enough, you could walk through the art and glass shop into the distribution room at the back. With heavy metal music blasting, you could purchase cannabis or magic mushroom chocolates. You could even stay and smoke to avoid standing outside in the snow. The Holy Smoke remained open for many years until court decisions ruled against them, forcing them to close.

In Roberts Creek, one ferry ride north of Vancouver, I struck up a conversation with a muscular, dreadlocked man at the Gumboot cafe. Having only a half gram of weed on me, I offered to share it with him and we walked to the pier and smoked my tiny joint. He then invited me to return with him and stay a few nights in his spare woodland cabin. Opening the cabin door, I was greeted by a sea of giant drying buds hanging upside down from strings stretched across the room. There was just enough room to access the pair of CDjs and he showed me how to use them. He then filled a big bag with buds for me to smoke. I slept with buds dangling around me and then spent the weekend trimming his crop in a big beautiful house with his family. I was paid $20/hr which eclipsed the $10-12 I was getting at the time as a landscape and garden laborer.

I moved onto a farm with a veteran cannabis grower who introduced me to his life's passion of cultivating cannabis genetics. I grew a crop of experimental outdoor varieties from his archive of seeds, with his help. I ended up trading 1 oz. of my crop for a Tibetan singing bowl. I also lived with an ethnobotanist, who lent me his collection of cassette tapes, introducing me to the heavyweights of the psychedelic movement, including a featuring Terrance McKenna and his peers at gatherings in Mexico and Hawaii. Terrance had an intense life-long relationship with cannabis and described it as the "country cousin" of the psychedelic scene.

Festivals

While exploring British Columbia, I attended some incredible music festivals. I worked as a harm reduction volunteer at Shambhala music festival three years in a row. I lead a team of a dozen people who were trained to work alongside the first aid and security teams to help attendees manage uncomfortable psychedelic experiences. I recall only once having someone overdose on cannabis: they had eaten too many strong cannabis brownies and needed somewhere to sleep and a bottle of water.

Another gathering I attended three years running was a multi-day event called "Intention". The event was held at the charming camp Elphinstone on the Sunshine Coast. It featured workshops throughout the day hosted by various talented participants, with music and dancing and feasting in the evening. At these workshops, I learned a lot of interesting things.

I learned how psychedelics were known as entheogens. The word "entheogen" is derived from Greek roots: "Entheos," meaning "full of the divine" or "inspired," and "genesis," meaning "to come into being" (Nichols 2016). Entheogens are often contrasted with recreational drugs, emphasizing their role in facilitating profound spiritual or mystical experiences rather than mere recreation or escape (Pollan 2018).

I learned about the power of crystals and lucid dreaming, chakras, and meditation. I learned about the power of intention when embarking on a psychedelic vision quest as well as the importance of integrating these experiences into your life.

I learned about the Mayan calendar and how seven years from now on December 21 2012, there would be a great alignment of zeros signifying the end and beginning of a great length of time.

I decided to perform a ritual to set a strong personal intention for my life. I ate a scooby snack as I carried a crystal amethyst wand to the shoreline where I could see the great towering mountains reflected in a relatively calm sea stretched out before me. I smoked a bowl of cannabis out of my glass sherlock pipe. I knelt down, and plunged my fist, gripping the amethyst wand as I plunged it into the icy, cold waters. I made the intention that for the next seven years up until December 21st 2012, I would work on developing one of the centers of consciousness as described by the chakra system.

The first year I would enhance my root chakra by focusing on work and improving my living conditions. In the second year I could find a partner to explore emotional and physical connection; and within that union proceed in the third year to apply my personal power to impact society. Then by using that power in year four for compassionate ends; I would follow up in year five by communicating this experience to the world. In year six I would naturally become a visionary by knowing my work deeply. Finally I would finish all of this off in the seventh year with the transcendental crown chakra ascension on December 21, 2012.

This provided structure for my own personal "hero's journey", that I had learned about from renowned author, Joseph Campbell (Campbell 1949). Campbell's work exploring belief systems around the world presented human cultures in sometimes surprising ways. I was intrigued by the image of the youth joyously celebrating their journey to the sacrificial temple. It redefined sacrifice not as a loss, but as a sacred, joyful contribution to something larger than oneself. These sacrificial heroes perceived their life as a gift being given back to sustain the world—a reciprocal exchange between human and divine.

To imprint the importance of my intention on my personal development I was determined not to remove my hand from the icy water until I could see a well defined dragon in my mind's eye. It would have to be projected clearly, as if it were real, up from out of the ocean in front of me and into the sky before me. Even as my arm grew numb, I squeezed my grip on the crystal and waited and watched star-sprinkled waters for my dragon. When he emerged, he was the most beautiful dragon that I had ever seen, like stained glass crafted out of amethyst crystal and tinted green against the night.

Dana Larsen

While I was on the Sunshine Coast, I had the pleasure of sitting in the back of a crowded living room with Dana Larsen. We were both attending the unofficial pre-screening of an unreleased Cannabis movie called *The Green Goddess*. He was smoking massive joints and generously sharing them. At the time he was editor for cannabis culture magazine, a publication that rose to infamy alongside Jodie and Marc Emery. Dana operated the Medical Cannabis Dispensary in Vancouver, one of the other early appearances of retail store-front cannabis.

Dana, like Ted and Chris, is an excellent public speaker. While running for the leadership of the provincial New Democratic Party, Dana spoke boldly and clearly in venues across the province about the continued harms of drug prohibition. Starting a group called Sensible BC, Dana led one of British Columbia's most successful signature gathering campaigns ever (Sensible BC 2013).

The campaign did not reach the passing threshold of 10% of registered voters in each of British Columbia's 85 electoral districts, or about two-thirds of the provincial population. They gathered over 200,000 signatures for cannabis decriminalization across the province in a short amount of time, illustrating how organized and widely supported cannabis law reform is. They showed our politicians that the people who support cannabis are politically active.

Another group called "Stop the Violence BC" led by researchers from the University of British Columbia added to the call for drug policy reform at the time. Stop the Violence showed the link between cannabis prohibition and gang violence (Werb et al. 2011). Guided by the best available scientific evidence, Stop the Violence BC called for regulation aimed at starving organized crime of the profits they currently reap as a result of prohibition (Stop the Violence BC 2011).

They spoke at one of our annual cannabis conventions at Vancouver Island University. It was also at this time that Washington and Colorado used their democratic strength to become the first of the states to legalize recreational cannabis by ballot vote.

Dana also writes cannabis fiction. His cannabis allegories built over familiar and popular imaginary worlds help to recast the image of cannabis in a positive light. *Green Buds and Hash*, *The Pie-Eyed Piper* and *Hairy Pothead* are among the titles on Potheadbooks.com. Dana and the Vancouver cannabis activist community impressively and frequently portrayed the reverse perspective of what I had been taught as a youth. Using their knowledge of cannabis and quick wit they engaged in many debates for cannabis legalization in the Canadian news media.

420 events at the Vancouver Art Gallery, hosted by the core *Cannabis Culture* crew were the largest cannabis gatherings I attended. Carefully delivered harm reduction advice was followed by fistfuls of joints thrown into the crowd. Dana often appeared alongside a talented cast of PotTV hosts. PotTV was one of the most prominent online cannabis communities at that time and now hosts a

growing archive of the many contributions made by the Vancouver cannabis community to the cause of legalizing cannabis (PotTV 2021).

A Dream

Another part of my exploration into personal growth was Lucid Dreaming, which involves practices that help to increase your awareness while dreaming.

One night I had a dream that I was visiting Ted's apartment and it was full of people. Many of them were older and rough looking, as if they had spent time on the street or in jail. I got the sense that one of them didn't like the look of me, I felt anxious for my safety and got up to leave.

Upon waking, I forgot about the dream until I was later visiting Ted's apartment: it was full of people, many of them similar to those that had populated my dream. As I started getting stoned I recalled the dream: there was a man telling a prison story who reminded me of my nocturnal antagonist. I felt uneasy for a moment but his story quickly hinged to the fact that he now had to permanently wear diapers to treat his medical condition. His humble laughter then released me from my anxiety. When I rose to leave, by coincidence, he left with me, saying a few kind words from what was a vulnerable, unwell, ex-convict.

This dream helped me come to terms with the prospect of working with people with difficult life experiences. It enabled me to replace the fear that I thought would protect me from danger, with a compassion for the strangers I would meet. Whatever danger I had come to perceive in people with a criminal past needed to be tempered with the knowledge that many ex-convicts experience complex challenges including ongoing medical conditions that lead them to make hard decisions that would help them avoid greater suffering (Binswanger, Krueger, and Steiner 2009).

My Sister, Ceri

At around this time, my younger sister Ceri was diagnosed with melanoma skin cancer after a bad sunburn caused changes to a mole on her neck. As my mother worked as a receptionist in a doctors office, the family closely followed the advice of Ceri's doctors. She underwent multiple surgeries to remove malignant lymph nodes, leaving her with a two inch crater in the side of her head, scarring down her neck and significant pain. She suffered serious and debilitating side effects from brain radiation therapy and steroidal anti-inflammatory medications.

These treatments failed to control her brain tumours. They also caused nausea, vomiting, and neurological pain so severe she was unable to put food into her mouth or swallow. They failed to prevent the cancer from spreading to other parts of her body. With chemotherapy and a schedule of drugs, she lost all her hair, became bloated and still suffered pain and insomnia. When the medical professionals could offer no more treatment options, we looked for alternatives. One of them was cannabis. I suggested that cannabis could help with the symptoms of her treatment based on things I'd learned at Hempology 101.

In 2006 my sister became a member of Ted Smith's Victoria Cannabis Buyers Club (VCBC) in order to obtain medical cannabis. The VCBC operates on a proof of condition mandate. This means that you need to provide verified medical documents that indicate you have a medical need; but you don't have to talk to your doctor about cannabis. At this time, in 2007, there were not many cannabis friendly physicians.

Soon after this visit my family and I bore witness to some of the miraculous effects of medical cannabis. A short time after smoking a joint she felt her appetite restored, she was then able to sleep restfully and began soon after to communicate clearly. She was able to join her family for dinner and movie night, enjoying trips to her favorite Chinese food restaurant.

My sister and I had consumed cannabis together in the past. We bonded in our teenage years by walking to the nearby park and sitting on a bench together to discuss our lives over a joint. She loved to swing on the swingset. I had shared with her my knowledge of cannabis use for chemotherapy treatment but she was told not to consume cannabis while going through the carefully monitored treatment regimes. Now that the doctors had exhausted all their options, she was free to smoke with me again.

Once we were sufficiently baked, our conversation would boldly but delicately wander toward the big question of her dire situation. What if she were to die? What was her idea of death? How would she want people to feel about it? How would she want us to remember her? I had seen a video by Timothy Leary on the *Tibetan Book of the Dead* (Leary, Metzner, and Alpert 1964), which emphasized making plans for your own death.

She was clear and compassionate in expressing that she would just want everyone else to be okay. She was calm, light, beautiful, and transcendent.

During the last weeks of her life, I witnessed the intense emotional turmoil that imminent death can bring to a family. The immensity of the sorrow dwarfed all other existing feuds. Grudges were forgotten and hearts opened. Even as her health declined, she was a continuous beacon of compassion for us all.

Try to imagine that someone you love dearly is going to die and has only a short period of time left to live. You could think of all the things that you would want to say to your loved one. As you say these things aloud sitting at their bedside, the medications your loved one has been given to ease their pain might make it impossible for them to connect with you. You might never know if they heard you or not. You might never be able to say goodbye.

(My sister at a restaurant)

If you complete this painful exercise you might realize that such a dire reality can befall any of your loved ones and that you should tell them how you feel about them now and often. This exercise can help you understand how valuable it is to have a pain medication like cannabis that acts while allowing the patient to continue on with their essential life functions, eating, sleeping and communicating.

I recall during this time returning home with a small vial of honey oil. Somebody had given it to me to smoke and I showed it to my brother. Little did I know that this very oil would become famous in the coming years for treating skin cancers and that if I had simply put some onto a band aid and placed that onto her mole, the outcome may have been different. The saga of Rick Simpson (see APPENDIX A) had not yet begun.

My sister's segment on *The Daily* on Shaw TV, where she shared her story and attempted to warn young people of the dangerous trend of tanning, won a media award in the Empowerment category in the Northwest Video Awards.

You can watch it on the Digital Timeline that accompanies this book.

Melanoma, unlike many cancers, is clearly visible on the skin. Changes in the shape, colour, or size of moles are potential indicators. Early detection is directly linked to a very high survival rate—close to 95 percent—if detected before the cancer spreads below the skin (Canadian Cancer Society 2021). Melanoma kills close to 20 Canadians a week. The most at risk are fair skinned, fair haired, blue eyed, and freckled, people of all ages. Melanoma is suspected to be related to U.V. exposure. In Australia, where the ozone layer is depleted, the rates of Melanoma are the highest in the world (Australian Cancer Council 2020). Someone will die from melanoma every hour (World Health Organization 2021).

She spoke out about the dangers of sun tanning and tanning beds and my mother helped lead a local campaign that successfully raised the minimum age required to access tanning salons.

After Ceri died, surrounded by my family, I stumbled out of the house and crumpled in the street. I dragged myself to the local park where we would swing on the swingset together and smoked a massive spliff. At 20 years old, she was just about to begin a scholarship at the University of Victoria to pursue her love of music. She sang every Sunday at a local church, as well as alongside a harmony chorus of women directed by my mother. She had the voice of an angel and a boyfriend and family who loved her.

My parents pledged to fight cancer and raised tens of thousands of dollars for the Cancer foundation through hosting dance parties, selling custom made pins, and amassing a large crowd of people to Walk for the Cure. After some time had passed, I returned to the sunshine coast and my work as a landscaper, building and maintaining gardens.

While visiting Victoria in the summer of 2008, I dropped by the V-CBC (also known as The Club), where I was hugged and asked to become their new baker. After the experience with my sister, I felt compelled to help others in similar circumstances. Even when it would mean moving back into the city and earning less money, I would do it because it needed to be done.

Making Medicine

The way the Victoria Cannabis Buyers Club was decorated like a living room, with art, magazines, records and books stacked around the walls, made the space feel like a portal back in time to the 1970's. Ted and Gayle dressed as archetypal nature loving peace activists with patchwork, tie dye and denim and 1000 different cannabis T-shirts.

It was a fun place to be with activities always being planned. Weekly hempology meetings were only one part of Ted's activism that also included game shows in front of the Ministry of Health, costume contests at the courthouse, cannabis themed caroling in front of City Hall, cookie giveaways and much more.

I began learning to prepare the Club's products from then Head Baker, Gayle Quin. I had met Gayle at the Hempology 101 circle. Gayle had come to my house some years before to teach a friend and me how to make our own *cannabutter*. She was the witchiest woman I had ever met. You could hear her cackling a half mile away and she would start up for no particular reason. She always

(Gayle Quin at Hempology 101)

had time to speak to every member of the club about their personal circumstances. On top of her knowledge of medicinal cannabis, she would recommend other herbs and healthy, witchy practices to whomever asked, myself included.

Gayle used her herbal medicine know-how to expand the club's products to include a whole range of topical oils and salves that combined cannabis with other wild-crafted herbs. She made lip balm, poultices, eye patches and more.

The bakery operated out of a separate location in downtown Victoria, about 2 blocks from the VCBC. Each day we would make 3 liters of cannabis vegetable oil at the VCBC and take some of it to be stored at the bakery.

We made our own Ghee by melting butter and 'clarifying' it by skimming off the non-fat milk solids, which become a foam on the surface of the liquid butter. We always used the highest grade of olive, hemp and grapeseed oil. With 3 liters of oil in a double boiler on medium-low heat, we would add either leaf or bud that had been ground and decarboxylated.

We used leaf that was donated by the club's growers who often had more than they could use. We would use leaf material from three different sources to include as many trace active compounds as we could. Each cannabis cultivar has a unique, limited amount of the total available cannabinoids and terpenes found in the species. By grinding and mixing them together we could create a product to deliver a larger spectrum of compounds. Contrary to the silver bullet approach of pharmaceutical medicine, that isolates compounds for specific actions, our herbal medicines utilize the shotgun method, providing a diverse array of ingredients to meet a wide array of needs.

The non-medicinal ingredients in our edible products also came from local, organic sources. One of our growers who lived on a family farm was so proud of the eggs he brought us that he suggested we show them to the judge as evidence of the high-quality of our products, bless his heart. Our recipe book became a central piece of evidence in the Crown's case against us. It has been available to view online since 2009. See APPENDIX B.

The recipe book contains a diversity of products with something to suit the different needs of the membership. Products are designed for appropriate times of day; to target a specific kind of relief; to be applied to a particular location; to take into account a wide tolerance range and to adjust for members' physical and mental histories and limitations.

In between learning to make the suite of products in our tiny apartment kitchen, I would spend a few days a week at the Club, infusing the oils and distributing cannabis products to the membership. Being a distributor (commonly known as a budtender) meant that I got to meet and speak with the club members who used the products. This gave me the opportunity to hear how the products I made were experienced by members. Their feedback would then be discussed and new products formulated to serve them.

Knowing that each day, hundreds of Club members' needs for appetite stimulation, sleep, and pain relief were being provided through the Club's products filled me with a satisfying sense of purpose. Although sometimes (assisted by crescendo from Elton John records) the feeling would spring back into literal tears of disbelief that this situation exists at all, and that I was under threat of being punished for assisting critically ill people eat cookies to live better lives.

An important lesson I learned as a medical cannabis distributor is to give people the benefit of the doubt by suspending judgment on their character. People who come across as mean or have a negative attitude when interacting may actually be suffering from multiple health issues. I learned that people with chronic illness are all around us, and that their mood towards me on any given day may be affected by their healing journey. I learned how privileged I am not to need medical cannabis. I practiced compassion.

I learned that cannabis has a very wide range of effects and those differ among every person. Members would share with me their experiences which were also wildly variable. While many found cannabis helped their condition, members with severe conditions tended not to experience much of the psychoactive effects reported by those with less severe ailments. From this perspective, the notion that people would seek to consume cannabis just to get high, something trumpeted by politicians at the time, did not take into account the experience of the most unwell people among us. The most unwell do not get high and they really need our help.

As the club's baker and a distributor, speaking to people about cannabis daily, I thought it my responsibility to personally test all of our products, including high dose edibles.

When exploring high dose edibles, I triggered the anxiety that is so common among edible cannabis experiences. 90% of the people who I introduced to edible cannabis through the VCBC had eaten a piece of party cake in the 70's, turned green and folded into the fetal position, never to touch another cannabis edible. It was part of the introduction to the VCBC that individuals were told about our low dose edibles that would help them reach a threshold of benefit without experiencing the side effects of home-made cannabis products.

When exploring high doses, at times I became anxious, felt ill and curled up in my bed. My anxiety around the death of my loved ones came to the foreground. There was no way in that moment that I could prove that my cat was not dead. I may never get to see her again and this created an immediate sense of intense grief. It was only improved as I began to urge myself to strongly commit that if by chance, she was still alive, that I would show her just how much I love her.

When she came happily trotting up to my window, I was intensely happy to see her. This same effect focused around my partner and parents on different occasions. Whenever I now recall the intense emotion felt during that experience, I feel a powerful focus toward honoring those people in my life that I dearly love. After a time, my anxiety ceased and I could eat as much as I wanted.

I was beginning to learn how to create and arrange electronic music, including the synthesis of sounds from different shapes or waveforms. After some hours spent arranging electronic music, I would eat a cookie or two and lay in bed. After a short time, an effortlessly composed symphonic music would begin in my mind that was more intricate and beautiful than anything I had ever heard.

To appreciate the subtle beauty of modern electronic music, I would prepare my bedroom for my experiences by installing surround sound speakers, lowering the lighting, burning some incense and lying on my bed.

At times, with music playing, I would relax my eyes and percieve the colour, opacity and shape of the waveforms flowing out of my speakers. I would watch the space in the center of the room where the audio from my speakers met to form a floating, transforming object composed of musical colours, textures and shapes.

ANALYTICAL TESTING

While I explored the qualitative effects of the psychoactive cannabis experience, the VCBC was honing in on their quantitative analysis. In an effort to increase the consistency of product dosing the VCBC sought to standardize methods for making them and test the results. At the time, a Vancouver specialist named Dr. Paul Hornby was the go-to source for analytical cannabis testing. These early reports we would receive were scientifically cryptic, requiring a challenging degree of deciphering and calculation.

Dr. Hornby began his work with cannabis as a hemp field inspector for Health Canada. He would take samples from hemp fields for analytical testing to make sure Canadian industrial hemp contained the required 0.05% THC. In the 90's, a doukhobor hemp farmer from Saskatchewan came to Paul with a product called 'Hempty', an industrial hemp leaf tea. The Doukhobors were drinking hemp leaf tea as a means to relax after a long day's work in the hemp fields. While the tea had little THC, it had plenty of CBD. The farmer was prohibited from selling 'Hempty' because CBD was illegal under the Canadian CDSA.

Hornby moved on to start Hedron Labs, which helped to test products for Vancouver's first cannabis dispensaries for cannabinoid content as well as undesirable contaminants. His work with standardized oral preparations of cannabis proved helpful to many patients seeking to navigate their use of different cannabis cultivars.

He was the first to analyze Haley's Comet, the high CBD cultivar that has helped patient advocate Hayley Rose avert her daily grand mal seizures. After observing over 4000 cases he developed a formula of suggested ratios of CBD to THC, as well as milligram

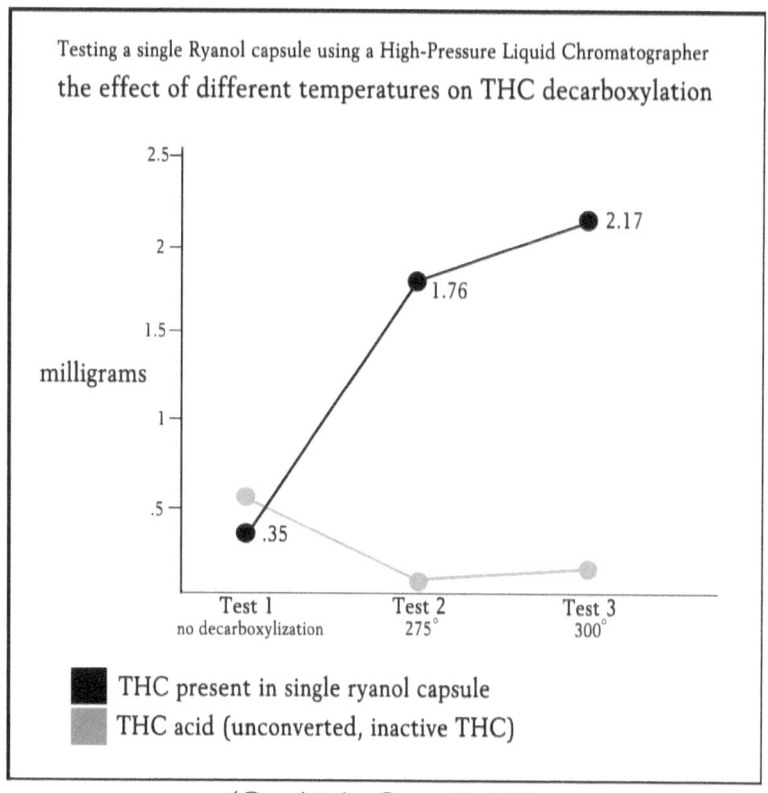

(Graphic by Owen Smith)

amounts, for patients with conditions including epilepsy, anxiety and multiple sclerosis.

Once we had access to Hornby's High-Pressure Liquid Chromatography, we began experimenting with our processes. In the previous chart, the left column shows how many milligrams of $\Delta 9$ THC are found in a single *Ryanol* capsule, while the bottom bar shows the temperatures used for the three testing sessions. An increase in activated $\Delta 9$ THC from .35 mg per cap with the original method to 2.17 after decarboxylation, is scientifically significant and has been reported as efficacious by the membership.

It was important to create low dose products to help people find their tolerable threshold and avoid unwanted effects. We standardized every part of our process to create similar strength products. Individuals would get to know each product through the 'start low, go slow' method. For a cookie that had an approximate dose of 25 mg. it would be suggested to start with a ¼ of the cookie (6mg) and wait up to 2 hours before eating any more.

Arrested

Leading up to my arrest I had plenty of time to think about the consequences of my actions. Ted had been challenging the cannabis laws for a decade and had argued the case for cannabis edibles to the BC Court of Appeal years before. He had been told that his submission, while interesting, was inadmissible due to a technicality.

He knew then that he would be coming back.

I remember reading about this in an early issue of the club's newsletter, the "Cannabis Digest", while sitting on a park bench in the church graveyard across the street from the courthouse, sun on my face, smoking a 4 inch spliff.

Every day at the VCBC, members with serious medical conditions would make it known how much they were benefiting from using the edible and topical products I was making. Ted's arguments made sense to me while I found the Canadian government's arguments mind numbing. The Prime Minister at the time, Stephen

Harper, was quoted as saying, "Drugs are not bad because they're illegal. They're illegal because they are bad." His Conservative government tried repeatedly to implement new mandatory minimum sentences that threatened 18 months minimum jail time for making cannabis products.

During the weekdays I would bake, and on weeknights I would make DJ sets to listen to at work. On the weekends I would go out dancing and DJ to sweaty dance floors at venues around Victoria.

The bakery itself was just a single room with a small kitchen on the second floor of an apartment building in downtown Victoria. Most of the apartment was filled by boxes full of parts for an unassembled board game. I sometimes used the boxes as places for my cookies to cool.

It was shortly after lunch while making capsules and listening to a song from one of my DJ sets (An-ten-nae – Ill, Acid Crunk EP Volume 5) there came a *bang bang* on the door accompanied by the stern announcement of "Victoria Police!".

"You have to let us in", one officer said.

"It's not my apartment", I told him.

"If it's not your apartment, You have to let us in", he repeated.

I would later recognize this as a 'knock and talk' or 'tap and rap' strategy from a Youtube channel called *Never Get Busted*. It's a clever way to say two things at once. "You have to let us in" could mean that I am legally obligated to let them in or it could mean that they cannot enter without my permission. In the half a second I had to think, I realized that letting them in was what needed to happen and with a sigh I opened the door, ready to accept whatever consequences that would follow.

"What have we got going on in here?" Asked the lead officer, Peter Gill.

"This is the bakery for the Victoria Cannabis Buyers Club, do you know Ted Smith?"

"Yes, I know Ted Smith" replied the lead officer as they looked around the apartment. It was the middle of the day so I was busy making everything at once. There were cookies cooling on a multi level cooling rack; butter melting on the stove; a tray of capsules was set out on the table in the center of the room. The fridge was full of ingredients and oil infusions including a number of non-cannabis infused oils (Arnica, Comfrey, St. John's Wort) used in topical products.

I knew they couldn't tell that these were cannabis products. In the recent past there had been a court case for the infamous Watermelon of Wreck Beach in Vancouver. Watermelon would stroll the nude beach distributing edibles until she was arrested by undercover police. In the trial, the police found out that there were no means available to test cannabis once it had been combined with food ingredients (Bains 2007).

"This is the bakery for the Victoria Cannabis Buyers Club", I repeated. I was determined to be honest while not saying any more than I had to.

"Okay, so if I ate one of these cookies, what would happen to me?" The lead officer asked.

"I can't tell you what would happen because they are not for you, they are intended for medical patients."

"Okay, but would I feel woozy? silly? Would I feel funny?"

(Cookies cooling at the bakery)

"I can't tell you what would happen for you but I can tell you that medical patients who eat these feel better: they get to eat, sleep and be free of pain."

I then started to remember my meditations from the graveyard where I had thought about this moment.

"I think you should know that these products aren't yours to take, but if you do take them, the consequences will be that very sick people will not be able to sleep or eat tonight, people will have seizures, they will be in intense pain, all because of the job you are doing."

I realized that I was about a foot taller than the police officer and my posture might be considered to be aggressive so I volunteered to sit myself down.

The secondary officer asked to see my I.D.

I had lost my wallet with all of my I.D. the year before while attending an all night mountain rave on the Sunshine Coast. I only had an old student ID card and some library cards so I handed them my wallet. The officer found a list of pay check totals on a small piece of paper. He asked if they were drug transaction records, I looked at him sternly and told him it was used to pay my taxes.

It was at this time that they noticed the remains of the joint I had rolled before lunch. Scissors, papers and about a .6 gram bud and some crumbles. I had totally forgotten it was there. This was enough for the officers to charge me. They could use the evidence of cannabis possession to launch a full scale search of the apartment. They called it in and soon a 3rd officer showed up. Turning my head I saw the face of David Bratzer peek inside the door.

Right next to the door was a poster I had made for the 10th Annual Cannabis conference held by Hempology 101 at the University of Victoria. David was a featured speaker at the event, representing the Canadian branch of L.E.A.P (Law Enforcement Against Prohibition). LEAP members add unique insight and authority to the voices against drug prohibition. David faced discrimination from his own police force. He would later be taken off the case due to his familiarity with our work.

Following David were a huddle of officers led by the

infamous Officer Laur. Laur had been involved with Ted's previous arrests.

"Well, I've seen a lot of grow ops, but this is my first bake op!", Laur exclaimed with a wry smile. He held up a stack of cardboard boxes. "Are these for carrying the baked goods?" The room was half full of these stacks of small white boxes.

"No, they're parts of a board game".

Hempology had acquired a large number of unassembled cannabis board games called "The Cultivation Game" that was slowly being put together on the weekends. He gave me a strange look. I told him what I'd told the others, that this was the bakery for the Victoria Cannabis Buyers Club.

The officers huddled out in the hall. I remained seated where I would have normally been filling capsules with infused veggie oils. A part of me still hoped I would be able to keep working.

Laur returned and charged me with possession and read me my rights. He explained that I would have to go downtown but also that they were glad I was compliant and would not handcuff me. The apartment would be searched and contraband seized as evidence.

They led me out of the apartment into the hallway through a crowd of a half dozen officers.

"Who lives here?" one blurted out with a hopeful authority.

"A sick old woman who has cancer", I replied.

As I exited the building, Ted Smith and another VCBC employee were in front. Ted told me that when we came out of the building,

I had my head raised high while the police were slumped over looking at their feet as they led me to the police car.

On the ride to the station, I heard the officers talking about the case, "they've been through this before" one responded.

"Can they even test for TCH… or THC or whatever in the cookies?"

"That'll be for JP to figure out."

JP refers to Jurisprudence or the Crown lawyers.

"So, what happens next?"

"I guess they gotta change the law."

Arriving at the police station, the officers told me I'd been given the rockstar treatment but now I would have to be put in handcuffs. I obliged and was led into the interrogation room. The room was cold, the seating was a three plank wooden bench, not very comfortable and the lighting was bright, the paint was egg white but covered with small black pock mark holes like from poorly mixed concrete.

It was now that my lack of photo ID would become the focus. They couldn't believe that I didn't have a driver's license. I explained that my BCID and passport were lost and that I was a bicyclist. Victoria is not a large town and there are lots of excellent bike trails to get around. I explained this to multiple sets of officers who came in at different times to ask me the same questions in different orders. In my student ID picture I was short haired, chubby and clean shaven. On this day I was skinnier, with a massive beard and long hair. They all had a laugh when I tried to smile the way I was smiling in my student ID.

They were glued to another idea. I could be a fugitive, on the run from the law, trying to conceal my identity as a serial criminal. They informed me that they were trying to get hold of Health Canada to ask if the location of the 'Bake Op' had a medical cannabis license under the MMAR (Marihuana Medical Access Regulations). If it did then they were unlikely to press charges. By some mysterious magic, when they asked me whose apartment it was, the part of my brain that was supposed to remember the name of my mentor, Gayle Quin, mysteriously turned off and I honestly couldn't have told them if I wanted to.

It wasn't until an old friend who was now an officer walked past my cell that my identity was verified. My friend Eric had been goalkeeper for a local soccer team that I formed with some friends that we called *The Blazers*. As the name suggests, the team was built on the principle of togetherness through smoking cannabis. We smoked at practice, we smoked in the changing-rooms, we smoked in the team huddle at half time and we won the league 3 years in a row.

"Owen, I wouldn't expect to see *you* in here" he said.

"Me either", I replied, "but here we are."

The lead officer then asked to confirm if he knew me. He confirmed and they left the room.

After many hours of waiting, I heard some voices down the hall say the word *marijuana*. I got up and walked to the door and put my ear against it. In that moment I felt a little like a Robin Hood character, straining to hear anything from the prison guards I could later use against King John. I could hear officers discussing what they were going to do with me. Health Canada still hadn't responded and they weren't even sure if they could test the evidence that they were seizing. It was up to Jurisprudence to assign charges.

A few doors down was the drunk tank that welcomed a few screaming, howling and cursing occupants. As a teenager I had drunk myself into a couple of jail cells, one time after wrestling and kicking a police officer. The state of mind that alcohol created for me sometimes led to violence for the fun of it and ended in pain and unconsciousness; while I'd contend that on the contrary, cannabis consumption ushers in peace culminating in pleasure and sleep.

My lunchtime buzz was wearing off but I was lucid. I felt out of place sharing a wall with the wild drunkards. The assumption of guilt that accompanies the prison cell environment was not able to permeate my adamantine sense of righteousness. I felt so little guilt that I thought it must have been visible to the guards. I accepted the offer of a phone call with legal aid. I was told to say nothing, but I'd already said everything I'd wanted to say.

Upstairs in the lobby, staff from the VCBC had arrived and were demanding to see me. Ted had been coordinating an immediate response to the event. He had spoken to the officers at the scene as they began to seize products from the apartment to bring to the station as evidence. The officers refused Ted's suggestion to turn a blind eye to the situation.

After about 8 hours and just before midnight I was released with a Promise to Appear notice. This confirmed that I had a court date before a judge scheduled for early in the new year. As I was signing the document, the accompanying police officer asked me what led me to this line of work. I told him that my younger sister had died of melanoma skin cancer and cannabis was the only thing that helped restore her essential life functions to eat, sleep and speak with her family before she died.

"I guess that's what it takes." I concluded. He didn't respond.

I walked out of the underground parking lot at the police station and onto the street. I was shivering as it was around zero degrees outside. About two blocks down the road a man asked me if I needed anything. I just yelled "No!" and sped back to the VCBC in hopes someone would still be around. I really needed a joint.

Still waiting at the club were a few of the staff and Ted. They had been busy smoking and immediately passed me a joint. They asked me about my experience and then passed me the phone. My romantic partner at the time was delivering cannabis to people's homes all over Vancouver Island. She told me that she was glad it was me, that I was perfect for this because I would be able to handle the pressure when others might not.

Ted gave me the next day off and filled a bag with my favourite bud. After I'd returned home and greeted my friends and two kittens, I got stoned and felt the weight of the day hover about me. I've only ever wanted to help people. The people who I help are very grateful. How could anyone want to stop me from helping these people? I struggled to understand and I cried.

CHARGES?

The police report read: 09-57421
(Search Warrant – Cannabis Growers of Canada)

"Last Thursday at around 3:00 p.m. our members responded to several complaints from tenants at 865 View Street regarding a strong skunky smell coming from one of the apartments.

Our officers attended and discovered that one of the apartments had been converted and was being used as a bakery to produce cookies, muffins, oils and other products for the Cannabis Society of Victoria. A 37 year old male was arrested and was cooperative. A search warrant was obtained and we seized numerous items of potential evidence in relation to drug trafficking.

This is a unique set of circumstances and we are working in conjunction with Crown Counsel to determine what charges would be most appropriate but initial investigation indicates there was no exemption from Health Canada to produce or supply marijuana for medicinal purposes."

I was informed that the errors in the report were for my benefit considering that the charges against me could potentially harm my reputation. Ted called for a press conference. Local news sites attended and the VCBC was full of members watching, listening and some even getting in front of the camera. A local news station put out a short video comparing cannabis to alcohol, gambling and tobacco and called out the law against cannabis edibles as hypocritical. The journalist asked the audience "If someone you know was suffering, would you want them to have safe access to something that might make them feel better?"

You can watch all of our Press Conferences on the Digital Timeline that accompanies this book.

The city's major newspaper, the "Times Colonist" reported that at the VCBC "Marijuana cookies cost 75 cents. No figures were given on how many cookies are sold, but bagged marijuana sales would range between $1.8 million and $2.6 million a year. About a dozen [VCBC] members operate the site."

We had doubts that charges would be pursued and thought it likely that the trial would not proceed. The crown had to consider the likelihood of conviction and whether it is in the public interest to prosecute at all. Given the recent history of medical cannabis rulings, even if I was found guilty, no one would expect a judge to punish someone caught making cannabis products for sick people.

The efforts by police to uncover if I secretly had an MMAR license were pointless given that even an MMAR licensee would be breaking the law if they were caught doing what I was doing. At the time, Health Canada actively encouraged people to ingest cannabis orally without pointing out that straining cannabis oil through a cheesecloth is a punishable offense. The MMAR application form contained a check box to report if you intended to ingest your cannabis orally.

From our perspective, this looked like Health Canada was putting people at risk by enticing them toward a dangerously vague definition in the law.

A few weeks passed before my promise to appear. When the day came, Ted and I walked the few blocks across downtown Victoria from Johnson street to the Courthouse. We checked the docket, my name was not posted; we asked the clerk, nope, nothing. We turned around and walked back to the VCBC, smoking a victory joint. They weren't going to press charges as they knew they would lose and didn't want us to take them down in court and the media. They would just maintain the status quo and make us an anomaly. We called a press conference.

Feeling victorious, we announced that our recipe book would be available online for anyone to read. In it were all of our methods, ingredients and proportions for making differing strengths of oil. By making this knowledge public, we could empower people to make their own products where they felt safe to do so.

After the one day break I had been granted after being arrested, I had returned to the bakery to continue my daily task of making the club's products. Now that the charges had evaporated, I felt even more secure listening to music at a *reasonable* volume, melting butter and making cookies. The building manager had contacted us after the raid to say that if he had known beforehand that it was us in the apartment, he wouldn't have called in the police. Regardless, we moved the bakery to a new location shortly after.

I was living in a community house at the time with a bunch of young friends. It was only two blocks from the bakery and was 4 stories tall and multi-colored. We called it the "Rainbow house". I had a room at the very top with a little balcony that overlooked the long gorgeous Victoria sunsets. I would often sit up there after work, smoking a 4 inch spliff and drinking a craft beer, listening to the latest Dubstep tunes blasting out of my bedroom window.

I hardly ever got any mail at the Rainbow House because I'd moved everything to paperless but one morning I decided to dig through the stack of shared mail that had piled up on the living room table. Every so often I would get a GST rebate check, but not this time, instead there was a thick envelope from the Justice of Canada. It had been there for about 2 weeks.

It contained the charges against me along with photo records of evidence taken from the bakery that day along with a new "promise to appear" date, that was scheduled only a week or so away. We regrouped, informing the media and bringing in a local lawyer to help us build our case.

We used this second press conference to announce the launch of our newspaper, the Cannabis Digest. Originally the club's membership newsletter, the Digest had grown to over 30 pages with art, games, events and ads for local cannabis businesses. At the time it was Canada's largest cannabis publication, given that the preeminent *Cannabis Culture magazine* had stopped printing after the (Owen, Ted & the Cannabis Digest) United States D.E.A. arrested publisher Marc Emery who later served five years in prison for selling seeds through its back pages.

Our lawyer, who was not familiar with cannabis law, looked over the paperwork. Ted had a clear understanding of the legal arguments and answered his concerns readily while beginning to explain our strategy.

The lawyer then looked at me, "I understand what you are trying to do but what I don't understand is why you didn't tell me about any of these other things."

"What other things?" I replied.

"Your record. You should have told me about your criminal record. It's going to be harder to make these arguments when the crown brings up your past."

"What? Let me see that."

He passed me the part of the file that listed a series of criminal offenses and convictions including assault with a deadly weapon and breaking and entering. They were recommending 4 months jail time. I skimmed to the top and read the name. It was the criminal record of someone with the same first and last name as me but with a different middle name.

Included in the package were photographs of the evidence in marked bags. As it turns out, while the police were processing the evidence, one of the jars of oil slipped and smashed on the ground, releasing about a liter of cannabis oil onto the concrete. Our oils contained liquid lecithin which is very sticky and tremendously hard to clean. Long after I'd left the building, the powerful smell of the cannabis oil would have permeated the hallways and wafted into every nook of the Victoria Police Station.

I handed the package back to the lawyer and he sent it back to the crown. This case was outside of his expertise so Ted kept looking for a replacement. The lawyer he had used for his previous trials had retired. It was at this time that some good fortune blew our way as legendary constitutional cannabis lawyer Kirk Tousaw moved to Vancouver Island. Kirk had represented a number of high profile cases including Marc Emery's extradition and a noble but failed attempt to legalize recreational cannabis through the Supreme Court of Canada in 2002.

On April 29th, 2010, we met Kirk at a cafe across from the courthouse for breakfast before my *Promise to Appear*. Ted explained the arguments and Kirk asked me officially if I was willing to put my freedom on the line for this issue. It had to be my uncoerced choice to fight the charges and raise the challenge instead of looking for a plea deal. I was game.

While representing the medical cannabis grower Mat Beren, Kirk had recently forced Health Canada to change the law to allow for licensees to grow collectively and to provide for more than just a couple of people. With Kirk and Ted in the huddle, we were all game to take on the backwards policy of cannabis prohibition held onto by the white knuckled Canadian Conservative government.

Charges

Officially the charges against me were Possession of cannabis; Trafficking THC and Trafficking cannabis resin. The possession charge was for the cannabis left on the table after rolling one for lunch. The trafficking THC and trafficking cannabis resin charges were essentially for the same thing: the jars of infused oil and the products I was making from them.

Schedule two of the *Controlled Drug and Substances Act* (CDSA) divided cannabis into a number of parts. You had the naturally produced cannabis resin, THC, CBD, CBN as well as synthetically produced Nabilone, Pyrahexyl, and DMHP (Controlled Drugs and Substances Act 1996). People arrested with cannabis extracts of all kinds would be hit with charges related to one or some of these supposed separate parts.

If a defendant built a defense up around a charge relating to cannabis resin, the crown could obfuscate the defense by bringing in charges for THC, CBD or CBN. This often worked to ensure the

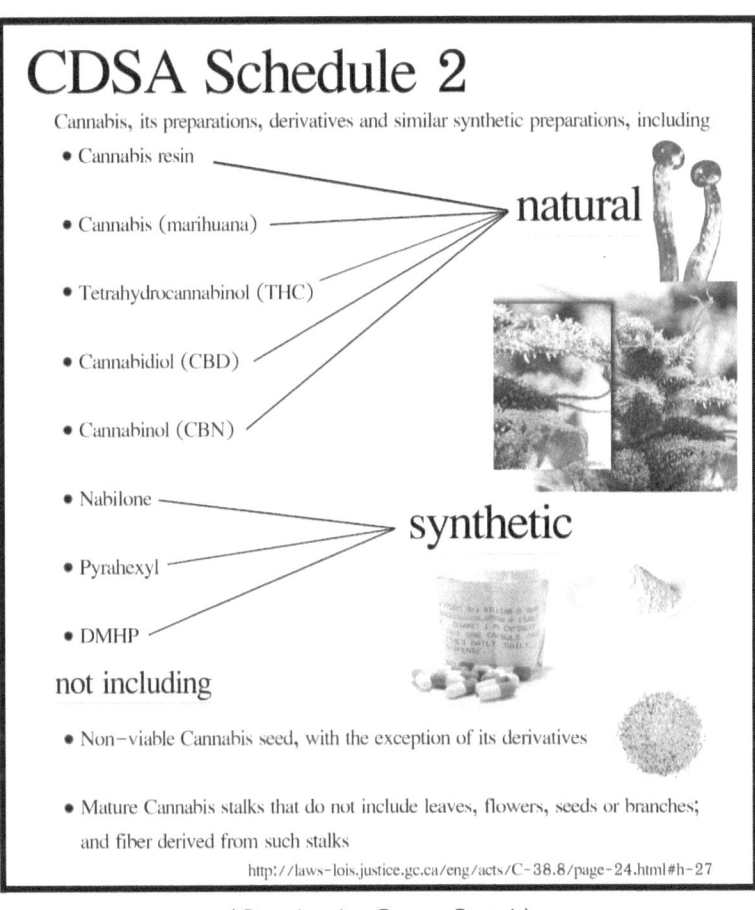

(Graphic by Owen Smith)

success of drug charges in court. We were well prepared for this with our expert scientific witness already selected.

At the Promise to Appear you must stand before the court and be read the charges and you must give your "Guilty" or "Not Guilty" response. I thought for a second. I had already admitted to being the club's baker to the police and I was essentially proud of my guilt, happy to tell anyone that I made cannabis products for sick people. I looked over at Kirk beside me. "Not Guilty" he whispered.

"Not Guilty, your honour."

There was a Times Colonist news reporter in the room. She followed us into the hallway and asked a few questions. Kirk disappeared around the corner of the long sterile hallway and reappeared half an hour later with news of our Judge and court date.

We returned to the VCBC where the back room served as the place where we could smoke joints and discuss strategy. Ted would be the first to take the stand. As my employer, he would be best able to explain the history and operations of the club and take full responsibility for my actions.

The crown would select QC Peter Eccles who had represented the government's position in previous similar cannabis cases. Eccles was a formidable opponent with great skill at grilling witnesses, turning pages of testimony to hot ash. To help us slay this dragon we invited one of the world's most prolific cannabis scientists: a little known man named Dr. David Pate.

Dr. Pate's research on cannabis is foundational to much of our understanding of cannabis today. His name appeared as a contributor to a large percentage of studies referenced by Health Canada in their cannabis "guidance to health care practitioners" document. He's also a really lovely and down to earth man.

We would gather four club members to speak about their medicinal use of edible and topical cannabis. It was important to have witnesses with supportive physicians. It was also helpful if their physicians had monitored their health after starting to consume cannabis. Four VCBC members were selected from a list of volunteers that had stepped forward: Sandra Large, Gina Herman, Ruth Arthurs and Gayle Quin.

With Ted leading us off, I wouldn't need to testify. I would only need to plead not guilty to the charges for the purpose of the Voir

Dire. A Voir Dire is a trial within a trial. Before the court could determine if I was guilty of the criminal activity, (that I had just pleaded Not Guilty to) we would use the Voir Dire to challenge whether the activity should be criminal in the first place.

We would select to be tried by a Judge alone. There was too much technical information to trust that a jury would understand the details and not get bogged down or confused. The judge could carefully deliberate and consider all of the information to create a clear coherent decision; at least that's what we were hoping.

If we won we could change the law forever: striking cannabis from the befuddled CDSA schedule and liberating the plant and all of its products for patients and caregivers across the country. If we lost, the crown would have new precedents to charge cannabis patients and caregivers with, and I would be led to testify in front of a Jury.

I had no compunctions about making cannabis oil for sick people, I was often reminded by grateful patients that I was doing the right thing. One of my colleagues at the VCBC was an AIDS advocate from Africa named Kamau. She kept a quote from Martin Luther King Jr. pinned to the back of the reception desk.

"An individual who breaks a law that conscience tells him is unjust, and who willingly accepts the penalty of imprisonment in order to arouse the conscience of the community over its injustice, is in reality expressing the highest respect for the law." (King 1963)

Kirk Tousaw

Kirk Tousaw is one of Canada's top cannabis lawyers. Born in the state of Michigan, Kirk has been an advocate for cannabis legalization since high school. He obtained a degree in Political Theory and Constitutional Democracy before moving to Vancouver in 2002. There he completed his Masters thesis on the *Malmo-Levine* case that challenged cannabis prohibition before the Supreme Court of Canada in 2003 (R. v. Malmo-Levine 2003). Malmo-Levine lost by a margin of 5-3, the only other time that cannabis has been judged by the nine. He became friends with Marc Emery: a meeting Kirk credits for helping boost his advocacy work.

He soon began working alongside John Conroy at *Conroy and Co.* where he helped with the success of R.v.Beren, a constitutional challenge to the production limitations on licensed medical cannabis growers (R. v. Beren 2009). Kirk defends cannabis growers, clubs, and individuals with recreational, medicinal or spiritual purposes: not because the *people* are bad, but because the *laws* are bad.

Kirk and his family moved to Vancouver Island in 2010, shortly after I was arrested and charged with possession for the purposes of trafficking THC. Ted Smith tracked Kirk down and invited him to help us bring another constitutional challenge to the medical cannabis laws.

After some consideration we elected to challenge the law that prohibits production and trafficking of derivative products as it is defined in the CDSA that is modified by the MMAR (now ACMPR). We argued that these laws violate Section 7 of the Charter of Rights and Freedoms: life, liberty and security of the person. We would argue on the behalf of patients, as in Canada you cannot be convicted of a law that is unconstitutional, even if that law doesn't apply directly to you. As an additional thrust for justice we would also attempt to find the government in contempt of previous court rulings, citing the gravely inadequate changes made in response to previous medical cannabis court rulings.

Up against the might of the Canadian federal government, Kirk's skill at asking questions would need to illuminate the compelling personal stories of the brave and courageous patient witnesses; the scientific detail of our expert witness, Dr. David Pate and carve through the testimony of the government's witnesses. With Kirk's help we would attempt to convince a Justice of the Supreme Court of BC that the restriction to "dried marihuana" is arbitrary, standing as a barrier to patients rights and that the restriction does not advance any legitimate goals of the government.

A positive outcome would instantly remove the barrier for patients in BC who would make their own medicinal cannabis products. Seeking to find the federal government in contempt was a long shot that we felt necessary. Kirk would also represent me if we went to a jury trial to weigh the merits of my actions.

Medical Cannabis Rulings

Over the past 20 years there has been a series of legal challenges that have changed cannabis laws to permit medicinal use.

1997: Wakeford v. Canada (Ontario Court of Justice) - Jim Wakeford, diagnosed with AIDS and suffering from severe nausea and wasting syndrome, was granted an interim (Section 56) constitutional exemption to possess and cultivate cannabis for personal medical use. This case set a precedent for future legal challenges to the medical cannabis regulations in Canada.

2000: R. v. Parker (Ontario Court of Appeal) - The landmark decision that first invalidated the cannabis prohibition. It concerned the case of an epileptic who could only alleviate his suffering by recourse to cannabis. The Court found that the prohibition on cannabis was unconstitutional as it did not contain any exemption for medical use.

2001: Marihuana Medical Access Regulations (MMAR) are introduced.

2003: Hitzig v. Canada (Ontario Superior Court) - This landmark case resulted in parts of the Marihuana Medical Access Regulations (MMAR) being declared unconstitutional. The Court found that the regulations infringed on the rights of medical cannabis users by unduly restricting access to cannabis.

2006: R. v. Krieger (Alberta Court of Appeal) - This case affirmed the right of medical cannabis patients to grow their own cannabis, ruling that Health Canada's refusal to grant an exemption for medical cultivation was unconstitutional.

2007: R. v. Long (Ontario Court of Justice) - Prohibition against cannabis possession in the Controlled Drugs and Substances Act deemed unconstitutional due to the absence of a constitutionally acceptable exemption for medical cannabis.

2007: R. v. Bodnar/Hall/Spasic (Ontario Court of Justice) - The Court followed the Long decision, holding that the prohibition against possession of cannabis was invalid and of no force or effect.

2008: Sfetkopoulos v. Canada (Federal Court of Canada) - The Federal Court of Canada struck down the federal regulations concerning the growing of medical cannabis by licensed producers. Prior to the case, a producer was prohibited from growing for more than one person.

2009: R. v. Beren and Swallow (BC Supreme Court) - The Court forced the government to allow for more than three licensed growers to share a facility and for a licensed grower to provide for more than one patient. Health Canada responded by allowing for four growers instead of three in the same space and for each grower to provide for two instead of only one patient.

2011: R. v. Mernagh (Ontario Superior Court) - The Ontario Court of Appeal overturned a lower Court ruling that would have legalized cannabis for all Canadians. The Court denied the argument that doctors were not participating in the program making it inaccessible to patients.

2012: Marihuana for Medical Purposes Regulations (MMPR) are introduced.

The Harper Conservatives

During this time, Canada's Conservative government was busy trying to usher in mandatory minimum sentencing for cannabis. They tried numerous times to pass bills that would escalate the penalties for growing, processing and selling cannabis. In 2007, shortly after I joined the VCBC, the Conservatives introduced Bill C-26, to go alongside their national drug strategy. Bill C-26 attempted to create a mandatory nine month sentence for growing one cannabis plant, along with 18 months for making cannabis cookies in any amount (Bill C-26 2007). The opposition parties slowed the progress of the bill, while activists mounted rallies in over 50 cities across Canada. C-26 died when an election was called in the Fall of 2008.

Where C-26 failed to reach committee, the next Bill called C-15 did reach the next phase of ascent. It would mandate minimum prison sentences for various "serious" drug offenses, including trafficking cannabis and cultivating cannabis for the purpose of trafficking. C-15 made no allowance for medicinal use, and could have easily snared compassion club operators and providers (Bill C-15 2009).

After failing to pass the bill through the house, the conservative government introduced the bill directly to the Senate the following year as Bill S-10.

S-10 was slightly different from C-15 and C-26 in that it raised the plant limit for mandatory minimum sentences from 1 to 6. This change is attributed to the intense focus of media and activists on the absurdity of a nine month sentence for growing a single cannabis plant. Growing less than five plants would still be illegal, but would not trigger an automatic mandatory minimum sentence (Bill S-10 2010).

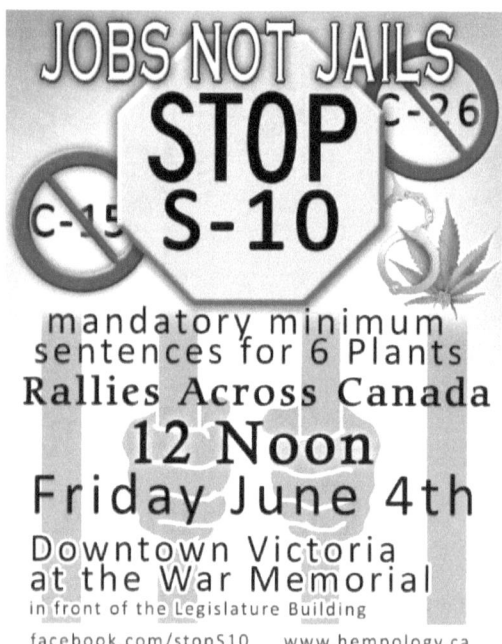

S-10 did, though, still contain an 18 month sentence for making any extracts or cannabis-food (worded as any marijuana product that isn't marijuana buds), which means baking a single pot-brownie and getting charged would result in a mandatory 18 month minimum sentence.

Every major study on mandatory minimum sentencing has concluded that it is extremely expensive and actually erodes public safety by creating hardened criminals out of functional, tax paying citizens. This policy disproportionately impacts families, turning parents into prisoners and children into orphans (Doob et al. 2009).

This is what we were up against: a government deeply entrenched and digging in its heels to make cannabis prohibition its political cornerstone. A persistent campaign to shore up their largely Christian voting base against the dirge of lazy hippies that the TV was so busy stereotyping. We knew we had a battle on our hands and that we were vastly out funded but that was no reason to stop.

Fundraising

We were grateful when Kirk Tousaw cut us a deal whereby we would pay in monthly instalments instead of an hourly rate. Given the length of the trial and the possibility of appearances in the Court of Appeal and at the Supreme Court of Canada, this would be a bargain.

Fundraising was an exercise in public education as much as a celebration of our continued incremental strategic success. Each event was an opportunity to show our city that the cannabis community is well resourced, creative and knows how to have a good time.

We hosted art auctions at local cafés showcasing the talented artists amongst our membership. We organized dance parties that featured some of our benevolent gardeners who double as DJs. We had raffles of "Guess the Gram" jars where members would try to estimate the total weight of cannabis buds in a large jar. We had a bake sale and put a donation jar at the distribution desk. We raised $15K through a GoFundMe crowd-funding campaign.

The majority of our fundraising would be done through the sale of donated cannabis by the club. We also received private donations from individuals and organizations including one licensed medical cannabis producer that asked not to be mentioned because it could affect their relationship with Health Canada regulators.

I attended a number of short scheduling hearings where we declared our intentions to challenge the law under the Canadian Charter of Rights. We were eventually granted four weeks in February 2012, just over two years after I was arrested, to make our arguments before the Supreme Court of British Columbia.

Part 2
The Trial

THE COURTHOUSE

The Victoria courthouse is a large square block building in downtown Victoria with entrances on all sides.

On the first day of court, a small crowd gathered outside the south entrance to the courthouse. Local media, a documentary film crew,

(VCBC friends and family outside the Courthouse)

about a dozen people from the VCBC, my parents and my girlfriend awaited my arrival.

I remember looking for the right entrance to use when a man in a full jean jacket and pants, with a long fuzzy white beard bushing out around his leather cap showed me the way. He was a VCBC member with the particularly grizzled appearance of an old biker but with a smile as gentle and pleasant as Santa Claus.

Upon arrival, I gave both of my parents a hug. They were nervous about the trial despite the confident attempts of their son to explain the complex arguments. My girlfriend was a strong pillar of support who graciously French braided my hair for the occasion. I told the news cameras that "a lot of people have been waiting a long time for this, this is a really important issue for a lot of seriously ill people." I wanted to keep my communications with the media simple and clear.

Voir Dire

Upon entering the courtroom, the detailed varnished woodwork and plush red velvet carpeting gave me a sense for the age and social status of the judicial system. It reminded me of a church or a royal court. The imposition of symmetrically spaced electric ceiling lights and the central console of clerk technology, gave the futuristic impression of *the Bridge* on a federation starship, from *Star Trek*.

The lawyers wore long black robes and white shirts with white ties. The prosecution was made up of two lawyers, QC Peter Eccles who was the lead prosecutor and K. Guest. Peter had a very confident, leonine and light-hearted demeanor at the beginning of the trial. I recall in his pre-trial court banter with Kirk that he likened his work to a crusade for the truth. He looked a bit like Elton John but with more facial hair.

Proceedings began with the general request of "all rise" for the honorable Justice Johnston. The judges appearance was one of relaxed focus behind his glasses and mustache. We began restating of the charges against me and my plea of "not guilty."

The Crown then asked the Court for an automatic publication ban. This would stop any news agencies from reporting on the case. We opposed the ban as we felt confident that if the public were to hear the details of the case, they would surely take our side on the matter. With the potential for a Jury trial at a later date, this would increase the chances of a well informed jury pool. The judge waived the publication ban as publication bans are put in place for the benefit of the defendant. Our desire to welcome reporters meant that such a ban would have no benefit.

At this point the judge asked all witnesses who were present in the room to leave until it became their time to give evidence. This is because hearing others testify could taint their testimony.

Trial Testimony

Over the next section of the book I will summarize the testimony of witnesses on both sides. The complete five volume deck of transcripts, that is the written record of everything that was said during the trial, is available online for anyone to access and listed at the end of this book.

Witnesses appeared in the following order:

Constable Colin Brewster - Victoria Police Department
Ted Smith - Victoria Cannabis Buyers Club Owner
Gayle Quin - Victoria Cannabis Buyers Club Employee
Dr. David Pate - Expert Scientific Testimony
Gina Herman - Victoria Cannabis Buyers Club Member
Sandra Carlson - Victoria Cannabis Buyers Club Member
Ruth Arthurs - Victoria Cannabis Buyers Club Member
Hanan Abromovici - Chief Science Officer, Health Canada
Eric Ormsby - Drug Approval Process Expert

Constable Colin Brewster

The first witness was called by the Crown. Constable Brewster from the Victoria Police Department (VPD) took the stand to verify and determine the value of the materials seized from the bakery. He had recorded a video walk through of the apartment and taken photographs on the day of the arrest.

He listed the exhibits one by one: lots of glass Adam's peanut butter jars, cookies, flat board game boxes, sandwich bags, empty egg cartons, an empty cap filling tray, caps, recipes, baking ingredients, a couple of cannabis posters, and my scissors, rollies and .8 of a gram of cannabis.

All of the cannabis samples had been sent for analysis and returned a month later having been positively identified with the cannabinoids: THC, CBD, CBN CBC and CBG.

The police officer had labeled our vegetable oil infusions as "Hash oil" which is a catch-all term for smokable cannabis oil with an approximate street value at the time of $20 per gram. After weighing the jars, the total estimated value was $800,000. Kirk's first job would be to show the court that these jars were not filled with "Hash oil" but vegetable oil infusions of various kinds and that none of them had a known street resale value.

The absence of flammable solvents in the apartment that would be necessary to make a concentrated, smokable cannabis Hash oil served as the first clue. The visible separation of oil and liquid in the jars through emulsification made it clear that the officer was mistaken.

A swing and a miss for the Crown's case.

Ted Smith

Having been on the stand a number of times before, Ted sat down with confidence and began to answer Kirk's questions in a free and open manner. Kirk began by asking Ted about the earliest days of the Victoria Cannabis Buyers Club.

While living in a van and hanging out at Sacred Herb, a hemp store in downtown Victoria, Ted met a woman named Leslie who volunteered in the AIDS community. She made cookies, brownies, and a salve out of cannabis and had great success helping people with HIV/AIDS. He also met Bonnie, a young woman who used cannabis and advocated for its medicinal uses. Bonnie inspired Ted to start the Victoria Cannabis Buyers Club (VCBC) but died before its inception.

It was in January 1996 that Ted started helping people with nothing more than a pager, a pamphlet, and a digital scale. He initially delivered cannabis himself, refusing to be paid except for the occasional joint and meal that would be shared with him. He ate from soup kitchens and food banks. In May 1996, he was invited to set up in the living room of a member, named Kathleen, who worked during the day, and was able to serve members until she got home.

Ted moved into an apartment on the top floor of a two-story red brick house in downtown Victoria, with cannabis cookies cooling on the window ledge. He provided medicinal cannabis products to people with permanent physical disabilities and diseases based on his understanding of the law.

The club's mandate was based on the *Morgentaler* decision, which struck down the abortion laws in Canada. Ted reasoned that if patients had the personal autonomy to have an abortion, then they should also be allowed to use cannabis. There was no legal precedent at the time that related to cannabis, so it was based on Ted's interpretation of the Canadian Charter of Rights and Freedoms.

In Nov. '96, Ted made a presentation to Victoria City Council, showing them a cannabis salve and informing those present of his plans to get a storefront.

(Ted speaks to the press)

In 1999, he gave away 101 cannabis cookies with the media and police watching, it was the first time the local press had been used to inform the public about eating cannabis for medical purposes.

The attention helped him grow the VCBC into a few hundred members, and Ted could now hire someone to help out. Serving only medical patients meant that Ted had a higher standard than most other weed dealers in town. He ensured that there was always clean burning herb available for those with compromised immune systems.

After being pressured by members who needed edibles, Ted started making the cookies himself with a couple of bags of leaf trimmings that were sitting around. Initially, his cookies were solid pucks that were packed full of ground leaf. They tasted powerfully like cannabis and gave the members equally powerful bowel movements. Some found this unacceptable, aggravating their conditions by bothering their stomachs. The new baker, Ted's friend Kathleen, began straining the leaf out of the butter with a cheesecloth, which greatly improved the overall quality of the cookies.

Membership at the club wouldn't pick up until around 2000 when Ted's activism with Hempology gained him media attention. He was arrested again, this time at the University of Victoria for sharing joints in the 420 Hempology circle and again a week later giving away 420 pot cookies at a rally downtown.

He was convicted of trafficking THC by a jury for the cookie giveaway and sentenced to 1 day in jail. He was given a $500 fine for trafficking joints at UVIC. His supporters organized a rally the next day where they easily raised the money to cover the fine.

Getting a Storefront

In 2001, a neighbor in the same building as Ted decided to set up his own operation selling cannabis, which led to a police raid. When Ted went downstairs to take out the trash, he was pulled aside by then Police Chief Darren Laur. The Victoria Police Department (VPD) had been staking out the place from across the street in the Revenue Canada building and had been watching Ted. They had tried to get a warrant from a judge to raid his apartment but could not because Ted required medical information from his clients.

Laur then suggested that Ted get a storefront due to the volume of traffic in and out of the building. So, on April Fool's Day 2001, he moved the club to 826 Johnson Street and opened Ted's Books. With no electricity, just two folding chairs, a coffee tray, and a candle, he began selling cannabis alongside some books, art, and pipes.

A year later, it was determined at a Victoria City Council business licensing hearing that the store could operate without the guise of being a bookstore since the police had recognized that they were turning a blind eye to its operations. The VCBC at this time existed as an unincorporated cooperative with Ted as the proprietor.

To become a member of the VCBC, a person need only obtain a medically authorized document confirming their condition and photo ID. Member sign up procedures took about 45 minutes and we always made extra time to answer questions. One of the main rules of the club was that patients' medicine was for personal use only, and any resale of the medicine would result in revoked membership.

Members were informed of the legal system and assisted in filing the forms to apply to the federal medical cannabis program, the Marihuana Medical Access Regulations (MMAR) to attain a legal license to grow and possess cannabis. Their membership card would not protect them from the police.

Raids and Court Cases

On January 3rd, 2002, Ted saw a member give his cannabis to another in plain sight which led to the member having his membership taken away. When the member made a scene about this, Ted called the police. Later that day police returned with the man who indicated to the officers that Ted had cannabis stashed throughout the space. The officer called in backup and a search and seizure took place.

Charges were sent a month later to Ted Smith and Colby Budda. Ted seized upon the opportunity to again use the media to inform the public about their activities.

Three more raids followed and four charges laid against staff. Half charges were later dropped due to a lack of evidence indicating that any of the staff had knowledge of or control over the club's operations.

In the 2004 *R v. Smith & Budda*, the first decision regarding the VCBC, BC Supreme Court Justice *Chaperon* concluded that "It is unsettling to contemplate persons with AIDS or who are undergoing cancer treatment being forced to go down to the illegal drug emporium ... from persons who are interested only in selling them drugs of unknown quality for a profit. But on January 3, 2002, but for compassion clubs such as Mr. Smith's, that was their only alternative."

In January 2005, Ted was involved in another trial resulting from police raids. This time the crown dropped the charges of trafficking cannabis and focused instead on convicting Ted of trafficking cannabis resin, using the food and skin products as evidence.

Before that trial in Jan. 2005, it had not occurred to him that cannabis extracts were not legally protected by the MMAR, and he had not prepared a defense to challenge the issue. Ted was convicted of trafficking cannabis resin by Justice Harvey, but given an absolute discharge, which meant he received no punishment.

Upset at the Harvey decision, his lawyer, and the regulations, Ted filed an appeal by himself. After reading his factum, the Department of Justice and Crown admitted that he was at least due a new trial, given some errors in law made by the Judge. Rather than proceed with a new trial, the Crown told the BC Court of Appeal to drop the entire matter.

When I was arrested in 2009, Ted saw that he had another chance to change the laws. When Kirk Tousaw moved to Vancouver Island in 2010 it took only speaking with Ted to keenly accept the case. Ted connected Kirk with Dr. David Pate who would be our expert witness and quickly found VCBC members willing to testify. Kirk and Ted made a powerhouse combination at meetings, firing off details of law that I will attempt to summarize in the following chapters.

Interviewed by a local newspaper after our promise to appear, Ted said,

"For us, this is now not only a legal campaign, but it is a health-care campaign that we get to go and highlight what we're doing and why and what the flaws in the law are. Because what this really boils down to is natural medicine against synthetics. They're trying to protect synthetic drugs and pharmaceutical companies with these laws, and it couldn't be more obvious than by making THC illegal in the plant form so they can sell Marinol." (Marinol is a synthetic-THC prescription pharmaceutical.)"

Ted, alongside other activists, has shown that legalization is not something that you ask for but something that you make happen by breaking the law in order to bring the problem before the legal authority.

Ted's Testimony

For the rest of his testimony Ted described the products that I was producing and the methods we used to produce them, including how to make the base oils. He introduced the product guide and recipe book. He explained how the prices of the products were always kept as low as possible and sometimes even subsidized by the cost of the dried cannabis. This encouraged patients who had previously only smoked cannabis to start eating it as well. I was being paid $12 per hour for my work.

Ted also shared the financial struggles they faced due to previous seizures and legal fees from previous raids, which led them to a current state of financial debt. He mentioned how growers would loan them cannabis to help pay off their debts.

Ted talked about my history and involvement at the club, and also spoke about my sister. He discussed the various activities of the Hempology 101 student club at UBC, VIU, and UVIC, including the annual conventions, lecture series, and textbook. He emphasized the importance of hemp and political activism, and the newspaper he published with my help, the Cannabis Digest.

Ted introduced into evidence the Proclamation made by the City of Victoria in 2002 for International Medical Marijuana Day.

He also introduced a letter from the former Victoria Mayor Alan Lowe to the Minister of Health Tony Clement, expressing his concerns about the legality of producing derivatives of cannabis.

THE CITY OF VICTORIA OFFICE OF THE MAYOR

March 20, 2006

The Honourable Tony Clement
Minister's Office – Health Canada
Brooke Claxton Building, Tunney's Pasture
Postal Locator: 0906C
Ottawa, ON K1A 0K9

Dear Minister:

On behalf of Victoria City Council, I am writing you regarding the issue of public access to cannabis for medicinal purposes. This issue most recently came to our attention when numerous citizens expressed their concerns to City Council.

Many of these citizens currently rely on marijuana for the purpose of pain management and have expressed an inability to access the Federal Marihuana Medical Access Regulation (MMAR) program.

The meeting highlighted the concerns of the adequacy and effectiveness of current Health Canada regulations governing distribution and access to this controlled substance.

While the previous Federal Government has endorsed in principle the efficacy of the medicinal properties of cannabis, adequate production and distribution channels do not appear to be in place. In the absence of this infrastructure, many Canadians will continue to suffer the debilitating effects of their illnesses without the benefit of effective pain management techniques.

Victoria City Council therefore respectfully requests an immediate review of current policies and regulations to determine where improvements can be made to ensure a better quality of life for those Canadians in need of medical assistance.

Sincerely,

Alan Lowe
MAYOR

c: The Honourable Vic Toews, Minister of Justice and Attorney General of Canada
Members of Council
Chief Paul Battershill, VPD
Ted Smith, Victoria Cannabis Buyers' Club
Linda Dabros, Director, Health Canada
Philippe Lucas, Vancouver Island Compassion Society and Vice-Chair, Downtown Advisory Committee

No. 1 Centennial Square Victoria British Columbia Canada V8W 1P6
Telephone (250) 361-0200 Fax (250) 361-0348 Email mayor@city.victoria.bc.ca

He then shared his correspondence with the new Minister of Health Ujjal Dosanjh's office, who made it clear that derivatives of cannabis were illegal. He argued that "making a plant legal but the crystals that form on the plant illegal defies logic."

However, Health Canada continued to claim that cannabis resin may pose a greater health risk than dry cannabis, without citing any study to support their assertion. Meanwhile, the College of Physicians was arguing that patients should not use cannabis because it is a smoked substance.

Health Canada's application forms for a medical cannabis license featured an answer box that applicants would check off if they consumed cannabis orally. In continued correspondence with Health Canada, Ted questioned how license holders could be arrested for producing cannabis resin or THC if they cooked with cannabis? The more the discussion progressed the more it became clear that Health Canada did not understand the cannabis plant.

Health Canada initially claimed that the intention of the regulations was never to allow individuals to make resins or hash oil because the process would take place before the plants were dried. However, Ted pointed out that almost all extracts, edibles, and oils were made with dried cannabis. After writing back twice to question this assertion, Ted received another letter that contradicted the previous one, stating that activities involving chemicals or other substances were outside of the law.

Ted eventually grew tired of the process as he was getting nowhere with the bureaucrats, who seemed to lack a basic understanding of the botany of the cannabis plant and its derivatives.

Cross Examination

On cross examination, the prosecutor Peter Eccles asked Ted how many members have federal licenses. While many of the members had obtained federal licenses, not all would be required to. Ted would grant access to any person with a permanent physical condition who could provide a signed doctor's diagnosis or in some cases a pill bottle or other documentation confirming it.

When asked about the source of the cannabis he provides, Ted assured him that he does everything he can to screen product from the club's growers including inspections and returning product that has any signs of mould. A mould spore could cause an infection in someone's lung.

Ted lived and worked in the Victoria Street community and volunteered with youth organizations. He was familiar with the health challenges that face this portion of the population. Being located in the center of downtown Victoria, the club was visited by some of the most unwell individuals in the area including those suffering from serious mental health conditions.

At times the Crown Prosecutors' questioning seemed to go nowhere as if he were just filling time and trying to sound informed.

He then tried to have all of Ted's testimony thrown out based on the premise that Ted was prone to give opinions that were not founded in fact.

Ted had made the assertion that all regulatory changes to the medical cannabis system were forced into effect by court rulings. The Crown pointed out that some minor changes, like the reorganization of the categories of access and changes to the number of doctors who were required to sign the forms, had come voluntarily. If Ted was being overbroad about this then perhaps he is confused about other matters he spoke to.

In response to the objection, the Judge used a botanical metaphor.

"If there is a trunk of relevance to the evidence I'm hearing, and the trunk of relevance has branches that are arguably relevant, when we come to why Health Canada may be amending its regulations from time to time, we're so far out into the leafy bits that I'm not sure why we're dealing with it."

Giving up on that line of reasoning, the Crown then introduced a binder of documents that comprised Health Canada's "Drug and Health Products; Information for Health Care Professionals." Which Ted had never seen before.

He was then asked to explain the club's finances. Most sales are dried cannabis. Price is around $7-10$ /gram. Purchases are limited to 1 oz per day. Purchasing is monitored. The store brings in about $6500 / day. 10% edibles. $5 minimum purchase. Keeps a profit margin of 20-25%. He would pay $2400-2600 per pound for the best cannabis. He doesn't pay GST/HST on sales however all the staff of the VCBC file personal income taxes.

The space in which the club exists is actually rented and insured as the Lacuna Book Exchange Society that Ted set up as a non-profit society. Lacuna is a term that refers to the unregulated, unprosecutable, unfilled space or gap that exists in a law, sometimes called the grey area.

Peter Eccles then asked if he could visit the club over the lunch hour to have a tour so he could look around and have some idea of what he's dealing with.

"I would be honoured," replied Ted.

This was a peculiar request; but given how smoothly the testimony seemed to go we were excited. We would have a chance to show the Crown Prosecutor through the club filled with members.

When we returned to the club at lunchtime we met Peter in the front lobby to begin the tour. At that moment one of the members who had been at the courthouse watching the trial approached the front desk.

"I've just been at the courthouse watching that pompous ass of a prosecutor."

She turned and he looked right at her with his eyebrows raised.

"Don't worry," she said, "I'm just about to get my attitude adjustment."

And smiling, she walked up to the distribution desk to buy herself some cannabis.

Peter Eccles was escorted by Ted and Kirk around the club ending up with his nose in a quarter pound bag of the nicest smelling cannabis you could imagine.

Returning to the courtroom, Eccles asked about the absence of clinical trials: Double blind, placebo controlled blue ribbon studies on cannabis. Research in Canada that sought to find benefits from cannabis for people with HIV/AIDS that was launched by a Liberal government had been canceled by the Harper Conservatives.

Ted and Gayle developed the products based on feedback from members. If somebody was requesting cannabis edibles without sugar or gluten, or looking for an eye-patch or a suppository, they would make it for them creating an array of cannabis products to meet each patient's requirements.

Ted would not accept membership cards from other dispensaries and jurisdictions in legal medical states because the mandates and requirements for entry differed greatly and kept changing.

During the First week of the trial, the local newspaper, the Times Colonist wrote a series of articles titled "Court urged to snuff out medical pot access"; "Mayor's letter to minister becomes evidence in pot trial"; "Nothing unique about dried pot, Court told"; "Trust a key ingredient of cannabis cookies"; "Cannabis cookies and lozenges ease my chronic pain, woman tells court".

These can be found on the Digital Timeline that accompanies this book with all relevant writings, media articles, videos and events laid out in chronological order.

PATIENT WITNESSES

The Patient witnesses Gayle Quin, Sandra Large, Gina Herman and Ruth Arthurs all volunteered to share their story with the court with complete awareness that they would be admitting to committing a crime. In Canada, you can avoid answering questions that might incriminate you but if you willingly incriminate yourself by telling the truth then you may face consequences. The risk that these women accepted is why I think they are the heroes of the story.

Gayle Quin, Medicine Woman

I owe my introduction to preparing cannabis medicines to Gayle Quin. Years before I began my work as a cannabis baker at the dispensary, I met Gayle at a series of Hempology 101 student club meetings at my college. Over the course of a decade, Gayle assisted the VCBC in expanding their edible and topical cannabis product line. Most of the recipes at the end of this book originate with Gayle Quin.

When she was preparing to testify, she had breast cancer that was aggressively spreading through her body. She had a mastectomy and had become frail. She was using high doses of cannabis oil, as well as other treatment regimes. We honestly did not know if she would live to take the stand. Even the female POC court police officer broke down in tears during her testimony.

I have paraphrased and summarized her story from her testimony.

When Gayle was born her mother was very ill and had to be kept on a specialized diet. She lost her twin at birth. She had her first operation at three months old to remove a growth on her abdomen that left her with scarring. She had chickenpox twice and all three kinds of measles. She suffered from frequent lung infections and colds.

At 13 years old her major health issues started to appear. Her first menstrual period brought her three days of hemorrhaging. The cramps were so bad that she could not stop crying or get out of bed and was unable to attend school. It was at this age that she first discovered cannabis through the help of her sister. Cannabis relieved her cramping to the point where she could stand up, walk, eat, function and sleep at night.

Gayle's first cannabis Garden was in 1974 when she was 13. When her mother found the plants, she threw them out because they're illegal. This confused Gayle because they were so helpful for her and having attended church regularly she believed that God had given us all the seeds and plants of the earth to use for food and medicine. So she just grew them further away from her mothers house, atop of a nearby hill.

At 16 Gayle was in a car accident that caused her lasting knee pain. Cannabis helped keep her life on track despite her injuries and severe, irregular menstrual periods. At age 17 she got married and at 18 became pregnant with her first son followed by another at 20. Her doctors started giving her a regular pap smear until at age 23 when she underwent a biopsy to remove the pre-cancerous cone in her uterus.

This helped temporarily but soon she began having chronic infections in her abdomen. She was diagnosed as having pelvic inflammatory disease and was put on antibiotics that despite a consistent increase in strength were ineffective. Between the infections and menstrual pains she was unable to properly look after her children and so requested a hysterectomy at age 24.

Her doctor, believing that her uterus had prolapsed, simply stitched her up and removed her appendix. She suffered for another year with the same symptoms using cannabis for pain relief until her doctor agreed to another operation and this time to perform the hysterectomy.

Gayle was always open about her cannabis use with her doctor. When asked if she smoked she told them that she won't smoke tobacco but she does smoke cannabis. He told her that if it helps then carry on.

After the surgery her menstrual cramps stopped and she started to feel healthy enough to go to school and get a job. She became certified as a long-term care aide at Camosun college and worked for two years in Victoria and six on Salt Spring Island.

While working at the hospital she started getting rashes on her skin. She then began developing chronic ear infections and was put back on antibiotics but the pain kept getting worse and so she was then put on morphine. The morphine made her foggy headed, masking her pain but not taking it away. She found herself unable to functionally care for others at work.

Gayle moved onto a herb farm and began to treat her ear infection with herbal oil drops combining mullein, St. John's wort and yarrow in olive oil. While her ears improved, her lungs began to deteriorate with regular infections. Her problems didn't end there: she would get asthma-like symptoms from smoggy air, the smell of certain foods started to trigger nausea and vomiting and was frequently fatigued.

Cannabis took the pain and the swelling out of her liver and helped her sleep, which gave her enough energy to go to work the next day. But Gayle's health challenges came in groups. She was diagnosed with mercury poisoning, chronic fatigue syndrome and fibromyalgia. When she was then diagnosed with Hepatitis C, doctors prognosis was grim, cirrhosis of the liver and death within 5 years.

Gayle was only 33 and her sons were teenagers. She was determined to fight for her life. She began taking a number of herbs, large amounts of vitamin C, and eating cannabis every day. She ate milk thistle regularly and made dandelion tea out of its roots and leaves. She returned to her doctor each month to check in and keep track of her progress.

Treatment options for her hepatitis C were unsuitable because of her sensitivity to chemicals. She couldn't use aspirin or regular toilet paper. She's allergic to bleach and other household cleaning products. Her fibromyalgia makes wearing clothes difficult, and even the pressure of a little bit of elastic makes her unable to wear a bra.

The mercury poisoning made her feel like she was chewing on tinfoil and it interrupted her ability to read and study herbs by affecting her memory. The government told her that it was a dental problem and didn't qualify for coverage so she paid to travel back and forth to see a specialist for treatments. Over time her mercury poisoning symptoms disappeared.

At first she couldn't walk and lived in her living room for six months in her pajamas. While confined to her home she developed her knowledge of herbs, kinesiology, acupressure, reflexology and massage. Eventually she began feeling a lot better and after 2 years her doctor concurred. Her liver swelling had reduced and she had started eating and sleeping regularly. Several years later she tested negative for Hepatitis C.

While her health was improving, her marriage was deteriorating as her husband had become extremely violent, causing Gayle to fear for her life. She moved to Victoria and was homeless, staying with friends when she could. She then learned her father was dying of cancer and moved to stay with her parents and help them cope.

The Ministry cut her off of her disability because she was partial owner of a property on Salt Spring Island. They wanted her to go home despite the imminent threat of physical abuse. Her husband would not leave and refused to get a divorce. She eventually got a court order to divorce him and divide the property.

She then noticed a lump in her breast. Having moved to Victoria she would have to find a new doctor. At the walk-in clinic she was asked if she smoked. Just as before she told her doctor "I don't smoke tobacco, but I do smoke cannabis."

"We can't help people like you," the doctor said, who then asked Gayle to leave her office. Gayle became depressed after this encounter and it took her a year to build up the courage to see another doctor. Her next doctor refused to follow up with her, claiming that her medical records had been lost. This setback was also depressing for Gayle.

While in Victoria she heard about the VCBC and the raids and court challenges that were reported in the news. She sought them out and became a member, offering to help as a volunteer by cleaning and making hand drawn posters.

She began working with the VCBC by greeting and processing members at the front desk. Gayle had spent time as a long term care aide and was practiced in working with the elderly including those suffering from dementia or Alzheimer's.

She started bringing her knowledge of herbalism to the club's edible products. She added lecithin as a fat emulsifier to help our bodies absorb cannabis better. She spoke with every member that she could, taking their feedback and developing new products that combined cannabis with other beneficial herbs.

Gayle insisted that all of the ingredients used in the club's medicinal products be sourced organically and locally where possible. She replaced the white flour with a healthier whole wheat blend. She started making Ghee, for healthier cannabis cookies, which involves clarifying butter of moisture and non-fat milk solids.

"A member comes to me one day and says, 'I really want to cut down on my smoking.'

And I say, 'Well, have you tried eating the Ryanols?' They're little capsules, a very minute dose of leaf suspended in olive oil. And I say, 'If you eat two of those in the morning and two more later in the day, experiment a little bit, most people cut their smoking in half.'

And three days later he came back, and he was just bubbly with me, and he said, 'I can't -- I can't believe that you were so right!'

He said, 'In three days I've cut my smoking in half. just by eating the Ryanols.'"

She also started to host the Hempology circles at Camosun college and UVIC on wednesdays. Ted had been banned from campus for a short time after an undercover police officer had nabbed him at UVIC for handing out roach joints.

It was during this time that I met Gayle, who spoke with ferocious calm from the center of the circle. I expressed to her my interest in learning about cannabis baking. A friend of mine who sold cannabis also wanted to learn how to make cookies so I invited her to my apartment and she taught us both how to infuse cannabis into butter with a double boiler, colander and cheesecloth.

On her third attempt to find a doctor, this time on a recommendation from a member of the VCBC, Gayle found an MD who respected cannabis. Unfortunately this doctor was not a qualified surgeon and could not help Gayle address the concerns over the lump in her breast.

This was difficult again for Gayle and the symptoms of her mercury poisoning had begun to return. She went to see a Naturopath who wrote a request for Gayle to get a mammogram. A doctor's examination confirmed the need for the mammogram which three days later revealed that she had cancerous lumps in her breast and lymph nodes. A surgeon performed a right mastectomy removing 17 cancerous lymph nodes in the summer of 2011.

This was 9 months before the start of our Voir Dire and we didn't know if she was going to live long enough to tell her story to the Judge. She began taking Vitamin C injections on the advice of her Naturopath, Dr. Neil McKinney.

She continued to eat cannabis every day, noticing that if she missed her edible cannabis dose her health would quickly deteriorate. For the bruising in her knees she applied cannabis and Saint John's wort infused olive oil twice a day. She consumed an olive oil infusion to help with her pain, reduce swelling and increase sleep. She smoked whenever she needed instant relief.

Some time after becoming a member of the VCBC, one fateful Halloween, Gayle and Ted became romantically partnered. They were quite the pair. Ted would come into the VCBC on all fours dressed up in a dog costume with a collar and Gayle would don an elaborate dominatrix outfit to walk him about. Her favorite dress up character was Wonderbud, a cannabis superhero she had created. Her cackle was something out of a Grimm's fairy tale and

(Ted and Gayle)

the perfect pitch to match Ted's booming guffaws.

Cross Examination

During her cross examination the Crown took issue with claims made in the recipe book and info pamphlets. Gayle was not qualified to give medical advice. The Crown sought to point that out by highlighting sections of the recipe book.

"Cannabis can be used to replace almost any type of allopathic medicine, from diuretics to antidepressants - ear oil; throat and salves that reduce tumors."

"Extracts have been found to be effective on everything from bacteria and fungi, to the herpes virus and staphylococcus."

And in the product guide where there is a list of conditions indicated to be helped by cannabis.

"AIDS, HIV, wasting conditions, affected immune systems, and cancer are all greatly benefited by ingesting cannabis. It is a smooth-muscle relaxant, stops nausea, stimulates the appetite, eases hot flashes and enables one to eat, and maintain their normal body weight."

He asked her if the VCBC screens for pregnancy or schizophrenia. They did not. The club's mandate to serve those with permanent physical conditions or diseases was the standard response.

Soon after she testified in the BC Supreme Court in 2012, the cancer returned and spread to her bones. Her condition deteriorated, finding her in hospital; but the last time I saw her I remember her dancing in her bed: the cheerful, good humoured woman who taught me how to infuse cannabis into oils and make an assortment of medicinal products.

(Gayle Quin relaxing in her bed at home)

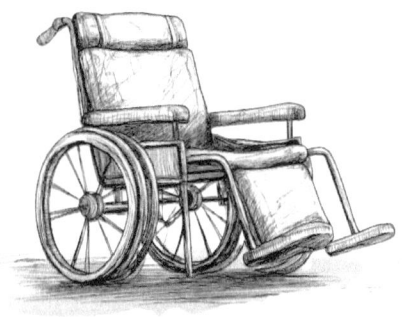

Sandra Large

Sandra is a wonderful, gentle, soft spoken woman who always cheers me up whenever I see her. She is in a wheelchair as a result of a severe motorcycle accident in 1975. Sandra suffered compression fractures and other physical trauma to the left side of her body, resulting in chronic pain, chronic headaches, and digestive problems. She still experiences these symptoms on a regular basis, and they have gotten worse over time.

On the witness stand, she recalls the accident, "A station wagon came on our side of the road, so it was either veer off into the gully and miss them or have them come dead-on into our front. Because we chose the gully, on the other side of the gully was a little bit of a lip, so when we went down into the gully I flew off the back of the motorcycle just like this and I remember watching the tops of trees come at me. I came to for a split second to see my left foot had gone around my neck and was facing backwards right here in front of me. And somehow my left arm got in there, so my shoulder's gone and so is the hip and so is the knee now. That is the result of that accident."

She explained that the accident caused her to be contorted like a pretzel, resulting in lower intestine issues that led to irritable bowel syndrome (IBS). IBS causes her pain and difficulty when digesting food, and she has been recommended a high-fiber diet. She also suffered a stroke in November 1995, which caused her to pass out and hit her face on a chair. Her blood pressure during the stroke was measured at a dangerous 210 over 108.

The stroke left her with a dropped left side, difficulty with stairs, and short term memory loss. She also suffers from migraine headaches, which start at the back of the head and cause nausea, vision issues, and pain. Additionally, she has osteoarthritis, osteoporosis, rheumatoid arthritis, and fibromyalgia, all of which cause chronic pain and stiffness. She notes that her conditions worsened after the stroke in 1995.

She suffers with sensitivity to light and wears dark glasses. Exposure to heat can trigger her seizures and heart issues. She suffers grand mal seizures and takes medication to abate them. She tried morphine for pain relief, but found it made her dozy and unable to focus.

Her understanding is that her condition will worsen over time, leading to decreased mobility in her shoulders and hips. When asked about her knee surgery, Sandra explains that the motorcycle accident caused significant damage to her cartilage, ligaments, and tendons, resulting in a 75% loss of feeling in one side of her leg.

Sandra also details her history of cancer surgeries, including a particularly invasive one that required her to be opened from armpit to armpit to remove a malignant tumor. She underwent surgeries in 1996, 1997, and 1998, followed by six weeks of chemotherapy, which led to hair thinning and stomach issues.

It was at this point that I lost control of my face and the memory of my sister's suffering joined with Sandra's story and I crumpled in my seat and cried.

She began to take opiates for intestinal pain but they eventually lost their efficacy.

She currently experiences drowsiness from Elavil and suffers from short-term memory loss and muscle spasms due to Mylan-Carbamazepine. Smoked cannabis and the edible product "Ryanol" help her manage the muscle spasms. Sandra also takes CO Citalopram, an antidepressant and uses Arthrotec for her osteoporosis.

She has now been a member of the VCBC for at least five years.

KIRK: Did you use edible products and lozenges when you first joined the Club, or was it mostly dried cannabis?

SANDRA: Mostly dried cannabis at first, but I was introduced to cookies by another member and found them very effective.

KIRK: What relief do the cookies and lozenges provide you?

SANDRA: They almost completely take away my fibromyalgia, reduce headaches, and eliminate the need for neck shots. They also numb the brain and alleviate a lot of pain.

KIRK: Has the use of cannabis products increased your quality of life?

SANDRA: Yes, it has allowed me to be more social and reduces my pain, which was previously debilitating for 11 years.

Kirk asked Sandra about her use of the product called Ryanol.

She takes eight capsules within a 24-hour period. This is the minimum amount she needs to achieve relief. She's never had delusions, hallucinations, or anxiety attacks, only relief. She doesn't feel a high or any sort of 'buzz' from Ryanol or cookies. They alleviate her pain and digestive issues. She doesn't feel high from smoking or vaping either but finds inhaling "Indica" varieties work best.

She doesn't like the taste of all the edibles but she doesn't make her own as she doesn't have access to the space, ingredients and equipment that she would need. Before she first visited the VCBC, she bought cannabis from the street. She was relieved that the VCBC offers a cleaner, more reliable product. No more rolling the dice with every purchase, she had accountability.

She uses a "Cannapatch", which is a cannabis leaf poultice for headaches.

"Ever find products like Ryanol from street suppliers?" Kirk asks.

"Never," Sandra replies.

"Any negative consequences?" Kirk asks.

"None."

Club employee Gayle Quin suggested she start taking lozenges for her diverticulitis, which Sandra believes helped her sidestep surgery.

She doesn't have a Health Canada license to possess medical cannabis. She spoke with both of her doctors. Both refused her. She is aware of the designated grower program but does not know anyone who could produce it for her.

She takes "Eight Ryanol capsules a day, a cookie every morning, and a mix of cookies, Ryanol, Stalkinol, and occasional smoking for the rest of the day, amounting to a half-ounce to three-quarters of an ounce every two to three weeks."

She can't always smoke cannabis due to high blood pressure causing what she describes as "electrical explosions" in her armpits. As a result, she's shifted to edibles. She also uses lozenges for throat infections and sore throats and uses the Cannapatch about once a month for headaches.

Cross Examination

Ms. Guest, the second Prosecutor, began the questioning.

"Ms. Large," Ms. Guest began, her voice steady but piercing, "you use a variety of cannabis products, correct?"

Sandra nodded, her voice slightly shaky. "Yes, that's correct. I use lozenges, cookies, dried marijuana, Ryanol capsules, and a Cannapatch."

"Quite a regimen," Ms. Guest remarked, flipping through her notes. "You even have a morning routine with these products, don't you?"

"Yes," Sandra confirmed. "I eat one cookie every morning. It helps me start my day."

Ms. Guest leaned on the podium, her eyes narrowing. "But do you know what's in that cookie?"

"No, I don't."

"And what about the THC levels in those cookies or the lozenges you consume?"

"I don't know."

"Let's talk about Ryanol capsules. They contain THC and grape seed extract oil, correct?"

SANDRA: "Yes, they do."

"But do you know the amount of THC in each capsule?" Ms. Guest pressed.

"No, I don't."

"And the Cannapatch?" Ms. Guest's voice was almost a whisper, but it carried throughout the courtroom. "Do you know its ingredients?"

SANDRA: "No, I only know that it works for me."

"So, you're essentially experimenting with these products, aren't you?"

SANDRA: "Yes, I rely on advice from VCBC staff and other members."

"Has this second-hand knowledge ever led you to change your self-medicating rituals?"

"Yes," Sandra said, "the staff at VCBC have been very helpful. I trust them, especially a staff member named Gayle."

"Would you consider changing your current regimen if Gayle suggested it and provided a valid reason?" Ms. Guest probed.

"I might," Sandra conceded.

Ms. Guest then shifted her focus. "You've made friends with Gayle and Ted, staff members at the VCBC, correct?"

"Yes," Sandra confirmed.

"Do you trust these staff members to make decisions about your health? Are you appreciative of the help you've received?"

Sandra nodded.

"And how much money do you spend at the VCBC each month?"

"I don't know," Sandra admitted.

The prosecutor leaned in. "Let's talk about your orientation at the Victoria Cannabis Buyers Club. It was conducted by a staff member named Spud, correct?"

"Yes," Sandra confirmed, "it lasted almost an hour. We discussed the benefits of different products."

"And does Spud have any medical training or qualifications?"

"No," Sandra admitted.

Ms. Guest brought up Jim, another staff member at the VCBC. "Jim was informed about your medical history through a doctor's form, but did he ask about your heart, liver, or kidney conditions?"

"No."

"And mental health? Depression?" Ms. Guest continued her line of questioning.

"He was informed, but he didn't probe further."

"Did he warn you about mixing cannabis with alcohol?" Ms. Guest pressed on.

"Yes, he did," Sandra confirmed.

"Interesting. Let's pivot to the risks of cannabis. You were warned about addiction and memory impairment, correct?"

"Yes, by Spud, another staff member," Sandra acknowledged.

"Do you smoke marijuana?" Ms. Guest's question seemed to hang in the air, heavy with implication.

"Every two to three days," Sandra replied.

"And did the VCBC discuss the risks of smoking, especially given your asthma?"

Sandra hesitated, then corrected herself. "No, they did not."

GINA HERMAN

Gina is the epitome of sweet, kind and gentle. She is a woman who almost laughs when she speaks to you, as if the joy in her heart wants to burst through every word. But Gina is also very stubborn and while she would giggle innocently at this fact, her stubbornness can extend from her eyes like laser beams, ready to burn a hole in injustice.

Gina is from London Ontario. She had spent every summer in British Columbia since she was a little girl and moved there when she was 16 with her brother and sister-in-law.

On the witness stand, Gina Describes the incident from when she was working full-time at a warehouse. She was in the packing department, checking boxes on a platform. She slipped, hitting herself on the steel line. Over time her pain resulting from the accident worsened, despite physiotherapy. She was married with two sons at the time of the accident.

She eventually found a doctor, who prescribed narcotics and prescription drugs, causing her to miss eight years of her family's life.

Her memory is not very good due to medications. She describes severe constant pain, with flare-ups that feel like electric shocks. Prolonged sitting and physical activities made her pain worse.

She handed in her driver's license when she was put on heavy narcotic drugs due to her injury. She is unable to drive or be a passenger in a car for anything other than short distances due to the pain medication. She undertook various treatments including an MRI during that time period. The doctors at St. Joseph Hospital pain clinic prescribed pain medication and other medications that she did not find helpful.

She was taking Oxycontin twice daily in the amount of 40 milligrams and Percocet in varying amounts. Gina's prescribed dose of Oxycontin rose over time from 40 to 240 milligrams to treat her chronic pain. Other medications include: Emtec-30 for pain, Nexium to settle the burning feeling in her stomach, Amitriptyline, Toradol, Ibuprofen, Naproxen, Celexa and Effexor, an antidepressant.

Gina explains that Nexium was for a disorder in her stomach, Amitriptyline was possibly to keep her calm, Toradol worked in injection form but not in pill form, Ibuprofen and Naproxen were used for swelling and arthritis but were not helpful, and Celexa was a depression medication. She confirms that her memory of the medications is not perfect as she was taking a lot of different drugs at the time.

He then asks if she knows the chemical composition of the drugs, which she doesn't, a sly look thrown at the Crown bench.

She experienced a number of unwanted side effects, including being medically drugged and having difficulty getting out of bed, which caused her to use a cane and bathroom aids. She explains that the drugs destroyed her and her relationship with her husband and two children, and she was no longer able to be an active and involved mother. To this day, she still feels guilty for not being able to be there mentally and emotionally for her children.

Gina explains that her move to Victoria was due to her husband getting a job there and her father already living in the area. Her husband found her a new physician, Dr. Sayad, to help wean her off her medication. She started treatments with Dr. Sayad in July 2006 and he continues to be her physician. An MRI exam in May 2009, showed that her condition had not improved. She wanted to wean off the painkillers as she had no quality of life and was unable to socialize or spend time with her children.

She joined the VCBC in 2009 as she was weaning off her medication. She had not previously used cannabis for medical purposes. She had a note from her doctor stating that cannabis would benefit her chronic pain, deteriorating disc disease, deteriorating sciatica, and arthritis. She has had chronic pain since being injured in 2002.

She needed to get off narcotic drugs and relied on products from the VCBC, including cookies, massage oils, and gel capsules. She obtained marijuana from the street prior to joining the VCBC in 2009 and did not have experience using edible or topical cannabis products before joining the club. She learned about edibles and their benefits during their first meeting at the club and currently uses them every day.

She also uses topical oils, which she applies to various parts of her body to help deal with pain. She has not experienced any negative side effects or allergic reactions from using cannabis. Due to the VCBC's mandate, her physician is aware of her use of cannabis products but did not have to prescribe them.

Gina explains:

"I just can't say enough good things about medical marihuana. I am able to get out now. I'm able to see my granddaughter. I am rebuilding my relationship with my youngest son as he was the hardest affected when all this started building up. And if I would have continued to be on the Oxycontin and the other prescription I was on, I truly believe I wouldn't be here today alive because they just kept putting me up and up and up on all these prescriptions."

"I didn't know whether I was here or there. I have my husband and I will never have the same relationship that we had before I got injured and on all them ridiculous narcotics that they put me on. My oldest son has not seen me yet off the narcotics. I talked to him last night on the phone and I have been telling him about this case and how strongly I feel about it and the reason why I feel so strongly about it, Your Lord, is I have a life now."

"You know, I am in pain every day. Some days I don't go out because of the pain, but the majority of the time I can get out for a couple of hours. I go for a morning walk every morning and then I go to see my granddaughter and have a little play with her. She's almost one. I can come downtown and enjoy —enjoy the inner harbour now."

"I felt bad because when I was so totally drugged up on prescription drugs people actually thought that I was a crack addict and I have never done anything like that before and it made me feel so bad that people -- that these prescription drugs -- and I grew up in a household where, my mom would say, you know, listen to the doctor. The doctor knows best."

"And it's very hard, it's still a very hard journey for me, but with a lot of very knowledgeable people within the VCBC and within the medical marihuana community I'm learning more and more each day. I'm always surprised at how much I am learning each day about medical marihuana."

"And for me, I'm living proof that I had pretty much lost everything due to heavy prescription drugs. I'll never have the same relationship I had with my husband. I'm trying to rebuild that with Thomas, my younger boy. And my older boy, he just roots for me every day and he says to me on the phone, long distance,

"Mom, I know I haven't seen you yet, but talking to you is so wonderful."

"You know, I can now talk to my six-year-old granddaughter in London, Ontario because I'm not starting a sentence and ending it way out in left field, where I didn't even know what I was talking about."

She described her withdrawal symptoms during the process of weaning off prescription narcotics, "Shaking, sick to my stomach, headaches, feeling like there were bugs crawling in my skin. I called it the heebie-jeebies. However, once I got into the VCBC and started eating the cookies … I seemed to be able to handle it as long as I had the cookie in me."

She explained her daily routine of making a pot of cannabis tea.

At this point the Judge stopped the questioning to ask counsel directly about her tea. If the cannabis tea bag is placed into the tea pot, the tea is legal, but once the tea is poured, what Gina now holds in her cup is illegal.

The Crown responded that once the leaf material is removed from the liquid, it would become impossible for an inspecting officer to verify that Gina was within her allowable possession limit.

The Judge did not look impressed.

From our perspective, this illustrated how the governments' concern over controlling cannabis patient consumption was over-riding patient rights to consume that medicine.

Gina expressed grattitude for the support and knowledge provided by the VCBC and its employees in helping her transition off prescription medication and obtain a federal medical marijuana license.

Gina had a designated producer who provided her with dried cannabis, but not edible and topical forms. She tried making her own topical massage oil using grapeseed oil in a crockpot, and the methods found in the VCBC recipe book.

She received no guidance from health Canada; she experienced no delusions or hallucinations from Cannabis. When asked if she'd experienced delusions or hallucinations from pharmaceutical products, she answered,

"Yes, I have. Quite frequently my husband and sons reported that if I was up and about I would start into a conversation and then not even within 30 seconds into the conversation, I would be somewhere else and they had no idea half of the time what I was talking about."

"Sometimes I would just be sitting there by myself and one of the boys would come in from school and I would have been talking to nobody but carrying on a conversation, by myself I guess."

Cross Examination

The Crown Prosecutor, this time, Peter Eccles questioned Gina about the difficulty she faced in relating to her family due to her chronic pain, and she confirmed that her youngest son even went to see her psychologist to understand why his mommy wasn't her old self.

"I would say 99 percent of the time, I have a good outlook on life. I'm glad that I wake up every day and that I can actually have a conversation with my husband, with my children, and with my neighbors. I couldn't do that before I got off the narcotics."

"After I got hurt, all of a sudden my whole life was shattering. I went from being a working mom, you know, going with the kids as I said yesterday, we were a very active family, basketball, baseball, going to soccer games, swimming. Camping was a big thing that we enjoyed with our boys and all of a sudden everything stopped dead. So, yes, I -- I will say I was very depressed. I'm sure if that was anybody else I think they would be pretty depressed too. All of a sudden your -- your life has stopped as you know it, as your children know their mom, as your husband knew his wife."

Gina goes on to discuss the soul-wearying effect of chronic pain and the stigma around it. She has had to learn to understand how most people who have not experienced chronic pain have difficulty accepting that people can need to use cannabis for relief throughout the day.

She believes that having a support system of family, friends, and psychologists is important, but acknowledges that it can be challenging to maintain optimism when so heavily medicated on pharmaceuticals. Her doctor, Dr. Sayad was a significant support for her, and requested that she bring products from the VCBC to him for his approval.

She still receives support from the staff at the VCBC as well as members who have similar problems with chronic pain syndrome. She knows that at the VCBC there is always someone there to assist them. She also uses a 'Vapor Daddy' device at home that she learned about through the VCBC. Gina tends to use more of it in the form of baked goods, topicals and teas. She smokes or vapes occasionally in the morning to alleviate pain quickly.

She now sleeps better at night. The only side effect she has experienced from cannabis is gaining weight from eating too much.

Ruth Arthurs

Ruth was the youngest of the patient witnesses, around the same age as me, a lovely, redheaded woman with bright eyes and a brave heart. Ruth and I are connected through social media and I recall the morning before her testimony, sending her the YouTube video link for the song "Strong" by Propatingz feat. John Jammin. If you listen to that song, you'll get a sense for the emotion that was passing through me during this part of the trial. Hint: it's dubstep.

Ruth is 32 and has two children aged six and ten. She was working as a youth counselor in Alberta and working on her social work diploma at Vancouver Island University, when she was in a motor-vehicle accident. It resulted in injuries to her neck, spine, and arm. She started experiencing dizziness, headaches, neck and back pain, and chronic pain after the accident. She describes her pain level at around nine on a scale and has affected her life significantly, including her ability to leave the house. She has had to get emergency babysitters because of it.

She has been in continuous treatment with prescription painkillers and various therapies which have been ineffective and sometimes cause negative side effects. She tried occupational therapy, psychology, head injury rehabilitation, speech therapy, and life skills, but continued to experience slow thinking, difficulty with sleep, pain and emotional distress.

Ruth had previously been a member of Dana Larsen's Vancouver Dispensary Society prior to joining the VCBC. Like all other members she sat through an intake interview which was thorough and lasted about 45 minutes. She was provided with a description of the products and warned about when to use them. She purchased dried cannabis for inhalation, as well as small gel capsules filled with oil, called Ryanols, which provide relief for her symptoms, including dizziness, nausea, and spinal pain. She finds the products to be convenient and effective in managing their pain, allowing her to function and participate in daily activities without ill health side effects.

Ruth carries Ryanols with her in a pill bottle, just like any other medication. She has never had negative side effects from them. She describes her experience with pharmaceuticals causing stomach pain and getting "whacked out" which became unbearable to continue. Her doctor supported her in obtaining membership to the VCBC, by simply providing proof of a verified medical condition. She has an application for a Health Canada license in process but is delayed, waiting for the authorization. She continues to experience the physical symptoms every day.

She also used topical products and oils sold by the VCBC, including a Cannapatch and does not experience a psychoactive effect or high from their use. She occasionally smokes cannabis to manage her pain and does not experience euphoric effects.

Cross Examination

The Crown Prosecutor inquired if Ruth had been informed about the addictive qualities of cannabis by the staff of the VCBC. Ruth does not believe cannabis to be physically addictive. She admits to smoking cigarettes, and occasionally having a bottle of wine and believes that cannabis causes psychologically dependency more like video games or fast food.

She understands that the VCBC monitors purchases to ensure that people are not abusing the system.

She consumes the club's cookies and Buddha Balls daily, with about five Ryanols per day to manage her pain.

She also mentions being hesitant to discuss her condition with others but found that many people in group therapies were medicating similarly.

Dr. David Pate

Our next witness would provide the basis for the scientific reasoning of our arguments. We would need to do some heavy lifting to explain to the Judge how cannabis works. Fortunately we had a good connection. One of the world's pioneering cannabis scientists was already familiar to Ted from a previous court case. Canadian doctor David Pate would fly up to join us from California.

Dr. Pate breaks all of his points down into simple terms for us to understand. I have paraphrased much of what Dr. Pate submitted to the court using the recorded transcripts but left some quotes verbatim to emphasize the nuances of Dr. Pate's understanding.

Expertise

Dr. David Walter Pate was qualified by reason of education, training and experience as an expert witness in the medicinal aspects of phytocannabinoids, (cannabinoids produced by the cannabis plant) and endocannabinoids (cannabinoids produced in the human body), as well as the pharmaceutical chemistry of these compounds. He was also qualified as an expert in the botany of cannabis.

Endocannabinoid System

Dr. Pate developed topical compounds for the eye based on the molecular structure of anandamide. Anandamide is an endocannabinoid that is structurally similar to the well known phytocannabinoid THC.

One way to imagine cannabinoids is as keys made to fit specific locks. Anandamide and THC are both keys that have been cut to open the same lock in your body. The locks are called cannabinoid receptor sites. There are more cannabinoid pathways being discovered, but the primary ones are called CB1 and CB2.

The receptor site's primary function is to regulate the sensitivity of the firing of the electricity across the nerve cell. As nerve cells fire, they send electrical information across the space between nerves known as the synaptic cleft. It's here that the cannabinoid receptors play a unique role. While most signals travel from A to B, cannabinoids will send signals from B to A, providing feedback between the two nerve cells.

As a class of compounds, cannabinoids have only recently begun to be understood. Dr. Pate believes that with enough study, cannabinoids could be as important a class of drug compounds as opioids. It is the most widely distributed type of receptor to exist in the human body located in the central nervous system and throughout the immune system. Dr. Pate found that synthetic copies or analogs of anandamide relieved pressure in the eyes in a similar way to THC.

THC and CBD had received some scientific scrutiny in the 1930's from UK based Lord Alexander Todd and United States chemist Roger Adam. It wasn't until 1964 when Jerusalem based researcher Raphael Mechoulam and his colleagues synthesized THC. Other breakthroughs such as the discovery of the receptor sites didn't happen until the 1990's.

One important difference between cannabinoid receptors and opiate receptors is that there isn't an accumulation of cannabinoid receptors in the lungs. Due to the opiate receptor sites in the lungs, too much of an opiate drug causes the lungs to stop working and leads to death. This difference is one reason why cannabinoids are relatively safe at very high doses and why there are no recorded cases of a fatal cannabis overdose.

HISTORY OF USE

Cannabis has a long history of use as a medicine and fiber crop in Asia going back thousands of years. Extracts of cannabis were part of the US pharmacopeia until the plant was made illegal early in the 20th century. The campaign to demonize cannabis was partially achieved through dominant use of the word marijuana. Doctors who were familiar with cannabis extracts were unaware that the word marijuana referred to the same plant.

After its medicinal use became widely outlawed, cannabis entered a few decades of obscurity. It was only the explosion in popular use during the 1960's that brought cannabis back out of the darkness.

BOTANICAL DETAILS

Dr. Pate's Masters Degree looked at what roles the compounds produced by the cannabis plant play during the life of the plant, independent of human interest. Cannabis produces trichomes: small resinous glands and microscopic thorns. These trichome structures are spread across the surface of the plant like hair. They are tough enough to stop larger insects from chewing through them and for smaller insects they become like sticky flypaper, entrapping them and stopping them from feeding on the plant.

Kirk presented some Macro photographs provided by Marcus "bubbleman" Richardson. The details of extreme close up Macro photographs of cannabis flowers were then described to the Judge by Dr. Pate.

"Cannabis is called a dioecious plant which means it has male and female flowers on separate plants. The male's role is just to grow up and shed pollen and the female's role is to catch it. This is done through a winded mechan-

ism normally, not necessarily an insect mediated mechanism."

"There are long feathery like projections from the flower which are optimized for catching pollen in the wind and these are called the styles. They have stigmas attached to them, and a stigma is the actual landing point and growth point of the pollen into the flower. The pollen tube goes down the style and into the ovary and the reproductive cells go into the ovary and a seed is formed."

"It's very crowded, but basically you can see those tendril-like structures. Those are the styles that catch the pollen in the wind and they disappear into this mass of green. If you look carefully, particularly on the right center somewhat lower in the picture, you'll see a pair of styles disappear into what looks like a little cuplike structure, okay?"

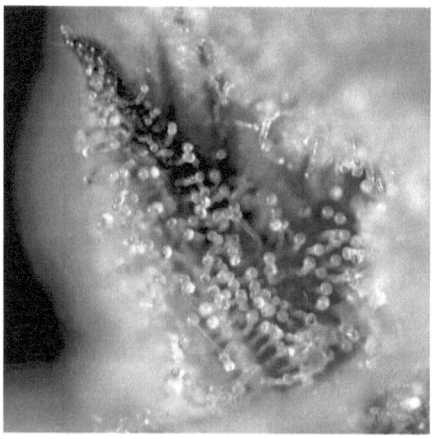

"That's called the perigonial bract or the bracteole. And that is actually a modified leaf that surrounds the flower which is interior to it, protecting it, and the surface of that bracteole is, as you can see, covered with glands. Those glands, if you look elsewhere in the picture, are stalked glands that are topped with a little reservoir."

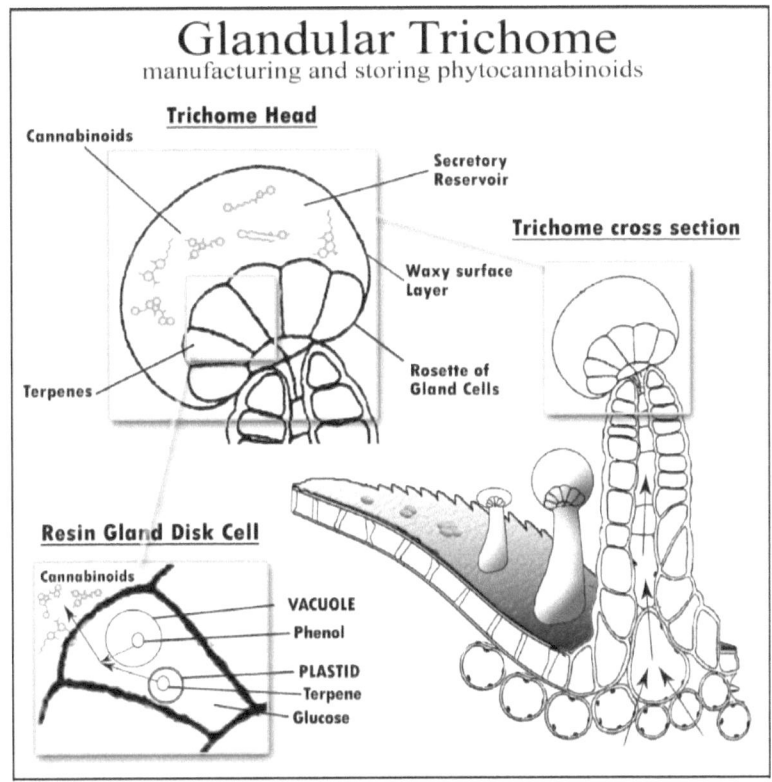

(Graphic by Owen Smith)

"Not only is it a reservoir, but at the bottom of the reservoir is the rosette of cells that form cannabinoids. They exude them into this reservoir which expands as a little apparent bead on the end of the stalk. It looks analogous to a golf ball on a golf tee to some degree. That's how these materials are through this mechanism both manufactured and stored."

Kirk then brought out another photograph with an even closer view of the trichomes.

Dr. Pate explained, "Trichomes are not entirely stable. The reservoir will break off. Even the trichome will break off the surface of the leaf and the reservoir will break off the tip of the trichome as well."

There may also be hydrocarbons of various sorts. Whether they're waxes, per se, it's hard to say. Certainly in the plant kingdom waxes are very common on the surface of leaves to inhibit transpiration of water. They are restricted in normal circumstances as much as possible to the stoma of the leaf which are  the little openings, pores in the leaf, that transpire oxygen, carbon dioxide and water.

The cannabinoids are, if you'll be consistent with our analogy, inside the golf ball, inside the glandular reservoir where they're exuded by the rosette of cells at the bottom of the reservoir. They're manufactured within the rosette of cells and then actively dispersed into the reservoir.

The colour of the trichome relates to the cannabinoid content remaining. The cannabinoids tend to polymerize. When they polymerize they acquire a colour, in this case a brown colour. Pure THC is clear, water clear, but if you were to take a little pipette and dip into a vial of it and wave it around for a few seconds, you would see it start to turn pink and eventually it would polymerize and turn dark.

There are at least three classes of trichomes themselves.

There's the large stalked ones that are the showy ones that you see. There are some very short stalked ones that you may not see and there are some ones that exist almost as blisters on the surface of the leaf. And I mentioned this to indirectly preface the answer to your question because there may be some cannabinoid interior to the leaf, but that may be hard to differentiate between some of the subtler forms of the trichome.

"The vast majority of the cannabinoids found in the cannabis plant are contained in the heads of the glandular trichomes."

There are also silicified, non glandular trichomes that are fairly large relative to the other trichomes and they're found on the underside of most leaves. They contain no cannabinoids or terpenes and are "purely mechanical defense" like a thorn and there's a couple classes of those as well. There's long ones and then there's the cystolithic trichomes, non-glandular trichomes which contain a little crystal of oxalic acid at their base which is perhaps unpalatable. It's speculative as to why it exists there, but the general thought is that all of these things are defensive strategies against insect predation or even mammals.

Accidental Hash

The heads of the trichomes can separate very readily from the remainder of the plant material. You don't even need that much pressure, just simply bouncing them on a screen or just dropping them on a screen at least will give you a few separations. It's a shedding process that happens easily and continuously without much mechanical provocation.

If a consumer obtains cannabis for example in a sealed package, puts it in their backpack and takes it home, then opens that package up, the mere agitation that occurs in that transportation process will cause some of the trichome heads to break off and collect in the pouch that it's in.

It's an accidental process, but you're going to get some of one and some of the other. It could be through a backpack experience. It could be through a postal experience. It could be simply shaking, you know, dropping anything. It's kind of a brittle, fragile phenomenon.

Cannabinoid Ratios

"It seems that the ratio of one cannabinoid to another is fixed genetically. The total amount produced is influenced by both genetics and environmental inputs, that is the percentage by dry weight. This can be attributed possibly to the production within the gland, but it also often has to do with the ratios of morphological parts that occur during different parts of the development of the plant."

"For example, the highest populations of these trichomes are on these structures immediately adjacent to the flower, and so a younger plant, it's not going to have as much cannabinoid by dry weight of the plant as a mature plant which has the mature reproductive structures having the dense populations of these trichomes."

"There's a suite of cannabinoids within the resin. Depending on the strain or 'bridal type' and within the geographic providence of that type, you can have a balance of various sorts between these several cannabinoids, primarily CBD, and THC, and past a certain point these ratios become fixed."

"The dominance of THC is primarily from plants genetically derived from tropical areas. While CBD is primarily from plants derived from high latitude temperate areas. Plants in between those two interestingly enough have a varying balance of the two. Low temperate plants from places like Afghanistan or Pakistan or Nepal, while certainly not tropical, have more THC than European plants and have more CBD than tropical, equatorial plants would have."

"Strains or 'bridal types' are varietal types like pink roses and red roses and white roses, that kind of thing. They're either land races that have been selected by native populations for various characteristics or they're wild types which are very hard to find, if you can find them at all, since this plant has had a relationship with humankind for millennia."

Terpenes

Terpenes in a lay kind of description are the aromatic components. You can have when you peel an orange, for example, or a lemon, a characteristic smell and that is the smell of the terpenes. One is even called limonene and it's the smell of lemons. And that is not restricted to citrus.

These terpenes are almost universal. There are terpenes called pinene for obvious reasons in terms of their piney smell and their occurrence in pine. Mints are well known to have these compounds and these are structurally identical to some of the ones in cannabis and in each case probably serves something of the same purpose in terms of insect repellency.

"Life is complicated and yet people in the pharmaceutical industry would like one drug, one effect. In herbal medicine you inevitably have multiple compounds and sometimes these compounds act in concert to modify the overall effect. In the earliest part of my involvement I thought terpenes were simply something that smelled nice. But it's becoming more apparent that the terpenes may actually have a role in the efficacy of the cannabinoids."

"This is a cutting edge area of investigation. What's intriguing with the thesis that terpenes may have synergistic or augmentative role is that with the endocannabinoids it's been shown that while anandamide and some of the few analogues of anandamide that are present in a body are efficacious in altering the body's function, there are other compounds that are related to anandamide which have no apparent action in the body. Yet when the inactive ingredient is added to the active ingredients (anandamide) they can influence their efficacy in altering the body's function. "

"In other words anandamide could have an action at a certain level, but anandamide and these other bodily components which in and of themselves are not active could accentuate that anandamide action. Now, if this is true, then it isn't that far-fetched to imagine that the phytocannabinoids themselves having their own action may be influenced by terpenes, which themselves may or may not have their own independent action. Even more intriguing is the fact that cannabinoids are partially terpenoid in their structure, so it's not as if the terpenes are completely foreign as a chemical entity to cannabinoids. Cannabinoids are molecularly partially terpenes."

Dr. Pate described the cross reactivity of THC and CBD. "CBD inhibits certain liver enzymes that metabolize THC so that if they're taken together may affect the course of THC through inhibition of those enzymes that may degrade the THC. In other words there's a well established mechanism possible"... for CBD to prolong the effects of THC.

SIDE EFFECTS

Dr. Pate stated unequivocally that the medical effects of cannabinoids have been well documented and that there's no reasonable dispute about them. The effects of THC are wide in range from anti-inflammatory to antispasmodic.

The psychoactivity of cannabis can, depending on your intent, either be a primary effect or a side effect. The term "side effect" is a term like weed, where in an agronomic sense of the term, weed has no meaning. It's more of a cultural term: if there is a plant in your garden and you don't want it there, it's a weed. And if it's making you money, you probably don't consider it a weed. And so side effects are similar in that side effects are non-target effects that drugs have and if you're looking for one effect and you're getting other effects, you consider them side effects and a nuisance like you would a weed in your garden. A side effect can suddenly be turned into a target effect by altering your intent.

"CBD is relatively non-psychoactive and primarily an anti-inflammatory."

There have been some studies in Brazil which show that CBD is as effective as some of the established antipsychotic medicines with none of the rather significant side effects that these established medicines have. The problem with CBD in that application and in other applications is that it's, as I understand it, metabolized fairly quickly so the dosages tend to be fairly high, significant fractions of a gram, half gram, three-quarters of a gram, quarter gram, something in that range. People in the pharmaceutical business like smaller doses if they can get it.

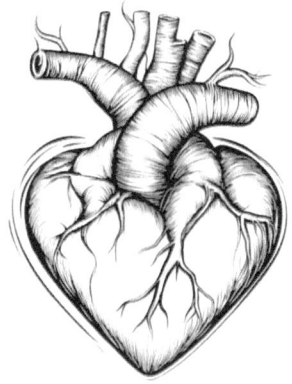

TACHYCARDIA

Tachycardia is more likely from inhaled cannabis as it creates a more pronounced spike of cannabinoid in the bloodstream. But a fast heart rate can come from a reaction to the plants psychoactivity, not necessarily from the cannabinoid's interaction with their receptors. If you're a drug naïve patient and you had an experience of being in an altered state that you're not used to, that can contribute as well.

Human Variation

People are all different in their metabolic outcomes. Just as we all have two eyes, a nose and a mouth, we have an inherent variety of each of those that allow us to recognize individuals as to who they are by sight instantly. Metabolism is like that as well. There are certain functions that are fundamental that everybody has, assuming it's not a pathological condition, but there are many sub variations on metabolism that make people more or less susceptible to certain things.

Now, just to make things more complex, plants themselves have various profiles of what they produce and how they produce them and the combination of the individual and their variability plus the plant and their variability make for a difference in what a particular strain will do for a particular person.

We have potentially different amounts of endocannabinoids, potentially different amounts of receptors, potentially variations in distribution of these receptors. There's many other factors, including the fact that cannabinoids may work by non-receptor mechanisms as well.

Concentrating Cannabinoids

When concentrating cannabis, what you're trying to take is the source of the active compounds and leave as much of what's called the ballast material away. There's not much in the way of immediate medicinal pharmaceutical properties to cellulose, to chlorophyll, to any of the other debris that may be on the plant so that if you can discard that through the process of selection of where the active materials actually reside, then it's of some advantage in some cases.

Methods of extraction fall under two broad categories, maybe three. One is simple mechanical isolation. The reservoirs are fixed to the trichome stalk and the stalk affixed to the leaf in an insecure manner. That might be functional from an insect predation standpoint, but that notwithstanding the fact is that these are easily separable. And so the purely mechanical means of separation allows a great deal of the ballast to be left behind. Ballast, I'm speaking of cellulose and chlorophyll and inactive bulk.

Then there is the extraction process where you isolate and concentrate resin using a chemical solvent and evacuate the reservoir of its resin. Then there are sort of hybrid approaches where you simply smash the mass in a mechanical way and the resin squeezes out and you collect it. That's sort of maybe a hybrid in between those two extreme techniques.

Separating resin heads can be achieved through a purely mechanical process that would yield a product that would be identifiable as still a gland or still a reservoir as opposed to a chemical extraction which would simply give you a tar.

Cannabinoids easily dissolve in fat and alcohol but not water. One can make cannabis food by simply dropping cannabis flowers into a bowl of muffin mix that contains some vegetable oil or butter. This wouldn't be as effective as extracting the leaf into oil directly and straining out the excess inactive leaf material.

Petrochemical solvents can also be used to evacuate the trichome of its cannabinoid rich resin. The volatility of the solvent allows the extraction technician to evaporate it and concentrate the cannabinoid resin far beyond what is possible with butter or vegetable oils.

These two main extraction processes (mechanical and chemical) were at the root of the confusion suffered by the police investigator who valued our vegetable oil infusions at the street value cost of chemical solvent extractions. A gram of basic cannabis concentrate was valued at approximately $20 while a gram of vegetable oil infusion had no known value.

As an illustration of this, on one occasion the VCBC was robbed during the night by an unknown burglar. Rocks were thrown through the window and thieves rifled through the shop until they found a large bag of vegetable oil infused capsules. The capsules were a very low dose and once the thieves realized that they created no marketable effect, the capsules were abandoned at a local laundromat and picked up and returned by one of the club's members later that morning.

Natural Contaminants

If it's not necessary to be there for the action to take place and it's a possible detriment, then why leave it in? Certainly we eat cellulose every day in our vegetables, so that's not so much of the problem unless you're on a restricted diet. But in the case of cannabis, some of those silicified trichomes that we talked about earlier are indigestible and their spike structure is designed to scrape and might possibly act as an irritant to the gut, especially if you have a raw gut with IBS or Crohn's disease. So it's plausible that getting rid of the cellulose and leaf material will do no harm and may be beneficial in certain cases.

The fact is, the active ingredients are found within structures that grow out of the leaf, that's the premise from which you operate. In the case of smoking, most of the fuel component of the pyrolysis comes from burning the cellulose. The cellulose in the leaf is only helpful in maintaining the ember of the joint. That pyrolysis produces heat from the ember which superheats the air drawn through the cannabis and both decarboxylates and distills the cannabinoids out the downstream end.

There are bits and pieces that are on plants because they're in open air conditions. They're not a laboratory artifact. They're an agronomic artifact and you get whatever is out there in the big wide world, insects of various sorts, some of them tiny and stuck to the leaf. Sometimes the plant absorbs various things such as heavy metals and pesticides, and moulds are a significant inhabitant of most plants and they particularly like the leaf.

There's nothing particularly attractive about the trichome from a mould's perspective. In fact, it may be repellant, but the leaf is where the nutrients are in the living specimen and so it would naturally be biased towards what I'm calling the leaf.

And I think one of the other significant considerations are the silicified trichomes that reside on the surface of the leaf and may be an irritant to oral ingestion.

I would say that, you know, it's a question of degree and getting rid of the leaf is getting rid of 90 percent of the bulk or more. And then getting rid of the trichome reservoir from the resin is maybe another percent or two, you know, so it's a point of diminishing returns. If you wanted to, you could then take the resin and isolate THC from that and then less bulk, but at every step there's a point of diminishing returns.

Decarboxylation

The THC compound which is psychoactive is actually an artifact of a natural product which has been heated. This natural product is the carboxylic acid form of THC, called THCA. It has a carboxylic acid group which is a carbon and two oxygens and a hydrogen in a typical configuration. And when you heat this natural product the carboxylic acid group goes away as CO_2 and water and gives you what we normally think of as THC.

This happens again, if I can use the term 'in situ' with a smoking process. The carboxylic acid form is more hydrogen bonded to each other, so it's not as volatile, but when it's decarboxylated it becomes more volatile and the super heated air from the heated ember of a joint or a cigarette volatizes it into the smoke stream.

It's immediately decarboxylated by heat during the smoking process. You have the heat of the ember in a 600 maybe or even 800 degree Celsius range which superheats air that passes through it and so everything immediately downstream from the ember is cooked and decarboxylated and liberated to volatilize into the smoke stream.

Localization

Topical cannabis follows a general pharmacological principle that you want to target the site of action to optimize the ratio of intended effects to unintended effects. In other words, if you can get the job done with a local application at the site where it's needed, then you don't have to have a large systemic dose in the whole body where it's not necessarily useful and may cause side effects.

Most pharmaceutical products, in the broader sense, are utilized within a range of routes of administration in which their usefulness is found. In other words, because of chemical or pharmacological properties, some routes of administrations are not applicable for some drugs, but most drugs are exploited through multiple routes of administration to maximize their utility in specific cases. With antibiotics, for example, you can have intravenous drip for someone who's really terribly ill and about to die of some sort of blood infection. You could have antibiotics in a skin cream to apply to a localized lesion that's infected. You could take oral antibiotics if you want systemic dosing where you either want to clean out the gastrointestinal tract which either is a desired or undesired effect.

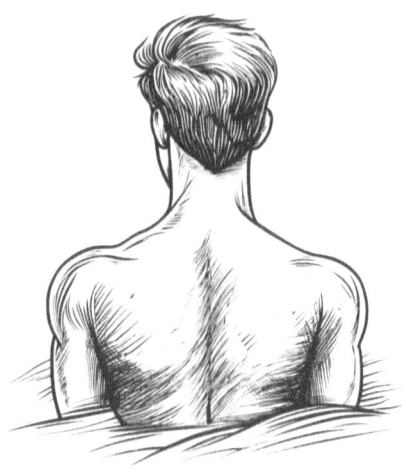

SKIN

Dr. Pate, through his expertise in pharmacodynamics, the study of the action or effect of drugs on living organisms, explained that because topical cannabis only minimally passes through the skin into the bloodstream doesn't mean it's ineffective. Cannabinoid ligands, like THC, bind to specific receptor sites in our bodies. CB1 and CB2 receptors have been located in nerve fibers of the skin, skin cells (keratinocytes), cells of the hair follicles, sweat glands, and other cells present in the skin. "Abundant distribution of cannabinoid receptors on skin nerve fibers and mast cells provides implications for an anti-inflammatory, anti-nociceptive action of cannabinoid receptor agonists."

Topical administration isn't going to give you a psychoactive effect unless you apply a huge amount of very concentrated material over a large surface area... It's such a non-toxic drug that if you were taking it as an anti-inflammatory it's not likely that you would get too much of the anti-inflammatory. At worst, I would conjecture that you might induce a localized irritation because cannabinoids can sometimes induce irritation locally, but that's a relatively minor drawback to topical cannabis.

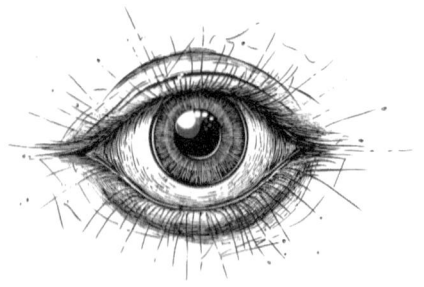

METHODS OF INGESTION

Basically you're trying to get the molecule into the bloodstream and so how do you do it?

Well, the easiest, the least painful and most natural ways to do it are through the available openings in the body. Inhaling smoke is a way to get the molecules from the plant into the bloodstream in a way that is very rapid and efficient. And it's probably a close second to intravenous administration which is the absolute quickest way to get something into the bloodstream as you might expect. Pulmonary administration is very efficient at that because there's a huge surface area to the lungs and it's intimately perfused with capillaries trying to optimize transfer of oxygen from the air to your system and that's of great advantage when you're trying to introduce drugs as well.

It could be argued that oral ingestion is probably the most natural way to ingest a medicine because it's analogous to eating. Topicals can be handy for rubbing on affected areas on the skin, either to apply to a lesion on the skin or to introduce these materials through the skin possibly to an underlying tissue.

The transmucosal is kind of an interesting variant on topical in that the mucosa of the body, particularly the cheek, under the tongue, and rectally, is highly perfused with blood, is thin and permeable. This is more so than the cornified layers of the skin would be and so that you get a faster acting effect and it's almost like oral, but it doesn't really go the whole route through the GI system, at least theoretically. In practice, some of it does.

These are general principles of drugs and even plant based drugs. Whole herbal drugs are restricted in some ways because they're solids. You can't do much more than smoke them or eat them, but if you can extract them, then you have more latitude as to how you can apply things.

One characteristic of pulmonary administration is a sharp spike in blood levels of the cannabinoids. They rise quickly in the bloodstream and they fall off fairly quickly. They have a short plateau and a quick diminution. That is more applicable to a malady of similar character, one of short duration, and usually perhaps acute onset where you need quick relief.

Glaucoma however is a life-long chronic condition and so treating it by smoking it is basically you end up smoking like a chimney every hour or two depending on the circumstance in the effort to maintain a plateau through a series of spikes. You can do it and a lot of people do and have treated their glaucoma in that fashion, but it seems a more natural fit of therapy to a malady to pick a route of administration that's going to establish the blood levels and then maintain them for a period of time so that the dosing is more infrequent. Oral seems to fit that bill.

And so with oral administration you have a slow spike: a slow rise which is not so relevant for a chronic disease, but a long plateau which is much more relevant. In the case of glaucoma you don't stop having glaucoma when you go to sleep and so if you want to maintain those cannabinoid levels overnight, then it's best to eat something just before you go to bed. Even if you smoke something just before you go to bed, you'd be good for a couple of hours but that's only a quarter of your normal sleep pattern. So if you eat something, you'd probably be good for most of that eight hours.

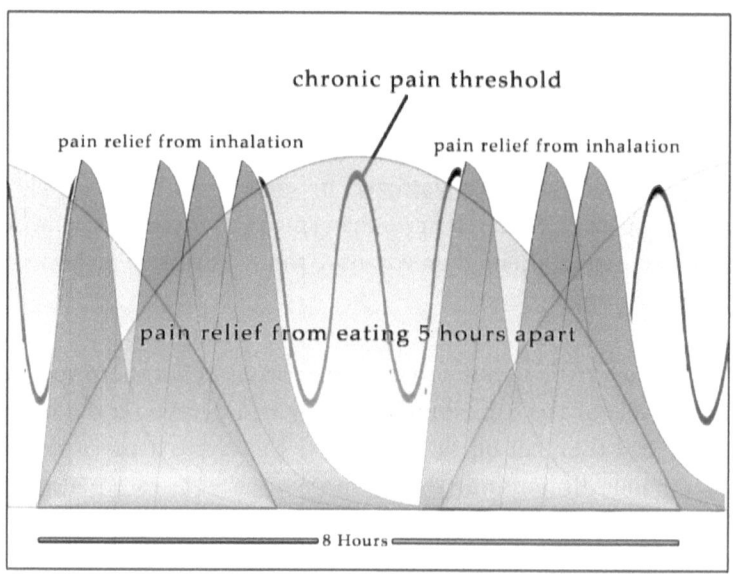

The chart shows the effective combination of eaten and inhaled cannabis for chronic pain management

(Graphic by Owen Smith)

If you're having pain on a constant basis, then constant applications are applicable, analogous to glaucoma. Sometimes you have a chronic pain condition, but you have what's called breakthrough pain where you have a particularly intense episode on top of the plateau that you already have and then you may want to smoke as well to address that particular breakthrough pain. So, you know, it could go either way. The general rule is, if you have a chronic condition you want chronic administration of a drug that ameliorates it; if you have an acute condition you want an acute administration of a drug.

For example, if you have a condition like migraine and it's going to come on quickly but it's not going to last you all day, then maybe you want something that's smoked, or at least inhaled in some fashion because you want the application of that drug right then, because if you can thwart the initial symptoms that you may be sensitive to before you actually get the migraine, you may be able to blunt the course of that phenomena. So, maybe the migraine duration is an hour or two, and you don't necessarily want to be dosed all day just because you had an episode that morning. So you tailor the drug administration to the requirements of the malady you're trying to treat.

With edible cannabis you're establishing a baseline level and if that's sufficient, so be it. But if not, a much smaller amount through smoking can push those blood levels in a transient acute sense - a quick onset and short diminution back to the plateau provided by the oral ingestion. In other words it's a peak on top of an already established plateau, but it's more transient in nature.

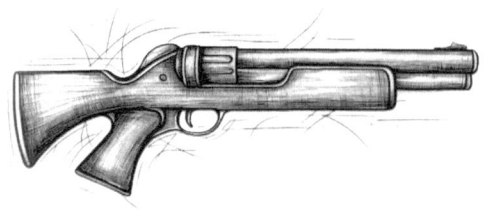

Sniper Vs Shotgun

There's a great divide between those who work with single pointed molecules and receptors and those who work with herbal medicines. It's been described as the difference between a rifle and a shotgun. One is more pinpoint and narrow, laser-like in its applicability, the other more broad and this has turned into something of a competition between the two schools. But in my opinion there are times when one is more applicable than the other based on what you're trying to achieve.

In many cases the herbal medicines have factors due to their complexity which help to prevent, for example, overdosing. This is because before you get to that point nausea would set in, whereas if you had somebody give you an injection of something you're along for the ride, whatever it brings and you can die as a result of too much of that one thing.

So there are different approaches and the single compound school which is predominant in a pharmaceutical industry doesn't like or trust the herbal approach because they see it as historical, old-fashioned, hard to control and multi-factorial. They like it clean, simple and straight, which is well and good except that that approach has its own inherent limitations and drawbacks which they probably would be reluctant to concede.

If you take a pharmaceutical approach with most drugs, there's a point at which people will die either because you can administer well controlled but not particularly regulable amounts of the drug relative to the patient's reaction. In other words if someone was in pain, there would be a normal dose of morphine you would give right off the bat to blunt that pain and let's say it's ten milligrams or 15 milligrams of morphine. And you would take it out of a bottle, put it in a syringe and inject it into the patient in hopes to alleviate the pain that they're in.

But that patient could be hypersensitive to morphine and this is notwithstanding allergic reactions, but just very sensitive to morphine and they could have serious consequences to that. They could stop breathing perhaps or inversely, maybe they're more immune to morphine than other patients and it doesn't have the pain relieving effect desired.

But that notwithstanding, a natural product in the previous example may prevent you from taking too much because, one, the routes of ingestion of a natural product don't include things like injection. They include things only analogous to food intake or air intake like smoking or eating and those tend to be a slower means to administer a drug. And so in the case of natural products, often the fact that they're in with other drugs and other components means that you get a bit of a warning as to 'this is probably as far as we should go' in terms of administering a drug.

Herbal medicine is a more forgiving kind of administration of a drug. It's not without its hazards, but it's not quite so hard and fast as a pharmaceutical preparation.

Relatively Safe

If those brownies that people were eating too many of contain almost any other drug, illegal or not, and they were overdosing in that fashion there'd be many people dead. The forgiving nature of cannabinoids allows a broader margin of error without serious consequence. If those cookies were dosed with heroin or barbiturates, people would be dead.

If you take five times more alcohol than you normally would need to achieve a psychic drunken state you'd probably be dead. You know, there are many drugs that have what's called a therapeutic index which is the ratio of efficacy to toxicity, which is maybe tenfold. Aspirin, for example, you can take two Aspirin and it'll work, but if you take 20 Aspirin you probably would have to go to the hospital. And in fact people often kill themselves suicidally by taking common drugs, Aspirin among them. But you could never achieve a successful suicide by taking cannabis.

There are some herbal medicines that are less tolerant of error than others. I would say if you want to draw an example out of the air, something like *digitalis purpurea* which is foxglove, a common actually decorative plant you see around, it's rather nice looking and it's used as a heart stimulant. And too much of it in a tea or too much of a more potent variety in a tea can cause you problems. It's not well controlled like many other herbal materials as far as the active ingredient contents.

With cannabis, it's not, although the same principles apply. The toxicity of the active ingredient makes the jeopardy minimal compared to, for example, going into a heart attack situation with digitalis by taking too much. Like I say, it's a very forgiving class of compounds, probably because the distribution of cannabinoid receptors is not heavily involved in vital functions in the brain.

For example with morphine, and I've alluded to this earlier, you can easily die from morphine overdose because first you go to sleep and if the dose is high enough you stop breathing and that's because the opiate receptors responsible for signaling breathing regulation in the brain are overwhelmed by the amount of morphine involved. But there's no breathing receptor regulatory mechanisms involving cannabinoid receptors, for example, so you don't have that jeopardy.

If it weren't for the fact that THC and the cannabinoids in general were so non-toxic you'd have many people in the hospital or dead from eating too much because often these baked goods are well endowed with the drug. And luckily it's THC and not some other drug which is more toxic because with THC you just wait it out. It's kind of overwhelming and uncomfortable, but nobody's ever died of it and that assurance in itself helps.

Start Low, Go Slow

I should introduce the concept of feedback loop in this context in that what we're describing is called self-titration. And for self-titration to be effective there has to be feedback information provided to yourself to make a decision as to whether to increase the dose or not. This is a temporal phenomenon in that if you're smoking some cannabis you inhale one breath's worth of cannabis and you wait a few seconds or a few minutes and you can perceive the blood levels rising by the effect that you're experiencing. You can know within minutes whether by that feedback mechanism, by that self-perceptive mechanism, you can tell whether you should take another inhalation or not.

Now, with oral ingestion you're talking about an hour, so that especially if the cookies taste good you may be tempted to eat a second one before the effects of the first one are fully perceived. And you know, that's an infamous story that you hear from a lot of people, "I know it was probably too much to take but it tasted so good." So there's the necessity to be careful with oral ingestion because the feedback loop to tell you whether that was sufficient is so long that impatience may set in and you may think well, it hasn't really achieved what I wanted to achieve when all you needed to really do was wait another 30 minutes and you would have found that that was quite sufficient.

Synergy with Opiates

"Sometimes it's been observed that cannabinoids will lower the dose of morphine or opiates needed to achieve pain relief. Sometimes it could be added to the maximum amount of morphine prudent to give and provide additional effect without the potential for that harm to be done which would otherwise be so when adding more morphine."

Dr. Pate was then asked to identify the different oil infusions by looking at the exhibit photos taken by the police of the items they seized from the bakery. He confirmed that "they alone could not result in death."

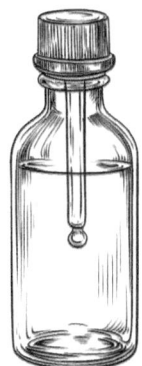

CLINICAL TRIALS

Cannabis has undergone a multiyear open label clinical trial by virtue of being in such popular use both medically and recreationally for an extended period of time.

Double Blind Clinical Trials are the exclusive practice for new molecules. You have to differentiate between new chemical entities and perhaps traditional medicines in the herbal sense.

Decades ago, when they started implementing these increasingly rigorous tests of drugs, they grandfathered in a lot of drugs that were in current pharmaceutical practice. They didn't want to take a whole pharmacopeia and have to reprove that these things worked. So in most cases they said well, we'll start right here and those approved drugs will be grandfathered in as approved because they always have been, but will require more rigorous testing of subsequent drugs.

There are probably residual drugs now on the market that haven't been through that process, but a lot of them have fallen by the wayside because there have been new and improved drugs to apply to the same maladies and so by attrition more and more of these drugs have been through the process.

Cannabis was in the pharmacopeia from the late 19th century, until it was removed in the 20th before the grandfathering process. Sativex, Navilone and Marinol are recent approvals.

Marinol is a pure synthetic THC product in sesame oil. Navilone is a THC analogue, which means it's a pure single compound that's similar in structure to THC. Sativex is a whole plant extract, 1:1 CBD:THC. Dr. Pate was head of the laboratory of a small company who developed the plants that eventually were used to manufacture Sativex and sat on the GW Pharmaceuticals board of scientific advisors.

Sativex is a modern version of those historical extracts that used to be in the pharmacopeia and this modern version has gone through that rigorous process and ended up in the same place, in the pharmacopeia more or less. The old style extracts were usually ethanolic extracts in a dropping bottle of some sort. You'd put a little in your tea or under your tongue. And the new version is the same extract in a spray bottle that you spray in your mouth. So let's say that the new version, Sativex, is the historical vindication of the old materials that disappeared probably before their time.

Blocking Research

About 70 percent or maybe three quarters of the studies done with cannabis are supported by the National Institute on Drug Abuse. And consistent with its name, you can tell they're not particularly sympathetic to the medical approach and they do not fund medical studies that seek to find positive effects.

What medical information we have gleaned usually is a side effect of the studies that have been done with an aim towards a predetermined outcome: frankly they work strictly in terms of trying to illustrate the harm involved in the use of these drugs.

For example, Donald Abrams, who is a well known researcher in this field relative to HIV/AIDS, did a study of potential toxicity between cannabinoids and HIV drugs. Collateral to that he did find some benefits from the use of vaporized cannabis in particular. But that wasn't the motivation for the study. It was a collateral benefit.

Conclusion

Philosophically, you have to ask what part of the plant is not a plant part. The trichomes are as much of the leaf as any other part of the leaf. Simply excluding the inactive parts of the leaf and taking the parts that are active of the leaf seems like an inefficient way to do things. It doesn't make sense scientifically to allow something and then disallow something that's intrinsic to what you've just allowed.

I'm not sure if I can make it any clearer than that.

Cross Examination

I will attempt to summarize the arguments made by the Crown Prosecutor and the answers given. I will skim over a lot that was either peripheral or repetitive. It was my experience sitting in the courtroom that the Crown's meandering jaunt of exploratory questions was extremely dull and I do not want to bore you or waste your time. If you are interested in the finest of details, you are invited to explore the transcripts.

The Crown Prosecutor first took aim at the peanut butter jars. "Peanut butter can be quite toxic to individuals with peanut allergies, can't it?"

He then pointed out that the consequences for marketing a therapeutic product that has no therapeutic purpose could lead to lawsuits and liability issues for a government that approved them.

He then took aim at our recipe book.

One of the methods outlined in the recipe book was to use a selection of starting materials from different plants to increase the likelihood of the inclusion of trace cannabinoids and terpenes. This shotgun approach was called out by the Crown as increasing the potential for variability in cannabinoid potency, meaning that our method of mixing three varieties together would lead to more variability in the final product. He compared it to how GW pharmaceuticals strictly use 2 cultivars to produce Sativex.

He then began to inquire if it is possible to identify a cannabis cookie by looking at it. The presence of cannabis scent does not determine the presence of THC because the terpenes that are associated with flavour also occur elsewhere in nature. A familiar skunky cannabis smell can be easily confused with many other natural phenomena. Skunk, flavourists would call it, is a note that smells musky among others.

It is impossible to tell the quantities of THC in a solution without laboratory analysis.

He then asked how much hemp one would have to smoke in order to achieve a desirable effect. Running the risk of asphyxiation, one would need in the order of a hundredfold the amount of hemp to cannabis to achieve a noticeable effect or as the prosecutor put it, "You'd end up with a joint that would make Cheech and Chong envious, wouldn't you?"

He then moved on to a key document prepared by Health Canada, entitled, "Information for Health Care Professionals."

He asked about the drug approval process being lengthy, difficult and expensive, particularly so for GW pharmaceuticals in producing Sativex, each phase of trials having a high attrition rate. Phase one would be more of toxicity testing and phase two and three would be more having to do with efficacy.

The Prosecutor then brought up the botanical product marketed under the generic name Laetrile. He explained how apricot pit products were flogged off onto the public as a cure for cancer. It couldn't be marketed as a cancer cure so it was relabelled as a vitamin in an attempt to do an end run around the Food and Drug Act Regulations that precluded selling it to the public as a cancer cure.

The Crown asked, "Are you aware that Steven McQueen shortly before he died tried Laetrile therapy for his cancer and it didn't quite work?"

Dr. Pate replied "No, I didn't know that, but at that point you have nothing to lose I suppose. If you're willing to substitute to the exclusion of established therapies, then you run the risk of progression of the disease. These are choices people have to make. Sometimes the established therapies are so onerous that people would rather have none or would rather have an alternative."

OTHER CANNABINOIDS

The Prosecutor asked about CBN.

CBN, which is also an artifact in cannabis, is not a natural product. It's a marker of the degradation of THC. It's reputed to have something of a sedative contribution to the overall effect. Also like delta-8 THC, it's a product which is formed as a result of exposure of the specimen to outside influences. It doesn't have an enzyme mechanism within the plant to manufacture it. Delta-9 THC upon exposure to air and light forms polymers and sometimes spins off a little CBN as a marker of that degradation.

You can influence the amount of CBN by the manner in which you abuse the specimen.

For example, if you're careful with it you'll have none. If you smash it into bricks or otherwise abuse the specimen, you're going to rupture the glands and the reservoirs that we spoke of earlier, spreading the resin about and exposing it to air and then of course that leads to accelerated degradation.

The Prosecutor then asked about the dangers of making hash oils. It is commonly known that using petroleum based solvents can produce gasses which are highly flammable and cause explosions when introduced to a spark.

He quickly moved on to question the validity of statements around the conversion of THC-a into THC. Waving in the field, a plant may be upwards of 90% THC acid. It is reliant on the process of harvesting, curing, storage and handling that determines how much and how fast THC-a becomes THC and in turn, how much and how fast THC becomes CBN.

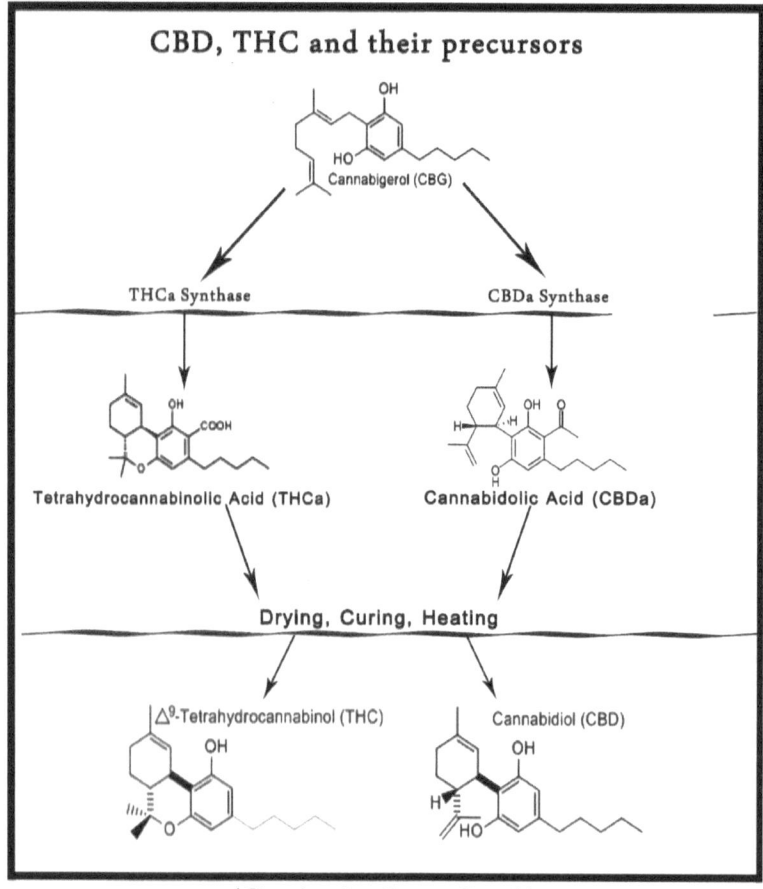

(Graphic by Owen Smith)

Smoking Cannabis

He then moved on to ask about the properties of cannabis smoke.

The smoke from cannabis cigarettes is chemically similar to that from tobacco cigarettes, however some investigators report that two potent carcinogens in tobacco smoke, benzanthracene and benzyo[a]pyrene, are present in higher concentrations in cannabis smoke.

The amount of tars in cannabis tend to be higher, but that's with a select specimen of cannabis that is available from the National Institute on Drug Abuse, and those are fairly low THC specimens. What they call low THC is about one percent and high THC is about three percent. So relative to modern standards these are extremely low.

Given the lower percentage of THC, individuals would need to smoke more to achieve a desired effect, consuming more tars.

More importantly, the chemistries of the two smokes differ. Tobacco has commonality with cannabis in that they're both cellulose products being ignited, being pyrolyzed. But the differences come to the fore when you're talking about not only the amounts of active ingredients, but the kind of active ingredients that are nicotine versus THC.

Nicotine in itself is a pure compound, and is a carcinogen. It's converted to a carcinogen in the body. It's there in approximately one percent by dry weight. THC, for example, is a very good free radical absorber. Free radical damage is implicated in carcinogenicity and its absorbance of free radicals and its inherent anticarcinogenic properties and its total presence being ten to 20 fold more than nicotine is another matter. There's also a third factor which I won't go too deeply into, but it has to do with the inherent radioactivity of tobacco. It has polonium-210 and lead-210 derived from the phosphate fertilizers used and if you look at various, even government websites, they'll attribute a sizable amount of carcinogenicity to the inherent radioactivity involved with tobacco smoking.

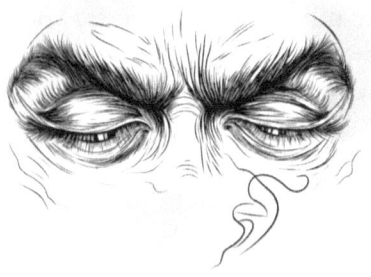

POTENCY AND TOLERANCE

The Prosecutor then asked about a practice where some individuals hold their cannabis smoke in their lungs for a prolonged time and proposed that these behaviors may worsen the negative effects. It was more of a statement than a question that Dr. Pate did not have insight to comment.

When asked about individuals building a tolerance to cannabis Dr. Pate replied, "that's been something of a controversy, but if drug principles hold generally for this drug and there's no reason to think they don't, then you would think tolerance would be something of a factor. It doesn't seem to be an extreme factor. Tolerance builds more quickly or more slowly depending on the type of drug you're using as an example. In this case it seems fairly slow.'

So-called high potency cannabis which I'll arbitrarily now define as something between 10 and 20 percent THC by dry weight has been available since the mid '70s, maybe even the early '70s but certainly the mid '70s. But it was considered much more of a connoisseur item and imported materials of lower quality were cheaper and considered more the staple. Extracts in the form of hashish or concentrated resin were available in the '60s and '70s and were intended to have high THC content.

So it's not as if these things didn't occur, but with time the lower quality materials have fallen more out of fashion and the higher quality materials have replaced them in frequency.

A person familiar with cannabis can visibly observe the density of trichomes to ascertain roughly how potent a cannabis flower sample might be. Sampling the product will give a better idea but ultimately, laboratory testing is required to pinpoint the potency accurately.

Rates of Onset

The Prosecutor then asked about the varying absorption rates of cannabis depending on how it is ingested, including smoking, vaporizing, and ingestion.

"I would agree with [edibles absorption rates] being slow and erratic, more on the slow and less on the erratic, but I would also contend that dosing is a little more reliable orally than it would be by smoking because there is additional numbers of parameters in terms of release of the drug from the matrix such as how you're smoking it... I would feel more comfortable with a known oral dose I believe than a smoked dose."

Prosecutor: "And one of the offsetting parameters for edible products is the fact that the consumer may not know or the manufacturer may not know exactly what's in there, correct?"

Expert Witness: "That's correct."

Prosecutor: "So you're eating a cookie that may have one, two, three, five, seven different strains, seeds. It may have any number of things infused into it. You have to trust the person who baked it?"

Expert Witness: "Yes, and you're along for the ride, whatever it brings."

Clinical Trials

The Phases of the clinical trial have to do with increasing population size, the cohort of people that are studied and phase three is the largest. And even at that there can be some effects that aren't noticed that are on a population several orders of magnitude larger in the general public domain. Clinical trials don't necessarily mean something is safe.

The classic example is Thalidomide. Thalidomide was a product that proceeded through clinical trials successfully, appeared safe and efficacious for the proposed use and then was discovered creating significant difficulties when administered to women who were pregnant in that their babies were born with significant birth defects.

With Thalidomide, the clinical trials had not included pregnant participants.

The prosecutor asked Dr. Pate about funding issues and the difficulty in conducting clinical trials. Pate mentions that the National Institute of Drug Abuse (NIDA) in the United States covers 70%

of funding for this research and selects for toxic research and against medicinal research. Most Western countries follow this trend.

Research

Dr. David Pate has helped G.W. Pharmaceuticals develop the oromucosal cannabis spray Sativex which passed laboratory testing and clinical trials.

Dr. Pate's extensive experience with laboratory research involves the "upstream" development of products with medical potential. Upstream development takes feedback from the patient and attempts to find evidence to support or refute the claims being made. For example, when a number of patients tell their doctor that a cannabis product is working for them, that product could then become the basis for laboratory research.

The next stage, which is considered "downstream," involves testing the molecule's toxicity and efficacy.

Dr. Pate passes on his findings to companies like GW Pharmaceuticals, who then take the product through the downstream clinical trial process, which includes designing the trials to protect the patients and minimize bias, as well as patient monitoring and follow-up. The extent of the follow-up depends on the stage of the trial and the type of patients involved. For early stages, which only involve testing for toxicity, there is usually only follow-up to make sure the healthy volunteers are still healthy after the trial. But for individuals suffering from a condition, there is an ethical obligation for follow-up.

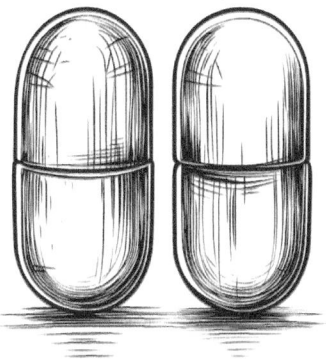

Placebo Effect

The placebo effect refers to a psychological phenomenon where a person's belief and expectation about a treatment can influence their perception of its effectiveness, even if the treatment itself has no real pharmacological effect. This effect is particularly relevant when dealing with subjective symptoms, such as pain, anxiety, or depression, where the patient's subjective impression of the symptoms is relied upon in clinical trials.

It is possible that the branding and marketing of a product can influence a patient's belief in its efficacy. However, during clinical trials, it is important to isolate and control for the placebo effect to accurately assess the pharmacological effectiveness of a treatment.

Subjective belief of the effectiveness of a therapeutic product cannot be objectively verified in a laboratory setting. It is based on the individual's perception and experiences. The placebo effect can play a role in this, where the individual's belief in the product can enhance its perceived effectiveness, but it cannot be confirmed through objective means.

Driving Ability

Dr. Pate is familiar with experimental studies observing driving ability, some of which are in the Netherlands, but the ones he has seen indicate no substantial impact on driving ability.

Adverse Mood Reactions

The Prosecutor described a series of reported adverse mood reactions, including panic, depression, delusions, and illusions. These reactions generally subside within hours of using cannabis and typically respond well to reassurance and support. He also mentioned a case where a 26-year-old man experienced acute delirium after unknowingly eating a very potent cannabis cookie

The Crown Prosecutor states "the evidence shows a strong link between heavy and prolonged use of cannabis and cognitive problems. Do you agree with this assertion?"

Dr. Pate replies "I would say that heavy and prolonged use of any substance can have negative impacts on cognitive functioning, so it is not surprising to see such a link with cannabis use. However, I would also want to caution against drawing strong conclusions based on just one study or body of evidence, as there can be many factors that contribute to cognitive problems and it is important to consider all the relevant information before making any conclusions."

He also mentions that the results of the studies do not seem to match everyday observation of populations and there hasn't been a marked increase in these problems despite an expansion of cannabis use.

Contra-indications

The conversation then shifts to the recommendations for individuals who should not take Sativex, including those with allergies, serious cardiovascular disease, history of psychotic disorder, and children under 18. Dr. Pate believes that the recommendations may be overly cautious, but those dispensing the product still have a responsibility to consider these parameters.

Follow Up

It is not safe or sound pharmaceutical practice to administer psychoactive drugs without any follow-up to individuals with compromised mental health. Such individuals may be in a biochemically imbalanced state and the use of psychoactive drugs could exacerbate this condition, making their symptoms worse.

This is one argument for the inclusion of physical locations for medical cannabis distribution as it provides the opportunity to gather data and monitor consumption patterns. These are important features of the operation of the VCBC.

Contaminants

Plant material used in making recreational cannabis can contain harmful compounds such as heavy metals, fertilizer residue, and pesticide residues, insect remnants or other undesirable substances, sometimes present in food products due to the nature of manufacturing processes. The difficulty of dealing with pests such as aphids and spider mites could lead to spraying pesticides on the plant.

Schizophrenia

They discussed whether cannabis could be a precipitating factor in developing schizophrenia, depression, anxiety, panic disorders, or poor psycho-social adjustment, particularly in those who begin consuming cannabis in early adolescence.

Dr. Pate responded that while there may be a correlation between cannabis use and these mental health issues, it is difficult to establish a cause and effect relationship. There could be other intervening factors. He is unaware of a corresponding rise in the prevalence of schizophrenia to match the rise in popularity of cannabis.

End of Testimony

It was apparent in the courtroom that the two government lawyers, Eccles and Guest were all over the map with their inquiries. It was hard to tell if they were unprepared and scattered or aiming for key points of law that were unforeseen to us.

It had been a solid showing by Dr. Pate. After we left the courthouse, Dr. Pate put on his rainbow cap and instantly transformed from courtroom scientist to cannabis wizard. Joints were lit and smoked along the sidewalk between the courthouse and the club, as was tradition.

Ted, Gayle, Dr. Pate and some of the members and staff from the VCBC met at a local vegetarian restaurant and enjoyed the buffet.

END OF WITNESSES FOR THE DEFENSE

When preparing for the next witness and equivocating over the admissibility of certain evidence the Judge reminded us all that we are in fact still in Canada.

"It's always an interesting thing to watch as counsel drift up to the edges and argue about whether or not they've had one skate on the right side of the blue line."

QC Peter Eccles

Crown Prosecutor Peter Eccles had been a gentleman throughout the trial. As the defense and prosecution gathered at different ends of the carpeted hallway outside of the courtroom, you could sense the tension between the lawyers. In the courtroom, they joked with one another and maintained a friendly rapport. At times while he was speaking, the Prosecutor held his back and leaned over the table, indicating that his back was sore. It was my immediate thought, and one shared by others in the room, that he would benefit from one of our cookies.

Witnesses for the Prosecution

While the stories of the patients as well as Ted and Gayle were very important, we knew that at the center of the battlefield would be a standoff between our expert witness Dr. Pate and Health Canada's chief science officer, Dr. Abramovici.

Like Dr. Pate's testimony, the following can get technical, but it's worth it, and will help you understand the strengths and weaknesses of the remaining arguments used to oppose cannabis legalization on the highest level.

I have paraphrased and summarized much of the testimony and provided quotes where I felt it was important.

Dr. Hanan Abramovici

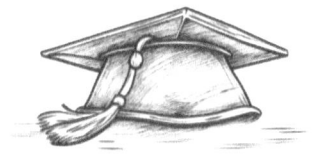

Expertise

Dr. Hanan Abramovici, holds a PhD in neuroscience.

His areas of expertise include molecular and cellular biology, protein biochemistry, pharmacology, physiology, neuroscience, and drug abuse research. He has been working as a Senior Scientific Information Officer at Health Canada since February 2010.

His job is office-based, involving the collection, analysis, and summarization of scientific and medical information on controlled substances and drugs of abuse, including cannabis. He wrote and reviewed a document available on the Health Canada website. The document includes 476 references and is called *Information for Health Care Professionals*.

He had to check all 476 references before footnoting them, which took about three months of full-time work. The purpose of the Information for Healthcare Professionals document is to provide the complete knowledge of scientific and medical literature on cannabis and cannabinoids to healthcare professionals, as well as the public.

He had been asked by Health Canada to assist in this case by providing a written report in reply to the report prepared by Dr. Pate.

More Study Needed

Hanan began by challenging the phrase used by Dr. Pate, "therapeutically active compounds." There needed to be more study before accepting this claim. He preferred the phrase "pharmacologically active" instead.

Abramovici would not accept that cannabis has any proven medical application, challenging Dr. Pate's use of the word "therapeutic." He only accepts the therapeutic benefit of cannabinoids when the focus is on cannabinoids rather than the whole cannabis plant.

He denied that anecdotal and laboratory research qualifies as scientific evidence wherever it supports cannabis' safe profile, yet later suggested the same kinds of research where a risk or harm was found.

Hanan confirmed that he was unable to find any scientific literature or studies to support cannabis efficacy for gastrointestinal conditions or transdermal delivery methods: "most of the cannabinoids would be trapped in the skin."

He declared the lack of scientific and medical information extends to adverse effects of marijuana-derived products, such as edibles and extracts. According to him, these too needed more study.

EDIBLE CANNABIS IS INEFFECTIVE

Abramovici held that without placebo controlled clinical trials there is no evidence that cannabis taken orally is safe or even works at all. He suggested that oral cannabis undergoing first pass metabolism on its way to the colon breaks down so significantly that it is ineffective.

He emphasized that oral doses are absorbed slowly, creating a longer period before one could feel the effects and opined that this would make it harder for individuals to self-moderate their doses. When asked if he agreed that oral ingestion produces longer lasting effects, he responded by saying it also produces longer lasting adverse effects.

In his literary review, Abramovici states that smoking is preferred over oral because the psychotropic effect or "high" occurs more quickly. Abramovici disregards that many patients use cannabis to help them to sleep, during which slow release is more logical than waking up once an hour to re-dose by inhalation.

The Crown suggested that to avoid this loss of medicinal content patients should grind their cannabis, wrap it up, and insert it in their rectum. While suppositories do work well, they are not, as the Crown suggested, wadded mashes of plant material inserted rectally. The Crown's position was insensitive to the point of absurdity.

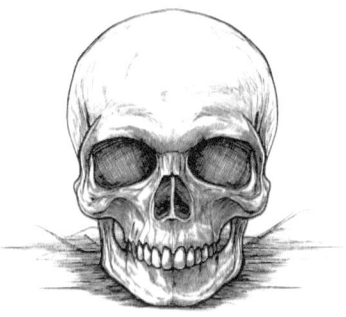

Adverse Effects

Hanan then began to list various adverse effects that he had reported in his affidavit including psychomotor and cognitive impairment. These effects could exacerbate a patient's existing condition.

Hanan stated that euphoria could be unpleasant for some individuals.

He then posited that cannabis use could lead to death through indirect causes such as impairment. Providing warnings about potential impairment is important, and ultimately, it is up to the individual to follow that advice.

Entourage Theory

Hanan challenged the statement about terpenes augmenting the effects of cannabinoids in an entourage. He pointed out that this was anecdotal in nature and lacking scientific support. Hanan denies the entourage effect has been adequately proven and states a need for more studies as well a recognition of its status as a theory.

He stated that there are no scientific studies to support the assertion that different strains produce different effects, or the idea that various compounds can produce synergistic effects and indicates that these might be good areas for a research scientist in the field.

Risks of Petrochemical Extraction

Hanan then discussed the risks associated with the petrochemical solvent extraction of resin from glandular trichomes. He cited articles relating to extensive burns suffered by individuals caught in fires that can result from these extraction processes but also noted that proper procedures can decrease risks.

Kirk rose in objection to the questioning on the grounds that it is outside the witness's area of expertise in pharmacology and the judge agreed and allowed the objection.

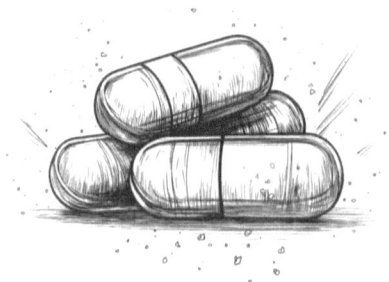

Standardization

A bramovici noted that non-standardized production methods are a concern when it comes to any therapeutic product offered for sale to the public.

As for standardized cannabis products, there is Marinol, Cesamet and Sativex. Marinol is a synthetic Delta-9-THC administered to patients suffering from HIV/AIDS-associated anorexia-cachexia, nausea, and vomiting, while Cesamet or Nabilone is a synthetic derivative of Delta-9-THC used as an antinauseant in the clinic. Sativex is an oral mucosal spray composed of botanical extracts from two different strains of cannabis sativa, its composition is well-characterized and stable from batch-to-batch.

Health Canada provides these monographs to inform healthcare professionals about their pharmacological and clinical aspects, including pharmacology, mechanism of action, clinical trials, adverse effects, and dosing.

Hanan then confirms that he will stand by his report and his written opinions refuting Dr. Pates' expert opinion.

Cross Examination

Poised like an eagle in his black and white Supreme Court robe, Kirk began.

LIMITED EXPERTISE

Dr. Abramovici has not conducted any laboratory work with cannabis or cannabinoids and has not published any papers on the subject. He did not receive any specialized training in cannabis or cannabinoids during his education. He is a member of the International Cannabinoid Research Society but has only ever attended one of their conferences.

Hanan has never presented on the topic of cannabis or cannabinoids, nor submitted any papers or posters at the International Cannabinoid Research Society conference. He joined Health Canada as a Senior Scientific Information Officer in February 2010. He has never worked in the medical marijuana access division and has never been involved in the processing, approval, or issuance of authorizations for marijuana possession. He has never reviewed any applications by patients to possess or produce marijuana for medical purposes.

He is unaware of most terms that refer to cannabis concentrates or extracts.

INFORMATION FOR HEALTH CARE PRACTITIONERS

Hanan began updating the Information for Health Care Professionals document in June of 2010 at the request of his superior at Health Canada, Ms. Desjardins. His main task was to read the old version of the document and the studies referenced in it before educating himself on where the science had gone since the previous version. He consulted online medical and scientific literature found in *PubMed* to educate himself.

Research into cannabis has been developing quite rapidly. The surge in interest in the field was sparked by the discovery of the receptor systems and the endogenous cannabinoids.

There are many thousands if not tens of thousands of studies on cannabis and cannabinoids that have been published on PubMed. The document for Healthcare Practitioners contains clinical studies, lab studies and case studies as well as anecdotal evidence.

Evidence

Anecdotal evidence can be supported or refuted by subsequent lab work or clinical studies. The absence of follow-up work on anecdotal evidence does not necessarily mean the reports are right or wrong, it just means the work has not been done.

Drugs may be developed through analyzing the scientific basis for a benefit suggested by an anecdotal report, followed by lab work and clinical studies. Clinical trial results do not guarantee safety once a drug is made widely available. Some drugs that were approved for marketing, were found later to have negative effects, such as the Cox-2 inhibitor Vioxx.

Vioxx, a non-steroidal anti-inflammatory drug used to treat inflammatory conditions and pain such as arthritis went through the clinical trial process and was marketed in Canada and elsewhere and is responsible for the deaths of over a hundred thousand people.

Dr. Abramovici continually expressed the need for "downstream" clinical trials for cannabis safety in the general population. Downstream development moves from producer to patient, involving human trials in clinical settings of substances that have shown success in "upstream" laboratory testing.

Abramovici confirmed that the government has stopped all research into medical cannabis, and drug companies are the only groups with the resources to perform them.

Employer Bias

As well as reviewing the Pate affidavit and the affidavit of Dr. Harold Kalant in preparation for the trial, Hanan reviewed two studies attached to Dr. Pate's affidavit, primarily authored by a Dr. Ethan Russo, who he knows is employed by GW Pharmaceuticals. Hanan submits that Dr. Russo's employment by GW Pharmaceuticals compromises the validity of any work that he might undertake.

Kirk Tousaw asked if scientists tend to want to please their employers?

Hanan responded that sometimes research findings do not necessarily align with the research institution's mandate.

Kirk asked what influences may affect an individual's perspective on research?

Hanan responded that Dr. Russo's perspective on the research may be influenced by his employment at GW Pharmaceuticals, which has a particular interest in certain realities. However, Dr. Russo is the current secretary of the International Cannabinoid Research Society who has published multiple books on the subject. Hanan had listened to Dr. Russo present on Sativex and adverse reactions at a recent ICRS conference.

Then came the following exchange:

KIRK: "Did you receive any directions from anyone at Health Canada with respect to your report or the testimony you're going to give today."

HANAN: "I did. I discussed -- sorry. I discussed my affidavit with my director at one point, yes."

KIRK: "Was that Ms. Desjardins?"

HANAN: "Yes. That's correct."

KIRK: "And did you provide a copy to her?"

HANAN: "Yes, I did."

KIRK: "And did she have comments to make on it?"

HANAN: "Very few."

KIRK: "Did you alter your report in any way based on those comments?"

HANAN: "Did I alter my report -- no, not really."

KIRK: "Well, no and not really are different answers."

HANAN: "No."

KIRK: "Did you prepare any draft copies of your report in preparation to give your testimony today?"

HANAN: "I may have, yes."

KIRK: "And would that differ from the affidavit that you've provided that's been marked as Exhibit in these proceedings?"

HANAN: "Yes."

KIRK: "And who, if anyone, did you share those draft copies with?"

HANAN: "I shared it with my director."

KIRK: "Anyone else?"

HANAN: "Legal counsel."

KIRK: "And you said your director had some comments, very few, but those comments did not result, I take it, in any alteration to the draft of your report, is that correct?"

HANAN: "I'm trying to remember now, sorry. It was a very, very busy week for me that week."

KIRK: "Take your time."

HANAN: "Thank you. She -- yeah. She had -- she had some comments on -- on my affidavit, yes."

KIRK: "And -- and as a result of those comments, did you make any changes to your affidavit?"

HANAN: "Yes, I did."

KIRK: "And what were those changes?"

HANAN: "Those changes were -- I would say those changes were probably paragraphs -- the last few paragraphs in the conclusions. Those were as a result of my discussions with Dr. Desjardins."

KIRK: "So when you say the last few paragraphs in the conclusions, you're referring to paragraphs 43 through 46 of your affidavit?"

HANAN: "Yes."

KIRK: "And in terms of substance, what did the draft say that's different from what the final report says?"

HANAN: "I believe those paragraphs were not in my original draft. They were added subsequent to my discussions with Dr. Desjardins."

KIRK: "And so paragraphs 43 through 46, your conclusions, did not appear in your original draft affidavit but just to be clear, they were added after Dr. Desjardins, your superior at Health Canada, provided you with comments, correct?"

HANAN: "That's correct."

KIRK: "And what was the substance of her comments?"

HANAN: "Those were her comments."

KIRK: "The conclusions were her comments?"

HANAN: "The conclusions came from my discussions with Dr. Desjardins."

KIRK: "I don't mean to be obtuse but what did she say, what were her comments and how are those reflected in this final draft?"

HANAN: "I think these were -- I'm trying to remember. Oh, I think I remember what -- okay. So these -- I think we had traded back and forth my original affidavit and these were paragraphs that she had put into the document."

KIRK: "So just to be clear –"

HANAN: "I -- I believe. I – Okay. I'm pretty --"

KIRK: "That's your memory of the event?"

HANAN: "That's my memory of the event, yes."

KIRK: "Okay. And so just to be clear, paragraphs 43 through 46 of your affidavit were, in essence, authored by your superior, Dr. Desjardins, and then you incorporated them into the final version of the affidavit?"

HANAN: "That's correct."

After this, Hanan was asked to leave the room while counsel discussed the revelation that the Crown's expert witness had allowed his superior at Health Canada to write his conclusions. It was clear that from here on his opinions were not going to hold much weight. That did not mean he could not still be useful to us.

Lead Prosecutor, Peter Eccles argued that since Dr. Abramovici reviewed the entire affidavit and swore to it, the opinions in those paragraphs were properly before the court, even if they were drafted by Ms. Desjardins. The court disagreed, stating that they may not have admitted those paragraphs had they known about Ms. Desjardins' involvement, as joint or corporate opinions should not be admitted into evidence.

Methods of Ingestion

Hanan explains that "Smoked THC will have a high spike in systemic levels, followed by a rapid decline, whereas oral ingestion results in a longer period of activity in the system, potentially benefiting patients with chronic pain who seek sustained relief."

They discuss the harmful effects of smoke, such as the presence of carcinogenic chemicals, ammonia, oxides of nitrogen, and hydrogen cyanide. The witness agrees that not smoking can minimize the intake of these compounds.

He then explains what happens to THC in the pot cookie that you just ate.

"Well, I believe the THC begins to be degraded in the stomach along with the rest of the food material. It then passes into the small intestine where it gets mixed with some enzymes released by the pancreas and the liver, and it begins to be absorbed in the small intestine. In fact, most of the absorption of nutrients occurs in the small intestine at different points, and from there the nutrients are absorbed by the portal vein, and then they go into the liver where those nutrients undergo a series of metabolic reactions, and then from there the nutrients, metabolites or compounds are distributed to the rest of the body via blood circulation. Then the remnants of the food get passed into the colon from where water is mostly reabsorbed into the body and it passes through the colon to the other side."

A patient may supplement their edible cannabis with inhaled cannabis, but it's important to note that Vaporizers are not necessarily cheap, the Volcano Vaporizer costs around $600.

They discuss Health Canada's quality control process that incorporates gamma radiation to control pathogens. Hanan admits that there are no studies that he knows of that show the safety of gamma irradiation for inhaled cannabis products.

Alternative Routes

The bioavailability of THC varies depending on the method of consumption.

Expect slow and unreliable absorption from oral doses in chocolate cookies with differential peak levels of cannabinoid producing potentially multiple peaks in the end user.

By spraying it in the mouth or cheek, peak plasma concentrations of both THC and CBD occur within two to four hours, lasting longer than when smoking. Blood levels of THC and other cannabinoids are lower when administered *buccally* due to slower absorption and rapid redistribution into fatty tissue.

Regarding topical THC, the witness explains that cannabinoids are hydrophobic, and absorption through the skin is limited. Some research has been carried out on transdermal delivery of synthetic and natural cannabinoids. There are cannabinoid receptors in the skin, and hypothetically, topical application could have therapeutic effects.

The witness confirms that they are unaware of any scientific evidence supporting the claim that topical administration is effective for inflammatory skin conditions or chronic joint pain.

Schizophrenia

Kirk: "You are aware that there has been both an increase in usage rates at a population level, as well as an increase in potency of what I'll call street marijuana available to the population over the last 20 to 30 years, correct?"

HANAN: "That's my understanding, yes."

KIRK: "And are you aware of any epidemiological or population-based studies that demonstrate a significant uptick in the rates of schizophrenia in the population over that same time period?"

HANAN: "What I am aware of is the studies that I've included, and those studies summarize the literature by doing a meta-analysis, and the that their conclusions are that there is an increased risk of developing psychosis among individuals who may not have a predisposition to the disorder as a function of usage and frequency."

KIRK: "But in response to my question, you're unaware of any studies suggesting or demonstrating that there's been an uptick or an increase in the rates of schizophrenia in the general population that would track the increase in both potency and use rates of cannabis in the general population?"

HANAN: "No, I'm not aware."

Cannabinoids

The conversation moved to the endocannabinoid system in human tissues, consisting of cannabinoid receptors CB1 and CB2, and the entourage of lipid compounds found in our cells that modulate endocannabinoid activity.

They also discuss the pharmacodynamic information on marijuana, focusing on THC and CBD. THC has psychoactive effects, while CBD lacks detectable psychoactivity and has high potency as an antagonist of CB1 and CB2 receptor agonists. The pre-clinical studies suggest that CBD has anti-inflammatory, analgesic, antipsychotic, anti-ischemic, anxiolytic, and anti-epileptic effects.

Finally, they briefly discuss CBN and CBG, two other phytocannabinoids, and their potential effects on the human body.

The doctor confirms that cannabinoids have potential therapeutic applications in treating various conditions, such as psychosis, epilepsy, anxiety, sleep disturbances, neurodegeneration, cerebral and myocardial ischemia, inflammation, pain, and immune responses, among others. The witness also discusses the pharmacokinetics of

THC, including absorption, distribution, metabolism, and elimination.

The potency of cannabis may be underestimated in some studies, as the conversion of THCA to Delta9THC is not always taken into account.

Tolerance

The development of tolerance to THC can occur with chronic use, leading to diminished psychoactive effects for some users. Increasing dosage is not as dangerous as with opiates. Cannabis pain relief can be similar in potency to codeine but works through a different pharmacological mechanism and does not depress respiratory activity, the leading cause of opiate related death.

THC is excreted via feces (65%) and urine (20%) and after five days, 80%-90% of the total dose is excreted.

Due to the complexity of pharmacokinetic and pharmacodynamic relationships, there is great variability in how different individuals experience the effects of THC. In studies, a range of 7-29 nanograms per milliliter is needed to achieve half of a high, but it is difficult to quantify exactly what half a high is.

Dosing

People may experience a subjective high at lower doses. Precise dosing schedules for cannabis have not been established, but there are some rough dosing guidelines.

Health Canada recommends a process of self-titration for patients who have never used marijuana before. This means that patients should start with a low dose and gradually increase it until they find the right dosage for their needs.

In some cases, a 10mg dose of THC was well-tolerated by patients, but a 20mg dose caused side effects like sleepiness, dizziness, difficulty coordinating movements (ataxia), and blurred vision.

What Cannabis Helps

Cannabis can be helpful for people with nausea, vomiting, wasting syndrome (a loss of appetite and weight), multiple sclerosis, amyotrophic lateral sclerosis (ALS), spinal cord injuries, epilepsy, and different types of pain, including cancer pain.

Non-cancer pain: cannabinoids have been shown to reduce sensitivity to pain in animal models, but clinical evidence in humans is lacking.

Post-Operative Pain and Neuropathic Pain: Short-term clinical studies suggest cannabinoids are moderately effective in reducing intractable central or peripheral neuropathic pain in individuals already receiving analgesic drugs, with side effects comparable to existing non-cannabis treatments.

Rheumatoid arthritis: A preliminary study on the use of Sativex, a cannabis-based medicine, shows potential benefits for patients with arthritis, which is a Category 1 condition under the MMAR (Marijuana Medical Access Regulations).

Headache and fibromyalgia: A randomized, double-blind, placebo-controlled trial of nabilone, a synthetic cannabinoid, showed statistically significant improvements in subjective measures of pain relief and anxiety in fibromyalgia patients after four weeks of treatment.

Movement disorders, dystonia, Huntington's disease: the potential role of the endocannabinoid system in Huntington's disease and the need for more research. The protective properties of cannabinoid-related compounds suggest that cannabinoids might help delay or arrest the development of the disease.

Parkinson's and Tourette's Syndrome: randomized, double-blind, placebo-controlled trials that showed improvements in motor and vocal tics and obsessive-compulsive behavior in Tourette's Syndrome patients treated with THC.

Glaucoma: Smoking or eating cannabis has been shown to reduce intraocular pressure, but these methods of delivery have drawbacks, such as short duration of action and unwanted side effects.

Psychiatric disorders: Preliminary evidence suggests that cannabidiol (CBD) may have antipsychotic and anxiolytic activity. There is a potential modulation of effects between THC, which has pro-psychotic and pro-anxiety effects, and CBD, depending on their doses. Abramovici notes that CBD's effects are usually seen in very high doses, which are not typically found in street marijuana or most strains of cannabis.

Hanan continued to highlight the need for more research on cannabinoids' potential benefits and side effects in treating various medical conditions such as Alzheimer's disease, dementia, inflammatory diseases, Crohn's disease, and cancer. Cannabinoids could be useful in treating inflammation and certain inflammatory skin conditions, though further research is necessary.

Cannabis has been found to inhibit tumor growth in certain types of cancer, although the effects vary depending on the dosage. In one study, THC was injected directly into tumors of *glioblastoma multiforme*, a form of brain cancer. This treatment inhibited the growth of cancer cells but required very high doses.

A separate in vitro study suggests that CBD may enhance the inhibitory effects of THC on human glioblastoma cell proliferation and survival, but more clinical work is needed to confirm this potential.

Contraindications

People under 18, those hypersensitive to cannabinoids, or those sensitive to smoking could be at risk of adverse reactions.

Due to potential drug interactions, particularly with central nervous system depressants, combining marijuana with alcohol or sedatives could be dangerous.

There is inconclusive evidence linking marijuana use and cancer, despite cellular and molecular studies suggesting that smoked marijuana could be carcinogenic. THC and CBD might have anti-tumor properties that could counteract the carcinogenic effects.

Smoking marijuana could result in negative histopathologic changes in the lungs.

THC & CBD SYNERGY

Hanan discussed a study published in the Journal of Pain and Symptom Management titled "Multicenter, double-blind, randomized, placebo-controlled, parallel-group study of the efficacy, safety, and tolerability of THC:CBD extract and THC extract in patients with intractable cancer-related pain." cited it in the "Information for Health Care Practitioners" document.

The study compared the efficacy of a THC:CBD extract (essentially Sativex) with a THC extract and a placebo in providing relief to patients experiencing advanced cancer pain. A total of 177 patients who were not experiencing adequate analgesia despite chronic opioid dosing participated in the two-week trial. Sixty patients were given the THC:CBD extract, 58 were given the THC extract, and 59 were given the placebo.

According to the abstract, the primary analysis of change in mean pain Numerical Rating Scale (NRS) score was statistically significant in favor of THC:CBD compared with the placebo, indicating that the THC:CBD extract worked in a statistically significant manner compared to the placebo.

However, the THC group showed a non-significant change. The study also reported that twice as many patients taking THC:CBD showed a reduction of more than 30% from baseline pain NRS score compared to the placebo group, while the number of THC group responders was similar to the placebo.

The study partially supports the hypothesis advanced by Dr. Pate and Dr. Russo that there is potentially a synergistic or enhancing effect between THC and CBD that may not be experienced in people taking THC alone.

Adverse Effects

Adverse effects from cannabinoids are typically dose-dependent and cease upon discontinuation of use. Adverse effects from cannabis are generally tolerable and similar to those seen with other medications, with rare acute complications manageable through conservative measures.

In "Adverse effects of medical cannabinoids: a systematic review," published in the *Canadian Medical Association Journal* (CMAJ) in 2008, The results indicated that 4,779 adverse effects were reported among participants, with 96.6% of them being non-serious. The most common serious adverse events were relapse of multiple sclerosis, vomiting, and urinary tract infections.

A book called "Science of Marihuana" by Iversen, which Hanan is familiar with, quotes a statement from the Institute of Medicine's 1999 report on "Marihuana and Medicine." The quote suggests that except for the harms associated with smoking, the adverse effects of marijuana use are within the range of effects tolerated for other medications. Hanan generally agrees with the quote but expresses the need for more clinical studies and epidemiological research to better understand the long-term effects of cannabis use.

Kirk questions Hanan on the use of the term "no scientific evidence" and whether it means no clinical studies. It appears that Hanan will discount certain types of evidence when discussing benefits but accepts them when discussing risks.

Re-examination by the Crown

The Prosecutor questioned Dr. Abramovici about the potential impact of the case on his employment and his job duties, to which Hanan responded that he had no idea.

They discussed an article that called for high-quality trials to further characterize safety issues related to the use of medical cannabinoids. Dr. Abramovici stated that he was not aware of the existence of such high-quality trials.

An article pointed out several concerns and limitations in the reporting of adverse events in published trials, indicating that they may be underreported.

Peter Eccles then asks about the establishment of the epidemiological link between tobacco and cancer, with Dr. Abramovici estimating it took about three decades.

Oral ingestion of cannabis and its slow and erratic systemic uptake is due to multiple factors, including digestion differences, food intake, and genetic differences in metabolism.

He cannot recall any specific clinical or preclinical studies to support the claims that cannabis can replace almost any type of allopathic medicine or that extracts are effective on everything from bacteria and fungi to the herpes virus and staphylococcus.

Neither does Dr. Abramovici know of any anecdotal studies reported or scientific literature supporting these assertions.

Eric Ormsby

The final witness came from Health Canada to explain the drug and natural health product regulations.

Ormsby's role in Health Canada since 2000 involves managing the Office of Science Bureau Policy Science and International Programs for Therapeutic Products. He has provided advice and assistance to Health Canada's Marihuana Medical Access Regulations (MMAR) Division.

He describes how regulatory oversight aims to ensure that drugs on the market are safe and effective for patients under recommended conditions of use. Drugs may be chemically manufactured or biologically derived, such as the Alzheimer's drug Reminyl which is derived from Narcissus plant bulbs.

The Federal Drug Regulations contain special rules for the approval of new drugs and provide a definition of "new drug" as per the regulations. Before this new drug approval process, there were many drugs in common use that became "grandfathered" drugs, such as aspirin. These did not require a full clinical trial process because they were approved before the Food and Drugs Act based on a history of use. Cannabis had been forcibly discontinued by prohibition in the early 20th century or otherwise one would have expected cannabis to have been grandfathered in as well.

Whenever a new indication is discovered for a drug it will need to pass through the regulatory approval process. The well known product Rogaine was originally a heart medication but is now marketed for hair growth, requiring a new submission for its new indication.

There are three methods through which Canadians can obtain drugs: clinical trials, the special access or emergency release program, and the submission and review process followed by a *Notice of Compliance*.

Cross Examination

According to Mr. Ormsby, Health Canada plans to remove Canadians' lawful right to produce marihuana for themselves or designate someone to produce it for them. The government has no plans to issue grandfathering of existing personal production license holders or the possible licensing of compassion clubs or compassionate dispensaries.

The Natural Health Product Regulation is a comprehensive scheme governing the manufacture, marketing, and sale of natural health products in Canada. Intended to ensure quality control, consistency, standardization, claims regulation, and other factors similar to what the Food and Drugs Act and its regulations do for pharmaceutical substances.

The FDA approval process has qualified the foxglove plant and its derivative, Digitalis, which is available to be used in Canada as a prescription drug to treat heart-related issues. The plant itself is toxic, and Digitalis poisoning can be lethal.

Daffodil (narcissus) bulbs are used to make Reminyl, with Galantamine as its active compound. The U.S. FDA's published an alert regarding its potential to cause mild cognitive impairment and higher mortality rates. Mr. Ormsby agrees that many plants have toxic effects.

Cannabis and cannabis extracts would fall under the NHP Regulation, but for their inclusion under the Controlled Drugs and Substances Act. The witness mentions that Marinol, Cesamet, and Sativex are examples of drugs that have received a notice of compliance because they require a prescription. There is no current discussion about amending the NHP Regulation to make it applicable to cannabis and cannabis extracts, as the intent of the regulation is to cover non-prescription drugs.

The process of drug development, including the high costs involved, the need for patents, and the goals of pharmaceutical companies can slow or stop a product's journey to market.

Final Arguments

The Crown argued that our members' medical decisions were unsupported by the science, that our members were driven to purchase by astute marketing skills that convince customers to prefer our "brand" of marihuana products.

They argued that our products were inconsistent from day to day and that nobody knows what is in them. No allowance should be made for this "slipshod and uncontrolled" approach.

No protection should be extended to the marketing of a glorified snake oil with claims it can cure all, including broken bones, to vulnerable and sick citizens. Accepting our request would create a new charter right: a subjectively based right to regulatory exemption.

There were other arguments presented by the Crown. Most of them are not worth trying to explain. Some of them drew the ire of the judge, who leaned across his desk and looked down at the Prosecutor through furrowed eyebrows as the pacing prosecutor ended his argument, flipping through pages of notes for his next point.

The crowns' final argument was that there would be no problem with patients making edible products so long as the leaf used remains with the liquid. This was so that a police officer doing a home inspection could guarantee that the amounts being stored were kept within the allowable personal use limits of the person authorized by the MMAR.

Our argument remained simple. These products are necessary to treat the medical conditions of these patients that we serve, and the government is doing nobody a service by preventing that.

THE DECISION

On Friday the 13th of April 2012, the Judge called the court to order.

THE CLERK: In the Supreme Court of British Columbia, this 13th day of April 2012, calling the matter of Her Majesty the Queen against Owen Edward Smith, My Lord.

"The clerk is now handing to counsel my written reasons for the ruling on this Voir Dire. For the reasons set out in that document, I have concluded that the restriction to dried marihuana in the MMAR is unconstitutional as it breaches section 7 of the Charter and is not saved by section 1.

The remedy for that breach is to remove the word "dried" where it appears in the MMAR and I so order.

Mr. Smith's application for a judicial stay of proceedings is dismissed, again for the reasons set out in my written ruling.

Mr. Smith is remanded to criminal chambers, 2:00 p.m., Wednesday, April 25th to fix a date for jury selection and for trial. Before that date Counsel will obtain dates for both jury selection and trial from trial scheduling."

(Owen and Coco outside the BC Supreme Court)

It took me about an hour to get my head around how we had just won the constitutional challenge, and yet I would have to return in nine months to face a Jury trial. Nevertheless on this day we had won.

Our Victory in the BC Supreme Court was likely to be appealed, if only to give the government more time to stall the decision from taking affect. The government would not be able to appeal the impact of the decision until after the Jury trial. For thousands of British Columbia medical cannabis patients producing derivative cannabis products became immediately lawful. The decision was met by a statement from the B.C. Chief Medical Officer, Dr. Perry Kendall: "By consuming cannabis in these ways, patients are able to avoid the negative health effects of smoking, which we know to be harmful to the lungs."

You can Read the Full Decision on the Digital Timeline that accompanies this book.

Here are some key quotes from the Judges Ruling.

[94] The court in Parker continued at para. 117:

[117] To summarize, a brief review of the case law where the criminal law intersects with medical treatment discloses at least these principles of fundamental justice:

(i) The principles of fundamental justice are breached where the deprivation of the right in question does little or nothing to enhance the state's interest.

(ii) A blanket prohibition will be considered arbitrary or unfair and thus in breach of the principles of fundamental justice if it is unrelated to the state's interest in enacting the prohibition, and if it lacks a foundation in the legal tradition and societal beliefs that are said to be represented by the prohibition.

(iii) The absence of a clear legal standard may contribute to a violation of fundamental justice.

(iv) If a statutory defence contains so many potential barriers to its own operation that the defence it creates will in many circumstances be practically unavailable to persons who would prima facie qualify for the defence, it will be found to violate the principles of fundamental justice.

(v) An administrative structure made up of unnecessary rules, which result in an additional risk to the health of the person, is manifestly unfair and does not conform to the principles of fundamental justice.

[102] The Crown says that the Charter does not protect a right to tasty cookies: someone who prefers to take their marihuana orally can eat it or bake the dried marihuana into cookies, in spite of some evidence that in its dried form, marihuana is not particularly palatable.

[103] The Crown's argument trivializes this aspect of the arbitrariness issue: the question is not whether constitutional protection is sought for tasty cookies, it is whether a prohibition against someone granted a permit to lawfully possess a medicinal substance that would be illegal but for the permit should not be restricted in how they choose to take the medicine unless the restriction serves a state interest that has more weight than the individual's choice on how to take their medicine.

[114] I conclude that the restriction to dried marihuana in the MMAR does little or nothing to enhance the state's interests, including the state interest in preventing diversion of a drug, or controlling false and misleading claims of medical benefit. I find that the restriction is arbitrary, and that its engagement of the rights to liberty and security does not accord with the principles of fundamental justice, and therefore infringes those rights.

[120] If the objective in question is to discourage diversion of medical marihuana into the illegal market, then Crown's argument that restriction to dried marihuana is fair and not arbitrary presumes that no laboratory analysis is needed to enable a police officer or other investigator to distinguish dried marihuana (which might not be in its whole leaf form) from any other dried plant which might also not be in its whole leaf form. If it is possible to distinguish chopped up, dried marihuana from other dried plant material such as might be found in most kitchen spice jars, it seems to me that there should have been evidence led on the point. I am not prepared to infer that it is necessary to restrict medical marihuana to its dried form in order to make enforcement of the drug laws possible. I am not concerned with making enforcement

of the drug laws easy if the cost of doing so puts the rights protected by s. 7 of the Charter at risk. In the absence of clear evidence that the restriction to dried marihuana is necessary, I conclude that this restriction is arbitrary.

[123] I conclude that the restriction to dried marihuana unnecessarily, and therefore to an unreasonable degree, impairs the security right to choose how to ingest the medicinal ingredients in the safest and most effective manner. Given these two findings under the second stage of the s. 1 analysis, I also find that it intrudes disproportionately on the constitutionally protected rights.

Established Scientific Facts

This will be a recap of many of the points covered during the trial that surmount to the scientific facts accepted by Justice Robert Johnston of the BC Supreme Court in April of 2012.

From Dr. Pate's evidence I accept:

• The active compounds of the cannabis plant are manufactured in cells at the base of, and stored in structures called glandular trichomes.

• The main active compounds are primarily tetrahydrocannabinol ("THC") and cannabidiol ("CBD").

• Generally speaking, the concentration of glandular trichomes increases as one moves higher up the cannabis plant, with fewer glandular trichomes near the root, and many near the top.

- Viewed microscopically, the glandular trichomes appear to be a stalk rising from the plant surface with a globular top. Dr. Pate accurately analogized this structure to a golf ball on a tee.

- These glandular trichomes contain resin, and it is in the resin where the plant secretes THC and CBD.

- The highest concentration of glandular trichomes is found on or near the outer surface of unfertilized female flowers.

- From the perspective of either a medicinal or recreational marihuana user, it is the contents of the glandular trichomes that are important.

- There are various methods for separating the glandular trichomes from the plant itself: one can agitate dried flowers from the marihuana plant over a fine mesh or screen, causing the glandular trichomes to fall off and pass through the mesh, leaving the host plant material behind; one can immerse the plant material in cold water, then strain the water through a fine mesh to capture the glandular trichomes.

- Both these methods remove the glandular trichomes intact, with the resin still contained inside.

- If the results of these methods of extraction are compressed, it is often referred to as "hash" if the dry sieve method is used, or "bubble hash" if it is wet sieved. If it is not compressed, but left in dry powdered form, it is often referred to – erroneously according to Dr. Pate – as "kif" or "pollen."

- Other methods extract the resin from the glandular trichomes: one might rub the flowers in their hands, then scrape the resin off the hand; one could soak either the trichome-bearing plant, or just separated trichomes themselves, in fat such as butter or food-grade oil, as the contents of glandular trichomes are fat soluble. The same applies to alcohol, as the glandular trichome contents are also alcohol soluble.

• The results of fat-based extraction methods are often referred to as "cannabis cooking oil" or "cannabis butter."

• Other methods involve using petrochemical solvents such as petroleum ether to take up the resin from the glandular trichome, then evaporating off the solvent. The results of the solvent-based extraction method is often called "hash oil."

• These methods result in separation of THC, CBD, and other potentially active ingredients called terpenes from the plant matter.

• There is no known medical utility to the plant matter that is left behind after the glandular trichomes, or their contents, are separated from the host cannabis plant, or in the glandular trichomes themselves after the resin is extracted from them.

• A caveat on that statement is the possibility that there may be some cannabinoid inside a leaf, not as readily accessible or as easily rendered as the glandular trichomes on the leaf surface.

• If the glandular trichomes containing the active compounds are not separated from the cannabis plant, a user can access the active compounds by smoking dried plant material with the glandular trichomes still attached.

• Release of the active compounds does not require heat as high as that produced by smoking, and an alternative way of inhaling the active compounds is through a vaporizer, which releases the active compounds at a lower temperature than smoking. Medical approved Vaporizers cost approximately $500.00.

• The medical benefits from THC include anti-inflammatory and anti-spasmodic effects, increasing appetite in those whose appetites are suppressed by medical treatments such as are administered to AIDS patients, and alleviation of nausea in those taking chemotherapy for cancers.

• The well-known non-medical effect of THC is its psychoactive effects, an unwanted side effect from a medical point of view, a primary benefit from a recreational user's point of view.

• CBD has some anti-inflammatory benefits, including some analgesic effects.

• There may be some potential antipsychotic benefit from CBD in high doses, but that has not yet been fully studied.

• The glandular head of the trichome also is known to contain terpenes.

• Terpenes are compounds commonly associated with aromas, for example pine or mint.

• CBD also has some potential to inhibit the metabolism of THC by the liver, thus reducing the body's ability to intercept and eliminate the medical benefit of THC.

• There are different mechanisms for getting the therapeutic components, whether THC or CBD into the body, and Dr. Pate described each.

• One can ingest the compound orally: if one were taking THC for gastro-intestinal conditions such as Crohn's disease or Irritable Bowel Syndrome this would arguably deliver the therapeutic benefit more directly to the site of pathology.

• Oral ingestion also has the benefit of prolonging the effects of the drug in the system, with the corresponding detriment of taking longer to build a therapeutic level of the drug than would occur with smoking, for example.

• Because of the slow build-up of the drug in the body, dosages are more difficult to manage, as it takes some time to determine when the optimum therapeutic level has been reached.

• Because orally ingested THC or CBD stays in the system longer, it would be better for someone with a chronic condition of pain or glaucoma, where some level of therapeutic dosage would remain while the patient slept.

• Smoking achieves a far quicker benefit, as the drug enters the body through the lungs and is dispersed rapidly.

• The level of THC in the body also declines much more quickly with smoked marihuana than with orally ingested THC.

• Smoking would be a better way to take a therapeutic dose in case of a sharp increase in pain or discomfort.

• Smoking also has harmful side effects associated with inhaling smoke which, although less deleterious than tobacco smoke, pose risks to health nonetheless.

• A fourth application or ingestion method would be to spray a solution containing the active compound under the tongue, called trans-mucosal. Its advantages include faster assimilation of the drug, like smoking, without the risks associated with smoking.

• There are some cannabis, or similar, products that have gone through the clinical trial process and become available.

• One is Sativex, an extract of the cannabis marihuana plant that contains THC and CBD in equal proportions, taken as an oral spray.

- Another is Marinol, a synthetic THC in a sesame oil capsule.

- Another is Nabalone, similar to Marinol.

- There remains a risk that a cannabis compound mixed with another drug, like an opioid or alcohol, can have worse results than either drug alone, and as well, the risk that the psychoactive effects of THC can adversely affect judgment, perception and reaction in those operating automobiles or dangerous machinery.

- Some research is being conducted on cannabis products, but a few clinical trials are needed to bring cannabis products to market.

- However one takes the active compounds in cannabis marihuana, it is unlikely that one will suffer any long lasting harm from an overdose.

- There is some potential for terpenes to have a role in the efficacy of cannabinoids, but this also needs much more research.

- The cannabis marihuana plant and its active compounds are unlikely to cause physical harm in themselves, unlike other drug compounds where taking too much can lead to death.

- It is not possible to tell by looking what the contents of a cookie might be, or what concentration of THC a capsule of oil might contain.

Part 3
After the Trial

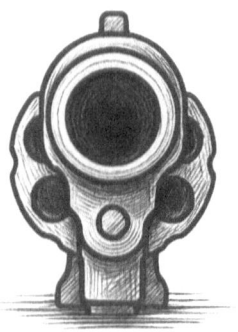

Taxes

As a result of Ted Smith's disclosure in the BC Supreme Court in 2012, that the revenue from the club was not being taxed, the Canada Revenue Agency visited the V-CBC. Ted had long been expecting the taxman to show up and considered it progress toward normalcy.

The CRA had seen the paragraphs of the judges ruling that indicate the untaxed revenue being collected by the VCBC. Ted was quick to clear up that the 25% markup on products did not go into his private coffers. He had always put all of the club's money into advocacy, activism and benefits for the members and staff. He had been declaring a modest income to the CRA as had his employees.

Faced with a $250,000 bill from the CRA, Ted decided to sell the club for $4200. It was then incorporated into a non-profit society by the staff and Ted was later voted in as President. At this time the club adopted a Point of Sale system with plastic membership cards. Despite paying full tax on their sales, the VCBC would continue to be outcast as an illegal clandestine cannabis shop. When asked about taxing an illegal business the CRA special enforcement division replied that if Ted were an assassin, they would want him to pay tax on every bullet.

Jury Trial

In April 2012, our argument for extracts had been successful in the BC Supreme Court, effectively legalizing medicinal cannabis extracts for federally licensed patients, and eventually their caregivers, in British Columbia. However, the judge ruled that my trial should proceed regardless of the constitutional victory because "society's interests in having the charges against Mr. Smith tried on their merits outweigh the violation of Mr. Smith's liberty right, at least sufficiently to deny him the judicial stay he seeks."

We assumed that because only about 10 percent of the members of the VCBC have federal licenses, we would still have some explaining to do. The rest of the club members have been diagnosed with permanent physical diseases or disabilities. With this large community of people standing behind us, each awaiting a chance to explain how at the end of their long painful paths they've persevered to find that cannabis works for them, we prepared for the Jury Trial.

The members would help us present the defense that it was necessary for me to break the existing law in order to prevent their ongoing suffering. The classic example of the defense of medical necessity is "*To steal a loaf of bread to feed one's starving family*" although in my case, nothing was stolen, and an entire community was benefiting. We reasoned that it would be difficult to find 12 people who don't have someone among their friends or family who knew about the benefits of medical cannabis.

Nine months later, on Dec. 21, 2012, I received a phone call from my lawyer Kirk Tousaw, revealing that the Crown did not believe they could convict me, promising an acquittal and canceling the Jury Trial. I invited my parents over to celebrate. They brought a bottle of champagne and we danced in my living room. This ordeal had been hard on them as the burden of understanding this complex issue is great. As much as they supported and believed in me, they were relieved I was off the hook.

Knowing the significance of this date on the Mayan Calendar, I had seven years before made it a special part of my personal growth plan. I planned to focus on a different center of consciousness each year for seven years, ascending the spine until the final *chakra*, referred to as the Crown. Having received the phone call releasing me from the grip of the crown prosecution on this auspicious date, the jubilation I experienced was met by electric shivers down my spine that reminded me of the icy waters I once plunged my hand into seven years before when I summoned my Dragon.

At the short trial in Jan. 2013, I was found not guilty after the new Crown Prosecutor, Paul Riley, chose to present no evidence. The Crown explained that because the Judge had ruled the law unconstitutional, their case was "significantly impacted" and by using the common law defense of medical necessity, I would surely win. The Judge didn't look impressed.

As a result, Kirk made a motion for dismissal, and the judge found me not guilty on all counts due to a reasonable doubt.

The Crown then entered their appeal and prepared to ask the higher Court to overturn Judge Johnston's decision and order a new Jury Trial, one where Johnston's decision would no longer exist. They did not appeal the solid scientific facts established by Dr. Pate during the Voir Dire. The Crown appealed on the basis that the law had been misinterpreted by the BC Supreme Court Judge. The Appeal hearing would be held at a later date by 3 judges at the BC Court of Appeal.

Being found not guilty was a personal victory but the issue of my relationship to the legal regulations would resurface a few weeks before the BC Court of Appeal hearing. Raising the issue of "Standing", the Court asked whether a person who is not in any way licensed under the federal regulations can be allowed to challenge those regulations in the first place?

The news of our trial had triggered a sudden bloom of illegal cannabis shops across Canada, providing all manner of edible, topical and extract products. The expungement of all of my charges was further encouragement and cannabis stores continued to multiply.

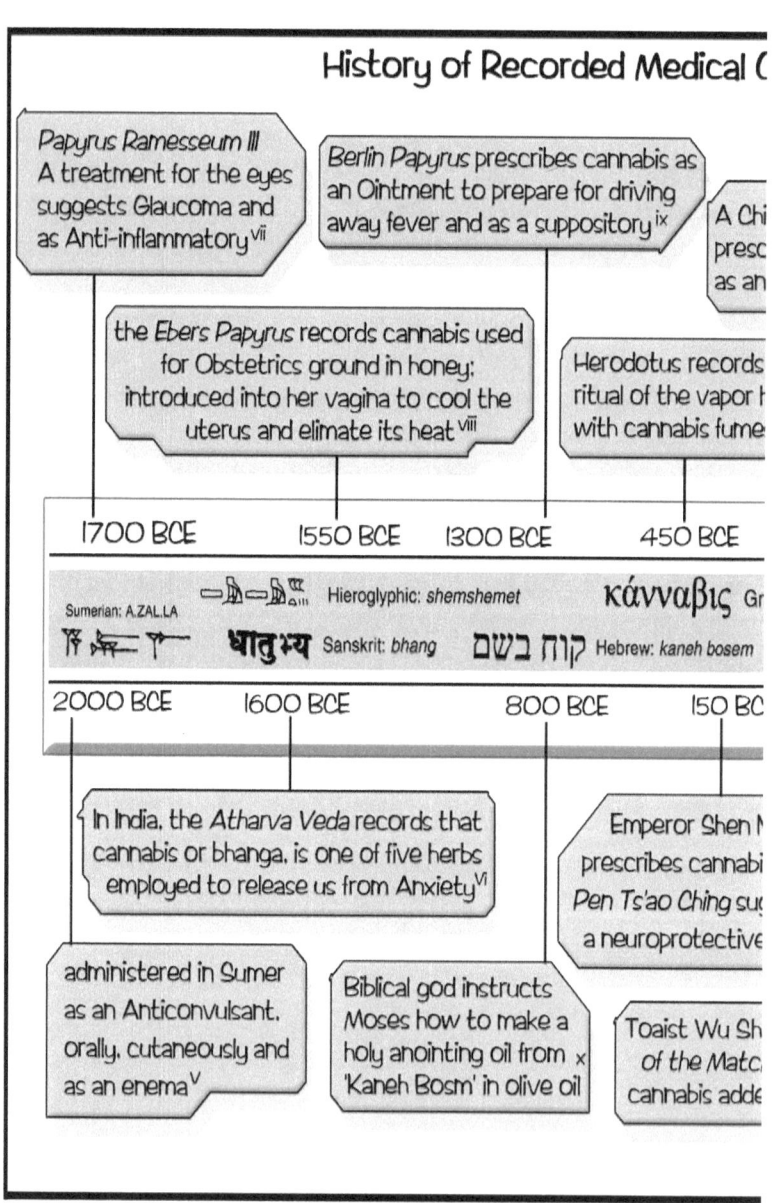

(Graphic by Owen Smith)

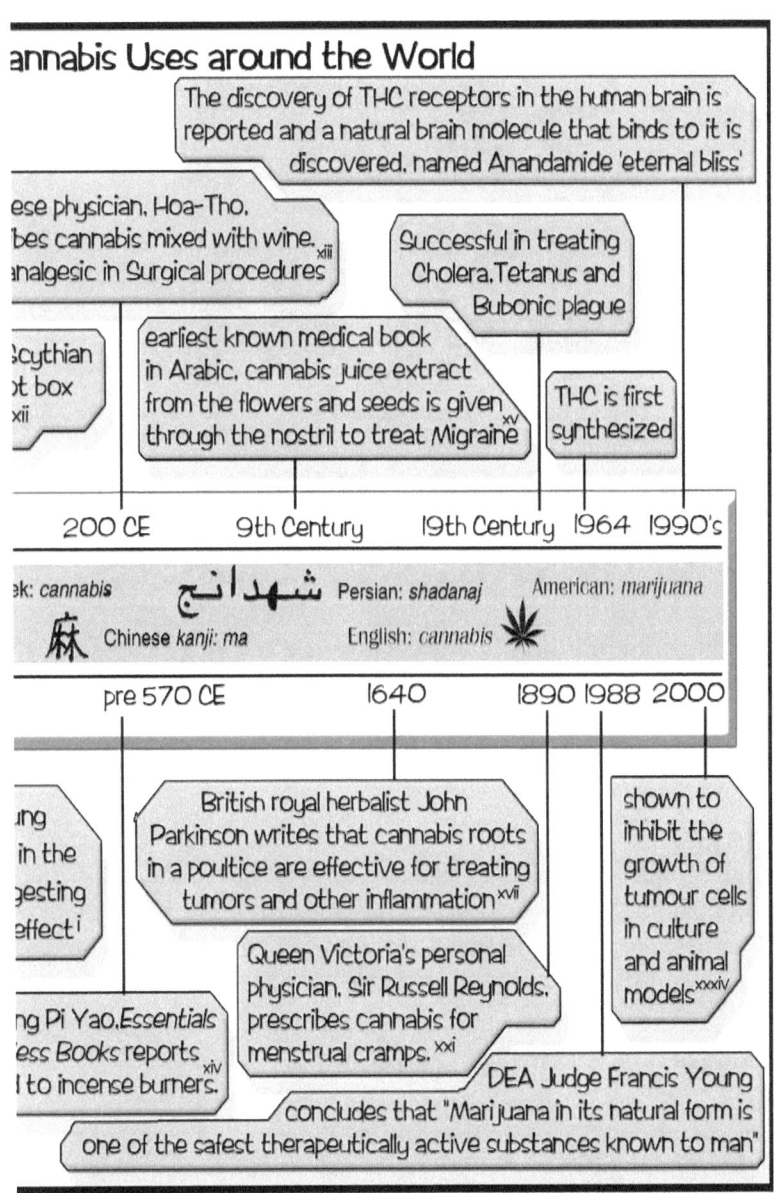

After the Trial 273

RECORDED HISTORY OF CANNABIS EXTRACTS

During the trial, I wrote an article tracking the historical record of medicinal cannabis extracts. I recall seeing the issue that this article appeared in, rolled up under the Prosecutors arm.

The government had repeatedly stated that due to the lack of double-blind, blue-ribbon, placebo-controlled, clinical trials, cannabis cannot be proven a safe medicine. Our expert witness, Dr. David Pate suggested that on the contrary, "Cannabis has undergone a multiyear open-label clinical trial by virtue of being in such popular use both medically and recreationally for an extended period of time, essentially hundreds of years."

The discovery of the endocannabinoid system has revealed a fundamental biological pathway, uniquely linking cannabis compounds to the health and homeostasis of all vertebrates throughout evolutionary history (Elphick and Egertová 2001). I will take you on a brief journey from ancient Taoist sages and Egyptian Papyri to the labs of modern scientists at L'Oreal: the history of cannabis extraction underscores the plant's enduring significance and presents much potential for our future with this versatile botanical.

BEFORE COMMON ERA

To advance our understanding of cannabis's potential as a medicine, it is helpful to look back through history at the many times and places this plant has emerged in local materia medica. Modern science is now exploring the neuroprotective qualities of a plant known to medicine makers for over 4,500 years.

Shen Nung (Shennong), revered as the "Divine Farmer" and patron of Chinese medicine, may be a figure rooted in Chinese folklore. The *Shennong Ben Cao Jing,* a classic Chinese materia medica, was compiled from earlier oral traditions around 200–250 CE. Recent archaeological discoveries lend credence to these ancient accounts. In the Yanghai Tombs near Turpan in northwestern China, researchers unearthed approximately 789 grams of dried cannabis buried alongside a light-haired, blue-eyed Caucasian man, likely a shaman of the *Gushi* culture, dating back about 2,700 years. The *Shennong Ben Cao Jing* notes that hemp grows abundantly, highlighting its widespread cultivation.

With wild cannabis growing in abundance, ancient medicine makers began to develop basic techniques to separate desired ingredients from the crude plant matter. In his extensive review, "History of Cannabis and Its Preparations in Saga, Science, and Sobriquet", Dr. Ethan Russo identifies three categories of herbal cannabis: Bhang, Ganja, and Charas. Bhang refers to a mixture of flowers, seeds, leaves, and stalks, often used to prepare traditional beverages. Ganja denotes manicured, seedless female flower buds, known for higher potency. Charas is resin collected by hand-rubbing live cannabis plants to gather the resin on one's hands or body, commonly known as hashish. Ancient methods of gathering Charas also include sieving plant material over fabric screens.

Clay tablets found in the ancient city of Nineveh represent the collected medical knowledge of Mesopotamia during the first millennium BCE. Some scholars interpret terms like A.ZAL.LA as references to cannabis, possibly used as an anticonvulsant administered orally, applied topically, and even as an enema. These ancient practitioners may have utilized various parts of plants to treat conditions ranging from impotence to epilepsy.

In nearby India, the early Ayurvedic text Atharva Veda exalts cannabis, or bhanga, as one of five sacred plants used "to release us from anxiety." The ingredients of the legendary Vedic holy drink Soma are hotly debated among academics. Author and historian Chris Bennett provides compelling evidence for the inclusion of cannabis in Soma in his book *Cannabis and the Soma Solution*.

Cannabis-infused drinks like Bhang have been popular for millennia. Bennett uses archaeological and etymological evidence to highlight cannabis as a consistent ingredient in ritual beverages. Techniques for preparing cannabis drinks evolved from simple methods of crushing and pressing oil from the seeded flowers of wild cannabis to advanced cultivation of female cannabis plants and mechanical separation of cannabinoids into forms like hashish.

Egypt provides rich insight into the medical practices of the ancient world from the extensive papyri that have been discovered and studied. Three notable entries are the *Papyrus Ramesseum III* which includes "A treatment for the eyes: celery; hemp is ground and left in the dew overnight. Both eyes of the patient are to be washed with it early in the morning." This could have been used to treat glaucoma or for the anti-inflammatory effects. The *Ebers Papyrus* records cannabis used for obstetrics: "ground in honey; introduced into her vagina to cool the uterus and eliminate its heat," further suggesting anti-inflammatory properties. The *Berlin Papyrus* prescribes cannabis as an "ointment to prepare for driving away fever" and as a "plaster." The Ramesseum Papyrus includes treatments some believe to involve cannabis, although much of the interpretation of these ancient texts remains a topic of scholarly debate.

It is still common in Egypt to use steam distillation to produce a hemp flower essential oil rich with therapeutic terpenes as a scent for perfumes, cosmetics, soaps, and candles, and to add sweetness to baked goods and candies. The essential oil possesses anti-fungal properties and can also be mixed with water and sprayed onto plants for protection. Although the varieties of cannabis used in today's products are low THC, this method could be applied to medicinal grade cannabis.

In some ancient Egyptian ceremonies, incense cones of Kyphi (kief hash loaded perfume) placed on the head would melt in the sunlight and by body heat releasing fragrant cannabis oil onto the scalp. In 2002, scientists from L'Oreal and the *Centre de Recherche et de Restauration des Musées de France* (C2RMF) collaborated to recreate ancient Egyptian perfumes using residues found in excavated vessels. French researcher Videault noted that the "perfume of the pharaohs" which included pistachios, mint, cinnamon, juniper, cannabis, and myrrh "will never be sold because some of the ingredients are illegal substances. In any case the smell is probably much too pungent for the modern world."

Greek historian Herodotus wrote detailed accounts of Scythian vapour hotbox rituals around 450 BCE. "First they anoint and rinse their hair, then for their bodies, they lean three poles against one another, cover the poles with felted wool blankets, making sure that they fit together as tightly as possible, and then put red-hot stones from the fire on to a dish which has been placed in the middle of the pole-and-blanket structure [...] the Scythians take cannabis seeds, crawl in under the felt blankets, and throw the seeds on to the glowing stones. The seeds then emit dense smoke and fumes, much more than any vapour-bath in Greece. The Scythians shriek with delight at the fumes."

Although our translations of these ancient writings are subject to speculation, it is apparent that the knowledge of cannabis was widespread throughout Ancient Egypt. It is a curious note that Moses, the leader of the Hebrew people, receives the recipe for a holy anointing oil containing large amounts of cannabis or Kaneh Bosm soon after leaving Egypt. This anointing oil was used for ceremonial purposes. The highly revered anointing oil is later applied topically by Jesus and his followers to fight epilepsy, skin diseases, eye, and menstrual problems.

IN THE COMMON ERA

In China, where some of the earliest advancements in hemp production occurred, physicians beginning with Hua Tuo (circa 140–208 CE) are believed to have prescribed cannabis mixed with wine as an analgesic during surgical procedures. The *Wushang Biyao* (Supreme Secret Essentials), a Taoist encyclopedia compiled around 570 CE, records the use of cannabis in ritual incense burners. Sinologist and historian Joseph Needham suggested that the founding scriptures of the Shangqing School of Taoism were written by Yang Xi (330–386 CE) during visionary experiences, "aided almost certainly by cannabis."

In a 9th century Arabic compendium of pharmacology, cannabis juice extracted from the flowers and seeds was administered through the nostrils to treat migraines, aching pains including uterine pain, and to prevent miscarriage. During this same period, the renowned physician and scientist Al-Kindi reported on its muscle relaxant properties in relation to conditions described as "the trembling."

One of the first great English botanists, John Parkinson, wrote in 1640 that cannabis roots used in a poultice are effective for treating tumors and other inflammations. He stated:

"The decoction of the roots easeth the pains of the gout, the hard tumors or knots of the joints, the pains and shrinking of the sinews, and other the like pains of the hips: it is good to be used for any place that hath been burnt by fire, if the fresh juice be mixed with a little oil or butter."

By the dawn of Western medicine, cannabis was being used medicinally in diverse ways for a wide range of conditions, including treatments for cholera, tetanus, and even the bubonic plague. One of Queen Victoria's personal physicians, Sir J. Russell Reynolds, stated in an 1890 issue of *The Lancet* that cannabis, "when pure and administered carefully, is one of the most valuable medicines we possess."

The popular method of directly inhaling smoke from crushed cannabis flowers didn't become widespread until after the introduction of tobacco from the New World in the 16th century. Initially, cannabis cigarettes were smoked as a treatment for asthma. Today, inhaling smoke or vapor from ganja flowers is a common method patients use to medicate, partly due to historical restrictions on cannabinoid research and the risks associated with processing cannabis under prohibitory laws.

The scarcity of accurate information previously isolated cannabis culture into small groups, hindering the development of comprehensive guides to cannabis medicine. The rise of the internet and discussion forums has provided a platform for the community to build upon their collective knowledge, despite the persistence of drug war mythology.

Cannabis prohibition drives gardeners to cultivate feminized Ganja indoors, in small spaces, for as much potency in as little time as possible, then either discarding or quickly processing the plant material into simple forms of Charas hashish. Due to legal risks and limited supply, when cannabis concentrates began to emerge on the Canadian underground cannabis market, they were valued at the same price per gram as 24kt gold.

Prohibitionists claim to protect society from high-THC cannabis, asserting that it is much stronger than in the past. However, the development of high-THC strains began in the 19th century when Western physicians like William Brooke O'Shaughnessy drew attention to its medicinal use. Some analyses from the 1970s indicate THC levels comparable to those found today. The recent increase in average THC content is consistent with the move toward controlled, indoor cultivation.

Modern studies of preserved trichomes in Morocco and Afghanistan have revealed that "Cannabis fields in [...] generations past would tend to yield equal proportions of THC and CBD." (Russo 2007) This challenges prohibitionist arguments, especially considering the promotion of pure synthetic THC medications, which have been shown to be less effective than whole-plant cannabis in medical applications. CBD interacts with THC at the CB1 cannabinoid receptor, potentially mitigating undesirable effects and offering therapeutic benefits.

IN THE MODERN ERA

Our modern era's war on cannabis has been declared a failure by numerous experts and organizations around the world. Criminal punishments have not effectively deterred individuals from seeking out this plant, which many consider to have significant therapeutic potential. In 1988, the DEA's own Administrative Law Judge Francis L. Young concluded at the end of a lengthy legal process that "Marijuana, in its natural form, is one of the safest therapeutically active substances known to man."

It is somewhat ironic that modern drug enforcement agencies celebrate successful busts by openly burning large quantities of seized cannabis, reminiscent of historical practices where cannabis was burned in ceremonial contexts, such as by the Scythians in ancient rituals.

Politicians and physicians often address the issue by highlighting the health risks associated with smoking, particularly the carcinogenic properties of combusted plant material. However, these concerns can be mitigated through cannabis extraction methods that provide safer consumption options. Providing refined cannabis products through regulated channels is a necessary harm reduction strategy.

Even basic techniques that separate the active ingredients from the plant matter can avoid these pitfalls, creating medicines that some consider superior to modern synthetic counterparts due to the entourage effect of whole-plant extracts.

Health Canada's attempt to regulate cannabis more like a pharmaceutical has been a slow and complex process, which some patients feel leaves them without adequate access to relief. The inherent difficulty in studying this complex and dynamic plant, especially for the purpose of isolating and synthesizing patented pharmaceutical products, lingers in the background of the Canadian Medical Associations' lament for more research.

In the late 1980s and early 1990s, scientists led by Raphael Mechoulam discovered the endocannabinoid system and the cannabinoid receptors in our brains, including the CB1 receptor identified in 1988. In 2000, a study in Spain led by Manuel Guzmán showed that cannabinoids could inhibit the growth of tumor cells in culture and animal models. As research expands in regions where cannabis laws are loosening, there is great anticipation about the potential healing benefits that phytocannabinoid therapeutics may offer.

A majority of U.S. states have enacted their own medical cannabis laws. A wave of support has followed the recognition of cannabis, particularly CBD, as a treatment for rare, severe forms of epilepsy in children, such as Dravet syndrome and Lennox-Gastaut syndrome.

Court of Appeal

On a cold December morning in 2013, 4 years after my arrest, I attended the BC Court of Appeal to witness the oral arguments of the two Crown Prosecutors and my lawyer, Kirk Tousaw, in front of three BC Appeal Court Judges.

Just two days earlier, we received a Memorandum from the Appeal Court Judges. Surprisingly, after four years of appearances and conferences, and two trials, the Memorandum requested that we discuss "Standing": that is, whether or not I have the right to raise the constitutional argument at all. It said:

"Specifically, the division wishes Counsel to address the question of how Mr. Smith's admitted trafficking in marihuana, when he has no authorization to do so in any form under the Marihuana Medical Access Regulations (MMAR), raises any question of the constitutionality of the restriction in those regulations on the form of marihuana distributed."

As I was healthy and did not require a medical cannabis license, I did not have a license to possess; as I am not a cannabis grower, I do not have a license to possess on behalf of a patient. Under the medical marihuana regulations there is no license to make cannabis infused vegetable oils to bake cookies, make lozenges, or fill gel capsules. It was my job to stand up for patients by providing edible products to those in bonafide medical need.

Before the hearing, our crew had breakfast with Ian Mulgrew, veteran columnist for the *Vancouver Sun*. Ian warned us that this experience would be excruciatingly boring and that the Court of Appeal likes to 'punt', avoiding any opportunity to make a final decision. The single row of seats at the back of the courtroom was full. The three Judges entered together, casting stern straight looks at the audience.

They began the day by addressing the "Standing" issue raised in their memorandum. They asked the Crown if I had the right to make the challenge, to which the Crown Prosecutor responded that there was a lot of precedent established that I did. Kirk agreed that the Supreme Court of Canada ruled in 1988 that no one can be convicted under a law that is unconstitutional even if their rights are not infringed.

When asked why I had not been prosecuted like any other drug trafficker, they stated the position that "after studying the reasons and assessing its case, the Crown concluded that the constitutional ruling significantly impacted on the Crown's ability to present its case to the Jury." The Crown repeated this point a number of times, even paraphrasing what I would have said on the stand in the Jury Trial.

They were sure that the Jury would be made aware of the Judges' constitutional ruling and would be obliged to decide in accordance with it. These arguments raised the question of the impact that the decision in our case will have on society. Unlicensed extract producers were now protected to operate their compassionate kitchens for sick people across the country.

Although most of the morning felt like I was watching *Boba Fett* brood over the chance to offer another carbonite statue to *Jabba the Hutt*, Kirk Tousaw offered brief but decisive flashes of reason. At the break, Ian Mulgrew gave his straight impression. "You're busted," he said, seeing the Judges' focus on the issue of Standing to be an avenue the Court may seek to use to dismiss the case altogether.

After the morning session dealt with the issue of "Standing"; the afternoon would focus on whether Justice Johnston erred in finding the restriction to dried marihuana unconstitutional. Legendary hash maker Marcus "bubbleman" Richardson joined us in the back row and took a few puffs of concentrate from a vape device.

The Crown lawyer Paul Riley claimed that having edible cannabis products is an unqualified choice of patients, which creates risks because it is an untested and illegal controlled substance. He posited that the trial Judge had underestimated the critical abilities that policies attain when working together in a synthesis of catalytic interdependence, namely the triple force of the Food and Drug Act, the Controlled Drugs & Substances Act, and the MMAR.

They read from the decision in R.v.Mernagh, where the Ontario Appeal Court judges stated "there is no right to prefer an illegal treatment over a legal one." Matt Mernagh had attempted to show that the MMAR program was an illusion because so few people could access it; we are attempting to show that the definition of "dried marihuana" that is provided to the program participants is essentially an illusion. Although a doctor must prescribe it, patients should have the choice to have their medicine refined from its inert plant bulk in order to ingest the medicinal ingredients in the safest and most effective manner.

They asserted that conventional cannabis-based products that have undergone regulatory approval, such as Sativex and Marinol, are available through prescription from a doctor, making homemade cannabis products unnecessary. Kirk later responded that the MMAR forms make it clear that before you receive a federal license to receive medical cannabis, "conventional treatments […] have been tried or considered, and have been found to be ineffective or medically inappropriate for the treatment of the applicant."

The Crown read parts of the VCBC Recipe Book and Product Guide and claimed that mild conditions that were listed, like itching, represented our criteria for membership and that this showed that club members weren't very sick. The Crown asserted that our patient witnesses hadn't met the standard for life-threatening illness presented in previous constitutional challenges.

Kirk had some time to read from the testimony of Gina Herman, who had bravely told her story to the court. Like many members of the VCBC, she has dramatically restored her quality of life with medicinal cannabis while reducing her dependence on prescription drugs and eliminating their harmful side effects.

Herb of Life

While I waited for the decision from the court of appeal, I travelled with my partner to Costa Rica. While enjoying the natural majesty that country offers, I wrote an epic fantasy adventure poem that mirrored my experiences with cannabis legalization. I wrote the story into 13 rhythmic and rhyming chapters that take 2 hours to read in full. The story paralleled all the events up to that point, and then continues by predicting what might come next. I often find that creativity is a good way to process stress, and this activity provided me with plenty of enjoyment and mental stimulation.

In my fantasy version of my life, not only did I predict we would win with three judges, but I predicted we would dominate completely with nine.

    A cacophony of hisses issued from the nine long necks

  and none of the ancient gods could have spied what would come next,

      in nine tiny bites it gobbled up the Kings high priest,

then a foul stench released and with each belch the smell increased

I then mused that this would give enough political force to an already sympathetic leader to result in widespread legalization.

A war upon a families love is one destined to fail,

and as popular as this plant was, their love for him would pale

in comparison, and as he'd sent so many of them to jail,

he gathered up his sense and between his legs he tucked his tail.

As silence fell across the crowd, he spied

his chance to tell the people that the Herb was legalized,

and this was wise, while his pride was damaged by the lies,

cheers filled the air and tears welled deep in people's eyes.

The Appeal Decision

We won the appeal by a two to one decision. The BC Court of Appeal dismissed the government's attempt to start a new trial however they gave the federal government a year to enact changes. This would delay the impact of our trial and continue the unconstitutional circumstances that threatened medical patients across the country.

The dissenting Judge made the case that I did not have "Standing" to raise the issue. While this was a curveball, we remain confident that I was within my rights. I should be able to raise a constitutional challenge to a law that threatens my freedom for providing cannabis health services to my community.

Not all Court of Appeal cases go to the Supreme Court of Canada. However, if there is one dissenting Judge in the Court of Appeal, the losing party is granted an automatic right to be seen by the Supreme Court of Canada. This would now escalate medical cannabis to the highest court in the country.

For Kirk Tousaw, this would be his trip to the SuperBowl. He would be joined by his mentor John Conroy and a flock of lawyers from across the country. Upon hearing about the appeal to the Supreme Court of Canada Kirk was quoted:

"I find it distressing that our government will spend buckets of tax dollars fighting against sick people's right to ingest physician approved cannabis medicine in the form of cookies. I look forward to the opportunity to defend patients' Charter rights before the highest court in the land. This is an historic moment because the Supreme Court of Canada has never heard a medical cannabis case."

INTERVENERS

One unique feature of the Supreme Court of Canada is the involvement of interveners. Interveners are third-party entities, i.e. other levels of government, non-profit societies, or industry representatives, that wish to provide the court with legal arguments to assist the judges with a perspective different from the defendant or federal government.

Our interveners were Santé Cannabis, the Criminal Lawyers' Association (Ontario), the Canadian Civil Liberties Association, the British Columbia Civil Liberties Association, the Canadian AIDS Society, the Canadian HIV/AIDS Legal Network, and the HIV & AIDS Legal Clinic Ontario.

Avengers assemble.

The Criminal Lawyers' Association (CLA) emphasized broad standing principles, arguing that even those not directly regulated, such as cannabis suppliers outside the official scheme, should have standing to challenge unconstitutional laws if charged under them.

The Canadian Civil Liberties Association (CCLA) focused on Section 7 of the Charter, highlighting that the threat of imprisonment alone engages liberty rights and shifts scrutiny to fundamental justice principles.

The British Columbia Civil Liberties Association (BCCLA) expanded on the concept of liberty, arguing it encompasses non-trivial medical decisions, not just life-threatening scenarios. They maintained that restricting these choices infringes on personal autonomy and that courts play a crucial role in ensuring state restrictions meet transparent, justified standards. They warned against defining liberty too narrowly, which could diminish the judiciary's role in upholding constitutional governance.

Perhaps our most impactful intervener was Santé Cannabis from Montreal as they brought the story of Mandy McKnight and her eight year old son Liam. Liam suffers from Dravet syndrome. Dravets is a rare and severe form of epilepsy that causes him upwards of 70 seizures a day. Liam was rendered catatonic from the regime of medications that his physicians attempted.

Before cannabis, he hadn't had a seizure free day in years. After consuming cannabis oil for a few days, Liam's seizures drastically decreased, and his health improved to the point that he could go back to school.

Mandy struggled to find a medical Doctor who would prescribe cannabis for her son. After being denied assistance by the Children's Hospital of Eastern Ontario, she had to fly to Edmonton to meet a Doctor who would help Liam attain a medical cannabis license.

Despite obtaining a license his mother was still breaking the law by turning his medicine into an oil for oral consumption. She would place a droplet of the homemade cannabis oil onto some coconut oil for him to eat.

With all this support on our side I felt confident we would win.

Supreme Court of Canada

In March 2015, I traveled to Ottawa with Ted Smith to attend the hearing in the Supreme Court of Canada. This would be the end of our 6 year quest to declare the Canadian medical cannabis regulations unconstitutional. We were hosted by

(Owen at the Supreme Court of Canada)

NORML Women's Alliance of Canada Director Kelly Coulter in the heart of downtown Ottawa, only a few blocks from parliament and the courthouse.

The night before the hearing, the MMAR Coalition hosted an event at a local Legion. It was well attended by patients and advocates from Vancouver to Nova Scotia. A bus load of advocates from around Ontario converted a coach into a mobile vapor lounge. It was called the Extract Express and loaded with dab rigs. It was a great pleasure to meet patients and advocates from across the country.

The Supreme Court of Canada is a formidable structure, fiercely stark from the outside, guarded by black metal statues of Truth and Justice. Inside, a large foyer boasts rare marble and finely carved wood. That morning it was full of medical cannabis advocates. The courtroom itself could only accommodate about 1/3 of the attendees who were otherwise able to view the proceedings from separate rooms in the building. Even these overflow rooms were full, something the Court officers told us has never happened before.

With John Conroy and an associated legal team accompanied by the lawyers for our interveners, there were a total of 11 black gowns sitting on my side of the aisle; only 2 crown representatives sat for the government. Supporters sitting in the courtroom could not help themselves but clap and cheer after the judges spoke, while Alison Myrden, one of Canada's first medical cannabis patients ate cookies and vaped in the center aisle.

The entire proceedings were broadcast live on *CPAC* and can now be viewed on the Cannabis Digest YouTube Channel and in the Supreme Court Archives.

Our Arguments

The Supreme Court of Canada, like the Court of Appeal, does not see new evidence, and so having all of the scientific facts from our trial unchallenged meant that we would only be arguing legal technicalities.

Our core argument remained that section 7 of the Charter – which protects life, liberty and security of the person from being infringed except in accordance with the principles of fundamental justice – is violated by the restriction to dried cannabis alone. We argued that liberty and security of the person includes autonomy

Ted, Kirk and Owen in the Supreme Court of Canada)

to make fundamental personal decisions, like health decisions, without interference from the state.

We also argued that liberty prevents the government from criminalizing patient conduct in this area. And finally, we argued that the restriction was arbitrary (because it harmed health instead of protecting it), overbroad (because it captured conduct that did not need to be prevented) and grossly disproportionate (because the harms done to patients grossly exceed any benefits that the restriction brings).

We asked for a Medical exemption for patients from the CDSA. We asked the court to remove medical cannabis entirely from the Controlled Drugs and Substances Act (CDSA). This would mean that cannabis for medical purposes would have no restrictions when in the hands of patients. In other words, patients can possess it, produce it for themselves and make any derivative medicines they want for their own use.

Government Arguments

The Crown continued to argue that the restriction to dried cannabis does not violate the charter and that we did not have "Standing" to challenge the law.

In similar fashion to the previous courts, the Crown's arguments were strained attempts failing weakly.

Here is an example "There's a recent case about access to um raw milk you know it's not healthy and causes health problems and so I want to have access to a raw milk Collective and the law that prohibits me from doing that is inconsistent with my section seven rights but the Ontario Court of Appeals said well no, um just because you personally believe that pasteurized milk has health concerns, there's no objective basis to your claim that that infringes upon your Liberty because there's no objective support for that..."

A justice interrupted him, "I don't want to delay you, you have a lot of ground to cover in a short amount of time, but I just want to signal to you that I'm not following this line of reasoning at all."

Later on Chief Justice Beverly McLachlan interrupted the Crown Prosecutor to say "Please refine your comments to things that really matter…"

As it appeared that the court was leaning in our favor, what shifted into focus was the remedy that the court would propose. If we were to win, would the law be declared of no force and effect or would the court give the government time to respond?

Thoughts also shifted to the greater impact that this decision would have on the legality of other psychoactive substances with medicinal value. If we were to win, we could be opening the gateway for other psychoactive drugs to become legal in Canada.

In the words of the Crown Prosecutor, "Under the legislative scheme, there are three means of obtaining access to a new drug for therapeutic purposes:

1. The new drug approval process.

2. Clinical trials.

3. The Special Access Program, which allows case-by-case authorization to use a presently unapproved drug based on demonstrated need by a physician in a particular case."

4. New Extra Regulatory Means: "On the approach the courts have taken, there appears to be a fourth means of obtaining access to a new drug in Canada: the extra regulatory means. You produce the drug, distribute it, and if you're prosecuted, you call evidence in court to prove on an anecdotal basis that someone believes they need the drug and that it helps them."

As you have read in the trial portion of this book, there were more scientific facts established for the medicinal value of cannabis presented in court than just anecdotal evidence alone; however the prosecutor does a good job clarifying the potential impact that this ruling could have on the future legality of other psychoactive plant medicines.

STANDING

Because I am not a medical patient, nor did I possess a license to support a medical patient, the question was raised again whether or not I had the right to challenge a system that I was not participating in.

Our Interveners rose to counter the issue.

Individuals and organizations can assert constitutional rights in the criminal context, as established in the case of R. v. Big M Drug Mart Ltd. (1985). The Big M case was a landmark decision in Canadian constitutional history. It established that individuals or entities, regardless of their personal situation, can challenge a law as being unconstitutional.

When there is a public interest in seeing an issue challenged, then there is value to individuals raising that challenge on behalf of other Canadians.

Big M Drug Mart, a Calgary-based drugstore, was charged with unlawfully conducting business on a Sunday, contrary to the Lord's Day Act. This Act, dating back to 1906, required most businesses to close on Sundays, reflecting a Christian tradition of observing Sunday as a day of rest (Lord's Day Act 1906).

Big M challenged the Lord's Day Act and won with a unanimous decision. The decision was significant as it was one of the first major interpretations of the Charter, emphasizing the importance of freedom of religion and the secular nature of Canadian law. It set a precedent that laws cannot compel religious observance and that the government cannot legislate on matters of morality or religion (Hogg 2007).

The Court held that any person or corporation charged under an allegedly unconstitutional law has standing to challenge the constitutionality of that law.

The Court held that any person or corporation charged under an allegedly unconstitutional law has standing to challenge the constitutionality of that law.

After the hearing our supporters gathered on the front steps of the Supreme Court. Kirk, Ted and I went to the CBC Radio Station in Ottawa and spent the day speaking to media over the phone.

A Letter to the Queen

"Her Majesty the Queen vs. Owen Edward Smith".

Despite this versus opposition displayed on CPAC for the audience at home, Queen Elizabeth II had about as much influence on the unfolding of our case as the Unicorn on the coat of arms above the judges heads.

If she knew more about this situation, I doubt that her late Royal Highness would concur with her counsel. If only in the privacy of her conscience, I'm sure she would agree that to make the contents of the teabag legal, but prohibit the tea in the pot is not a sensible restriction. The prosecutor for the crown, Paul W. Riley was recently awarded with the 'Queen's Counsel' distinction, allowing him to wear a silk robe in court. Although he looked good, the Judges expressed that his arguments were composed of "lawyer words", and incomprehensible lines of reasoning.

Having been born and raised in England, I decided it would be proper to write to the Queen and inform her of how her symbolic role was being represented to sick and disabled Canadians.

(Kirk Tousaw in the Supreme Court of Canada)

Your Majesty,

I am writing to you today as a British citizen living in Canada about a serious matter of dignity that threatens permanently disabled and diseased individuals. There are tens of thousands of Canadian patients whose maladies have exhausted the faculties of conventional medicine and for whom medical cannabis has been prescribed. These patients are only permitted this plant in its dry form and are prohibited from producing any other forms from it.

In 2009 I was arrested and charged for producing cannabis based medicinal products for these sick and disabled people. In response, I sought legal protection by raising a challenge based on the Canadian Constitution and Charter of Rights and Freedoms that you signed into law the year I was born. This challenge succeeded in 2012 and I was soon-after acquitted of all charges. An appeal was launched by the government, which was ruled in my favour in

2014. In response to another appeal, I recently attended the Supreme Court of Canada in Ottawa.

During the nationally broadcast hearing in the Supreme Court of Canada, the subtitle bar read Her Majesty the Queen Vs. Owen Edward Smith.

As I wait for a decision from Canada's highest court, I would like to explain my position in hopes of contributing to your understanding of this particular issue. Patients in Canada who are permitted dried cannabis are at risk of being arrested and jailed for making anything out of it. Take a cup of tea for example. After placing the herb into a teabag and lowering it into the teapot, the tea that is poured into the teacup is prohibited. I am sure you would agree that to drink out of the teapot is not common sense, but that is the law in Canada.

It is the law that the dried herb be consumed in its entirety. This goes against the established botanical opinion that this enforces the unnecessary consumption of contaminants that are a serious concern of critically ill patients. Patients with cancer, hepatitis C, HIV/AIDS, neuropathic pain and life-threatening seizures who find relief using medical cannabis cannot legally make or obtain the suitable medicinal products that will help them to sleep through the night. The government has asked that the court overturn the two previous rulings to send me back to face another trial.

My mother raised me to have the compassion that would lead me, if necessary, to risk my freedom to help those less fortunate. Although we are opposed in the public eye, it is my sincere belief that as a symbol of the kind-hearted people of England, you would see my point of view.

I have the honour to be, Madam, Your Majesty's humble subject.

Owen Edward Smith

SUPREME COURT OF CANADA DECISION

During the time leading up to the decision, I left the VCBC to focus on the Cannabis Digest. I moved to a beautiful 15 acre property on the Cowichan river with my partner in the middle of Vancouver Island. We named it "The Shire" for its idyllic green mounds and little bridges. There was a 3 acre man-made lake in the center of the property that we stocked with trout. We built organic gardens and housed chickens, ducks and alpacas. We experimented with cannabis infused wines, ports and cordial.

These things helped keep my mind busy and away from the pending judgment. I've known since the beginning that we had the opportunity to win big, but if we lost, then that loss would be just as large. I felt my life teetering on a precipice and I couldn't help but to turn my attention to nature.

From time to time I would read over my epic poem, in which I had imagined the justice system as a metaphorical hydra (giant sea serpent with multiplying heads) devouring the toady king's advisor in one bite. Tired of hearing the illogical arguments repeated over an issue so simple I could only envision absolute and unequivocal victory.

As I rounded the pond, I heard a strange sound and looking closely at the grassy shoreline I saw a toad that was being eaten from behind by a snake. The snake was halfway through the job, causing the toad to issue a squelching sound in desperate attempts to get a breath. The snake, noticing me, leaped from the shore into the water and swam away with the toad in its mouth. The head and front arms of the toad were still moving and the creature looked like a mythic four eyed two armed serpent swimming away across the pond.

I took this as a good omen.

I received a phone call from The CBC (Canadian broadcasting company) a day before the decision was due. I told Chris Brown about Mandy McKnight, and that they should tell her son's story of overcoming deadly epileptic seizures using cannabis oil. Tell Canadians how she has been at risk of arrest and losing her child for doing the only thing that is keeping him safe from deadly seizures.

On the night before the decision was released, I traveled down the island to Victoria and stayed at my best friend's house, a doctor of traditional Chinese medicine, and slept on the floor. When I woke, I checked my Facebook messenger and there were messages from my mother and from other mothers who I knew.

It was my mother who was the first to inform me that we had won the case with a unanimous decision and that the law had been struck down immediately.

Then I read the sincere gratitude of some of the parents with children who have epilepsy who would be able to go about their day without the fear that they may have their child taken away because of this essential medicine.

Here are some key quotes from the Decision.

"The evidence amply supports the trial judge's conclusions that inhaling marihuana can present health risks and that it is less effective for some conditions than administration of cannabis derivatives. In other words, there is no connection between the prohibition on non-dried forms of medical marihuana and the health and safety of the patients who qualify for legal access to medical marihuana."

The prohibition on possession of non-dried forms of medical marihuana limits the s. 7 Charter right to liberty of the person in two ways. First, the prohibition deprives S as well as medical marihuana users of their liberty by imposing a threat of imprisonment on conviction under s. 4(1) or s. 5(2) of the CDSA. Second, it limits the liberty of medical users by foreclosing reasonable medical choices through the threat of criminal prosecution. Similarly, by forcing a person to choose between a legal but inadequate treatment and an illegal but more effective one, the law also infringes security of the person."

"Everyone has the right to life, liberty and security of the person and the right not to be deprived thereof except in accordance with the principles of fundamental justice."

"The evidence demonstrated that the decision to use non-dried forms of marihuana for treatment of some serious health conditions is medically reasonable."

"Smith has standing to challenge the constitutionality of the MMARs. Accused persons have standing to challenge the constitutionality of the law under which they are charged, even if the alleged unconstitutional effects are not directed at them, or even if not all possible remedies for the constitutional deficiency will end the charges against them.

At no point in the course of these proceedings did the British Columbia courts or this Court issue a declaration rendering the charges against Mr. Smith unconstitutional. In fact, following the voir dire, the trial judge refused to grant a judicial stay of proceedings. Despite this, the Crown chose not to adduce any evidence at trial. As a result of the Crown's choice, Mr. Smith was acquitted. We see no reason why the Crown should be allowed to reopen the case following this appeal. Mr. Smith's acquittal is affirmed."

With my acquittal affirmed, I briskly walked about 20 minutes in the Victoria sunshine downtown to the VCBC, which was enough time to center my thoughts. I was expecting a full day of media including a live national television interview.

MEDIA STORM

The VCBC was packed with cameras and members and staff. We arranged a special WiFi strengthening device nearby. The lights and cameras were steered toward me. Here is the transcript of my national television appearance.

INTERVIEWER: "Joining us now from Victoria British Columbia is Owen Smith, the plaintiff in this case. Owen was charged with trafficking for baking pot cookies for a medical marijuana Club in 2009. Owen, great to have you on. First of all I guess congratulations are in order. You've taken this all the way, you have won, your thoughts on the news today?"

OWEN SMITH: "Thanks for having me on. It's certainly exciting news for some of the most vulnerable people in our country, some of the sickest people who haven't been able to respond to the conventional medications that are available, they are going to be able to use medical marijuana in a safer and more effective way without worrying about the law."

INTERVIEWER: "Give us a little more details on that because some people might not know a lot about this medical marijuana situation, some might say why can't they just smoke pot? Why is it important to be able to have oils, cookies, brownies, etc? Can you explain that?"

OWEN SMITH: "There are a number of reasons and Health Canada has always allowed people to eat brownies or cookies as long as they stuffed the dried marijuana in it and chewed it all down, which is unnecessary as the resin heads, as you can see (holding a plate of kief hash) are easily separated from the rest of the plant."

INTERVIEWER: "And you know Health Minister Rona Ambrose has said today that she's outraged by this decision and that the government thinks that cannabis has never been proven safe and effective as a medicine, what do you say to that?"

OWEN SMITH: "Well, Rona Ambrose should know that her fight on marijuana is really a fight against families, especially those who have children with epilepsy and to fight against a mother whose child is seizing I think is a fight that you're not going to win."

INTERVIEWER: "In your news conference, you got personal, you talked about your sister and her fight, her medical issues and how this helped her, tell us a little bit about that."

OWEN SMITH: "My sister died of melanoma skin cancer when she was 20 and she used cannabis to help fight the effects of the chemotherapy, it gave her the ability to eat, sleep and communicate with her family where the conventional treatments and the disease had taken that away."

INTERVIEWER: "And just quickly Owen I mean you've won this case so will you continue to bake and sell pot cookies?"

OWEN SMITH: "I'm currently making a recipe book and that should be published as well as an instructional guide on what it means to make a cannabis extract and all about our trial."

The media stories were typically short and simplified attempts, with little success, to explain the details of our constitutional arguments. The news focused on the absurdity of children smoking to abate their epilepsy, when an edible oil is obviously more suitable. This story was guaranteed to connect with compassionate citizens who were previously unaware of the horror these families go through.

The media repeated that the court had permitted patients to choose one form over another. It should be made clear that making an extract is not a trivial choice for patients, but a logical process one undertakes to achieve the sought after benefits, and avoid unhealthy contamination from potentially hazardous material. The reports that patients can now eat their cannabis instead of just inhaling it are not precisely true. Patients were previously permitted to eat their cannabis as long as they ate all of the plant material too.

The greatest part of the media storm was the Rosemary Barton Power and Politics interview with Mandy McKnight and representatives from the three major political parties. It was on this grand stage that Rosemary Barton asked the Conservative representative over and over again, why their government opposes a working treatment for an epileptic child. He could not answer. I had never before seen a politician so mortified to defend a party policy they had spent six years supporting all the way to the highest court in the land. His only defense was ignorance.

A number of follow-up stories with Mandy and Liam and other parents spread quickly across the country. An article by the Vancouver Sun titled "Cannabis oil hailed as 'a miracle' for epileptic son" spoke to Liams suffering 80 grand mal seizures daily, despite everything that was being done for him by medical professionals. After using cannabis, his seizures have minimized to the point where he has up to 10 seizure free days in a row.

After all of the media, and hearing the government's response to the ruling, I felt the need to immediately make a music video featuring original music I had made. The video is called Rona Ambrose Outrage remix and you can find it on the Cannabis Digest YouTube channel.

Government Response

The landslide decision from the Supreme Court of Canada is now a landmark in the landscape of Canadian cannabis litigation. The facts that we assembled form a fortified field position for further advancements against the forces of cannabis prohibition. While the drug war wages on, the battle of R v Smith is finally over.

The ruling went into effect immediately despite the government's request for a 1 year suspension to buy them time to create new regulations. The government now had to respond immediately as the ruling rendered the law of no force and effect. This lack of any law would mean there could be no charges raised of this nature until a new law is announced. All other charges that related to cannabis processing being reserved for the result of my ruling were dismissed.

About a month later the government issued a broad section 56 exemption that was followed by amendments to the medical cannabis regulations through the revised Access to Cannabis for Medicinal Purposes Regulations (ACMPR).

The CDSA was changed to make use of the term "cannabis" to refer to all substances listed under Cannabis in schedule 2 of the CDSA: Resin, THC, CBD, CBN. "Cannabis oil" now means an oil, in liquid form, that contains cannabis or dried marihuana.

The terms of the exemption stipulate that THC content must be diluted to 30 mg/ml. This low concentration oil will not be suitable for all medical patients. It would require that a patient who needed a dose of 100mg would need to consume arbitrary filler in order to achieve their dose. This is the new arbitrary line drawn by the government between patients and their medicine.

When announcing the exemptions, Health Canada also stated that dispensaries are unequivocally illegal. The government had moved the line to include the majority of medical cannabis patients, but not the most seriously in need, who require in-person service, higher strength products with more concentrated doses.

Industry Response

When I read that the government were allowing Licensed Producer's to sell derivatives in response to my Supreme Court Ruling, my first thought was 'fire up the chocolate factory!' Upon further reading it doesn't seem that the old Hershey plant at Tweed will be making anything so exciting. Tweed (later Canopy Growth) announced their upcoming Oil Extract Products on the same day, but their exemption will not allow their cannabis oil to contain any external flavours or scents.

The potency of these products would also be limited to 3%. This limit had nowhere been established by the evidence in our case. It only aligned with our very weakest potency product, Ryanol.

The inclusion of cannabis derivatives in the menus of Licensed Producers and retailers signaled hopeful news for the industry. A market report predicted that licensed producers could potentially double their market value without adding any production capacity, and little capital and operational expenses.

The industry would now have new product categories that they could make their own, with analytical tools and precise milligram doses in the foreground. This could help to reduce the stigma associated with cannabis use by bringing it into line with more familiar products available to the public.

The good news was also celebrated by licensed patients who grow their own cannabis and who previously had to break the law to make their own oils.

At the same time as our case, another cannabis trial was in motion to protect the right of medical patients to grow their own medical cannabis. A coalition formed around what was called 'the Allard injunction', a Judge's decision that effectively protected all cannabis growers in the medical cannabis system who would've had their licenses taken away by the changes being brought in by the Harper Conservatives.

The ability to grow one's own plants is an essential part of a person's capacity to provide their own cannabis, edibles or extracts. While the person may still harvest dried cannabis buds, they could use the leaf material that would otherwise be wasted to create oils suitable for edible and topical application. If patients lost their ability to grow their own cannabis, then they would essentially be restricted from making their own medicines.

While the licensed companies would be limited to providing products with a 30 mg per gram or 3% potency strength, those growing at home and producing their own products would not have the same limits.

The only major restriction placed upon registered patients was to ban "any organic compound that is highly flammable, explosive or toxic, including (but not limited to) petroleum naphtha and compressed liquid hydrocarbons, such as butane, iso-butane, propane, and propylene." This restriction was in part a response to the rise in popularity of poorly processed butane honey oil and has been partially responsible for the rise of Live Resin and freshly frozen solventless extraction.

You will find descriptions of different kinds of cannabis extraction techniques in the first Appendix of this book.

Any product resulting from an alteration in the chemical or physical properties of dried or fresh marijuana can now be created. The authorized person is also permitted to possess any product that is derived from an altered product, for example, lozenges made with an infused coconut oil.

Making an extracted cannabis oil is as easy as pouring dried material soaked in vegetable oil through a sieve. Dr. Pate's expert botanical evidence during my trial made it clear that cannabis extraction is so easy that it is often performed accidentally. The resin glands grow and swell while dangling at the tops of their brittle stems, awaiting that faintest agitation to release them from their fibrous host. By discarding the inert plant material, patients are free to consume their medicinal products in a safer and more effective way.

Hayley's Comet

Following the trial I had the pleasure of interviewing a number of medical cannabis patients about the impact that it had on them. Cheryl T Rose is the mother of Hayley Rose, one of the oldest and highest functioning survivors of Lennox-Gastaut Syndrome (LGS), a rare and severe form of epilepsy that causes multiple types of seizures, and delays cognitive and behavioral development.

Cheryl is one of a chorus of parents who are desperately seeking to expedite cannabis policy shifts, as their children risk suffering severe developmental setbacks from their continuous seizures. After trying over 22 different anti-epileptic medications and still having up to 40 seizures per day, Hayley finally found relief in a cannabis cafe in Vancouver by using a vaporizer.

Since 2008 Hayley has used medical cannabis to reduce her seizure activity dramatically and allow her to live a functioning lifestyle. Cheryl is concerned that the cannabis provided by Licensed Producers will be inadequate to treat her daughter's condition. After trying other CBD cultivars with limited success, Hayley found one in particular was successful in treating her seizures.

Hayley's Comet is a patented cultivar with a 1:1 THC:CBD ratio that was found and tested by the late Dr. Paul Hornby in Vancouver with the intention of making it available to all patients.

Licensed Producers now offer cultivars with a similar cannabinoid profile but Cheryl and Hayley, like many other sick patients, simply cannot afford to purchase their medicine at current prices.

Fortunately, Hayley retained access to her personal source of cannabis through the Allard injunction which allows her to produce at a low cost and maximize the yield by making a decarboxylated and concentrated cannabis oil which she eats 3 times a day. Cheryl Rose lamented the lack of education available to parents about how to produce cannabis oil for their children. She is very grateful for the one-on-one help she received from dispensaries around British Columbia, some in Vancouver now carry a strain in her name, Hayley's Comet.

Cheryl is excited to see Licensed Producers make oils and include the milligram dosage along with the Cannabinoid ratios on the labels of their product so that parents can know how to properly treat their children.

To help fill the gap between their experiences and the desires of the medical establishment they founded the Hayley Rose Research Foundation to perform group studies of whole plant cannabis medicine. Advocates launched a campaign to raise "funds for a pediatric research study of the Hayley's Comet strain on seizure disorders in children ages 10-18 years of age."

In the United States these kinds of efforts by parents are paying off as one by one States are now passing laws to specifically allow CBD rich extracts where medical marijuana is still illegal for anyone else. Alabama passed "Carly's Law," named for three-year-old Carly Chandler, and the Georgia House passed the "Haleigh's Hope Act," named for four-year-old Haleigh Cox. Each is intended to provide CBD-rich oil for children.

This positive change in medical cannabis law continues to advance on the heels of tragedy. Utah Governor Gary Herbert signed "Charlee's Law," giving people with intractable epilepsy access to CBD-rich cannabis oil, unfortunately only after its six-year-old namesake had passed.

Unfortunately, Haley's Comet would not be legal in these states focussed on CBD only, keeping many of the benefits cannabis offers out of reach of these families. For more information I highly suggest watching the multi-part series WEED by Dr. Sanjay Gupta.

(Cheryl and Haley Rose)

Alex and Gwen Repetski

After the trial I was invited to speak at an industry conference in Toronto. I received grateful embraces from some more of these parents including one Alexander Repetski, the father of three year old Gwen.

Alex's daughter Gwen was diagnosed with intractable epilepsy at 3 months old. After 9 traditional therapies were tried, Gwen was still experiencing major seizures as well as consistent subclinical seizure activity. Subclinical seizure activity occurs without the physical shaking that is commonly recognized, "it's like your brain is being scrambled", which was preventing Gwen's natural development. At 6 months old she suffered major side-effects from her steroidal injections, gaining 11 lbs. in 10 days, almost doubling her body weight. As any parent of an epileptic child will tell you, if a treatment holds the promise to end your child's ongoing seizures, it is worth a try.

While researching her condition, Gwen's father Alex discovered cannabis. He found evidence dating back over 150 years that reported cannabis as an effective treatment for seizure activity. Alex found studies showing the antispasmodic properties of cannabinoids and research affirming the general safety of its use. He presented his findings to the team of doctors that were taking care of Gwen. After some difficulty being heard, one doctor took the time to read the studies that Alex provided and was convinced that cannabis wouldn't hurt her. He agreed to help Gwen access the MMPR.

Alex found Avidekel. Avidekel is a high CBD strain with a content of 0.3 – 0.9% THC and 16 – 18% CBD originating from Tikkun Olam in Israel. CBC cultivars like Avidekel produce little to none of the psycho-activity that is commonly associated with cannabis. Avidekel is tested for contaminants before being sold to Alex in dried form, at which point he extracts the cannabinoids and tests his final product to ensure an accurate dose.

He admits this is a laborious process and would like to be able to purchase what is needed instead, but he does find some security in monitoring the whole process himself. It doesn't require a chemistry degree but some basic understanding is important. He dissolves the concentrated cannabis into avocado oil before administering a precise number of milligrams of each cannabinoid in a specific milliliter dose orally with a syringe.

Gwen hasn't had a seizure since the second day of her treatment. EEG's have continued to show no subclinical seizure activity. She is currently 80% through the process of weaning herself off of her previous conventional treatment, Valproic Acid (which didn't offer the seizure control or benefits they have seen with cannabis). Alex says that his detail-oriented process and the measured administration of mg. doses of cannabinoids in an edible oil makes sense to her physicians. Although she is still non-verbal, her doctors are pleased with her progress and continue to monitor her situation. Side effects from her cannabis use appear to be negligible.

Since the seizures have stopped, Gwen has restored her natural ability to learn skills, drastically improving her quality of life. She is now able to crawl, to walk with assistance and perhaps soon to run. In fact, in a recent conversation with Alex I learned that Gwen just recently stood up by herself for the first time. Gwen is now able to engage with her family, "her brother thought until now that baby sisters don't bother you." He's quickly learning otherwise.

Until the Supreme Court Ruling came down in June, Alex was ready to fight for his daughter in court. He was thankful for our victory and feels the ruling has lifted a weight from his shoulders. Sometimes breaking the law is necessary to prevent the suffering of another human being. In such cases as these, the risk of punishment is far outweighed by the rewards of compassion. In the words of this heroic parent, "you have never lived until you have helped someone who can never pay you back."

(Gwen Repetski)

The Road to Legalization

It is no coincidence that a few months after our historic victory in the Supreme Court of Canada (R. v. Smith 2015), the Liberal government began the process of legalizing cannabis. As this book illustrates, the road to legalization was a lot longer than Justin Trudeau's campaign trail: it was, in fact, a gradual erosion of state power over the choices of Canadians.

It began with AIDS patients fighting for the right to dignified care and quality of life challenging the government's authority to regulate who can access medicinal cannabis. Over time, these grassroots efforts, embodied by figures like Ted Smith and Canada's first compassion clubs (Lucas 2008), exposed the limitations of the government's ability to regulate bodily autonomy. They stood up for those who could not stand up for themselves, and in doing so, chipped away at the systems of control that had been in place for decades.

It was by order of the Court that the Liberal government first started down the road to legalization with their first attempt at medical cannabis regulation after Terry Parker(R. v. Parker 2000).

When further court rulings found the program inaccessible, more amendments were ordered. Could one person help a group of people? Could a group help another group?

The government's responses to court rulings were always minimized. Rather than fully embrace cannabis reform, the state made incremental adjustments, allowing small increases in the number of people who could grow together, or the number they could grow for, from 1 to 2, or 2 to 3. This incrementalism, a hallmark of hegemonic power, was a strategic move to maintain control while appearing to respond to legal and public demand.

Even when giving a guilty verdict, courts often granted an absolute discharge to defendants, meaning no punishment was issued despite the guilty verdict. These rulings acted as signals that the courts, unlike the government, were beginning to align with the evolving public sentiment around cannabis. For advocates like me, this was enough of an invitation to keep pushing forward.

After attempting to introduce mandatory minimum sentences for growing a single cannabis plant, the Harper Conservative government continued the trend of losing to medical cannabis patients in court. Each ruling in favor of patients, like my friend Mat Beren's absolute discharge for operating a large medical cannabis grow-op near Victoria (R. v. Beren 2009), contributed to the growth of legal consciousness in Canada. These victories weren't just legal, they were symbolic wins for the entire cannabis community, fostering a collective understanding that cannabis is a matter of healthcare and bodily autonomy, not criminal deviance.

After the Johnston decision in lower court, all other charges relating to extraction and the medical cannabis program were delayed, pending the final ruling in my case. As our case progressed and more people joined in disobeying the law by opening clubs across Canada, our challenge grew from a legal battle into a direct confrontation with decades of societal moral panic and legal norms.

We were, in essence, using the courts and the media to challenge the legitimacy of a hundred years of cannabis prohibition.

The mainstream media could not be safely relied upon. They always included a pun in the headline but left important details out of the article. Because they could not inform the public to our standards, we did everything we could to self-publicize our journey, growing the Cannabis Digest website and quarterly journal from its humble roots as the clubs newsletter, distributing 10,000 copies of the newspaper nationwide. Our work was helping to shift public understanding of cannabis from something deviant to something necessary, further reinforcing the feedback loop between public opinion and court rulings that had been set in motion.

Some members of the medical establishment responded reasonably to our ruling. They could now view cannabis not as an untouchable subject due to the abomination of smoking, but like herbal medicine, with its topical and edible comparisons.

Individuals signing up for the federal medical cannabis program began speaking to their doctors about all of the different products that they needed to support their health: including edible oil and topical products as well as how much dried cannabis was needed to produce those. I spoke with one woman who had obtained a license for 150 grams of cannabis per day to be consumed in various forms. This would allow her to grow around 750 plants.

The new legal grey area created by our victory in 2012 didn't just change the legal landscape, it triggered an economic transformation. Hundreds of cannabis dispensaries and ancillary businesses opened across all major cities in Canada.

This surge wasn't just a legal consequence, but a shift in the political economy of cannabis. What was once an underground market began to formalize, driven by the growing demand for edibles, extracts, and other cannabis products. Small businesses, fueled by civil disobedience and consumer demand, flourished in this gray area, creating economic opportunities that governments and law enforcement could no longer ignore. Cannabis prohibition was no longer just a social or moral issue, it was becoming an economic one, as cities struggled to balance enforcement with the realities of a booming industry.

Dispensaries were multiplying. In Toronto, the city tried everything they could to shut them down, even placing concrete blocks in front of one. It was too popular-the blocks were quickly removed. Later, Vancouver and Victoria began issuing business licenses for cannabis dispensaries, citing our case as justification, despite their remaining provincially and federally illegal (City of Vancouver 2015).

Access to these dispensaries varied. Some like the Victoria Cannabis Buyers Club required proof of a permanent physical medical condition, others required Health Canada paperwork and some required no paperwork at all.

As enforcement waned and competition between stores grew, there became more incentive to provide cannabis to anybody above the age of 18. These were ostensibly the first adult-use cannabis retail stores in Canada.

The movement once dubbed "Overgrow the Government" had evolved into a massive collective act of civil disobedience.

Some of the excess produced by medical cannabis gardeners found its way onto the new dispensaries' shelves, helping financially support the medical patient while feeding the surge in product quality and availability. This led to an economic boom that created many small businesses providing a variety of edible and topical products. Brands emerged in retail and processing. In Victoria, we had a 'Cannamall' that featured two vapor lounges; a dispensary; a high-end extracts shop; a consultancy and a lovely little edibles shop run by two sweet sisters.

With hundreds of cannabis dispensaries operating in almost all the major cities across Canada, cannabis quickly became a hot issue on the local, provincial, and federal levels. According to moral psychologists like Jonathan Haidt, public opinion plays a critical role in shaping both moral landscapes and political action (Haidt 2012). As more Canadians began to view cannabis not as a threat but as a helpful and necessary resource, politicians, including members of the Liberal Party of Canada, were forced to align with these new values. The consistent judicial support, combined with this evolving moral sentiment, created a feedback loop that pressured lawmakers to adopt more progressive legislation.

While distributing copies of the Cannabis Digest newspaper to Vancouver dispensaries, I stopped in at Cannabis Culture HQ. Climbing the stairway lined with historical cannabis art, I slipped into a meeting in Jodie's office where a group of activists and "Young Liberals" were discussing the motion to introduce a bill to legalize cannabis. This initiative eventually rolled up to federal

(Owen's car full of *Cannabis Digest* newspapers)

Liberal leadership and became the foundation for Justin Trudeau's election promise.

As stories related to our court challenge, like the McKnights, the Roses, and the Repetskis, started to make their way across Canada's media landscape, Justin Trudeau was touring the country in his bid for Prime Minister. His announcement was a surprise to many, but not us.

Given the government's history of incremental changes in cannabis policy it was predicted that the initial legalization regulations would be restrictive. Despite its positive momentum, opposition to legalization was persistent and well funded. The Conservative Party launched attack ads against the Liberals plan. With the war for public support in its electoral throws, the ongoing parallel news story of cannabis helping the sick, the elderly and even epileptic children provided a *mithril* coat of protection to the Liberal's election promise. Once the Supreme Court of Canada delivered its headline ruling, the Conservative arguments appeared as hot air and reefer madness.

When it came time for the election, I volunteered my graphic design skills to a strategic voting campaign in support of anybody but the Harper Conservatives. Justin Trudeau won the election in a landslide, obtaining the majority government he would need to legalize cannabis.

Legalization

Once legalization was on its way, the underground dispensaries, edibles companies and growers began to shut their doors to wait for their application for a legal licenses to be processed.

To commemorate the transition I hosted an event called "The Last Harvest of Prohibition." I invited Producers, retailers and processors to come to The Shire and set up their wares in a mini market. I organized music and catering for the day and we had a bouncy castle and fireworks. Hip hop versions of the Lord of the Rings theme song were heard across the small rivers and brooks, across the softly wooded rolling hills and wide, grassy meadows.

I invited the president of the BC Craft Cannabis Association to speak and she echoed the concerns that legalization must bend to include those who have suffered under the heavy hand of cannabis prohibition and reward those who have taken the initiative to develop their cannabis dream into a sustainable and successful business.

The people who grew, processed and distributed cannabis before it was legal took material risks to develop their skills and advance this important occupation despite being vilified by authorities. The

people who were harassed, arrested and made to serve time in jail deserve a social equity program to make legalization accessible.

The event was first intended to be the launch event for the new and improved Cannabis Digest Magazine. Unfortunately the financier had disappeared a few weeks earlier, leaving the country along with our written agreement and our unpaid contractors.

Ted Smith did not attend because he had become full time care aid to Gayle who was struggling with cancer and confined to her bed at their home. Gayle died the following year.

With the Cannabis Digest going dark, I was forced to leave the Shire to work in the city. My long-term relationship had suffered from all of the stress of my career and we decided to amicably separate. The stress of losing my job, home and relationship was strong enough to cause my first hemorrhoid during the launch party.

The cannabis marketing agency I had formed with some close friends was broken by the departure of the financier for the Cannabis Digest, and then bound in a legal dispute over money. I took a role as the General Manager of a group of adult use dispensaries that were aiming to transition to the legal market. The owner had been getting robbed and I helped to secure his business with the help of my father who specialized in security systems.

On October 17th, 2017 I had my photo taken cutting a cannabis cake on the bar of the Vapor Lounge I was managing on Salt Spring Island, BC. Unfortunately Vapor Lounges, places where cannabis culture had thrived, would not be included in the new legal framework. Our lounge had a door connecting it to the dispensary; doors to other businesses would not be permitted either (Government of Canada 2018a).

Soon after I found out that the man I was working for had not been paying suppliers, he then refused to pay me and I quit.

This business, among many others operating with a municipal business license, would close their doors upon request from the regulators while their applications were in progress. It did not reopen.

The chain of experiences had taken a psychological toll. I was depressed. The intense effort of legalizing extracts for patients had left me changed: transformed in ways that made it harder to relate to my peers. I wondered why people didn't care more about affecting change in society. I felt like the Hanged Man of the Tarot: suspended between worlds, having glimpsed a deeper truth, but left alienated in its wake. It was a psychological elevation, but also a disconnection.

I began to treat my loneliness with a variety of illicit substances: LSD, cocaine, MDMA, ketamine, GHB. My health began to suffer, and I struggled with addiction. Eventually I suffered an injury that made me unable to walk. I began physical and mental therapy and I began to let go, one substance at a time. Eventually, I had quit tobacco, alcohol, even coffee. All that remained was cannabis (predominantly edibles), a healthy diet and exercise. Far from a gateway, cannabis became my exit. It helped me sleep, eased my anxiety, and supported my healing.

Labeling theory suggests that individuals who were once branded as criminals or outcasts under cannabis prohibition may now find themselves excluded from the very industry they helped to create. (Becker 1963).

In hopes of advancing my career by addressing the many problems facing legalization from within, I accepted a role with one of the new global cannabis companies in their social responsibility department. Legalization would proceed for a year before edibles were introduced to the Act. The Cannabis Act amendment brought in a 10 mg per package restriction on the potency of orally ingested cannabis (Government of Canada 2019a). This matched the restriction introduced in the new medical cannabis program, the Access to Cannabis for Medical Purposes Regulations (ACMPR) (Government of Canada 2016).

While in the legal industry I helped create educational materials about edible cannabis safety; trained sales staff on the fundamentals of extracts and spoke with hundreds of new legal cannabis growers, processors and corporate staff. I helped set up funding for *Cannabis Amnesty*, an independent, not-for-profit organization dedicated to righting the wrongs caused by decades of cannabis criminalization in Canada, particularly its impact on racialized and

Indigenous communities who are over-represented in cannabis arrests.

As the excitement around legalization faded, the company I had joined shrank dramatically in size: my department was liquidated and I was laid off. I formed a consultancy called "Ethical Growth" and spent some time independently working on social responsibility initiatives. As efforts to establish a plastics reuse program failed to gain funding and my work with a BC First Nation was halted by an election, I landed on a Hemp farm for 6 months before rejoining Ted and the crew at the VCBC.

The VCBC was not able to comply with the Cannabis Act due to the 10mg limit, the continued prohibition on medical cannabis distribution centers and consumption spaces. The VCBC continues to operate without a federal or provincial license. As one of the sole remaining medical cannabis distributors it has grown to serve over 9000 members adopting patients from compassion clubs that have closed in Vancouver and Montreal.

(Ted during a CSU Raid)

Legalization introduced provincial government-run cannabis companies. The provincial governments have been given the authority to sell cannabis and make up the regulations surrounding its sale (Government of Canada 2018b). This has allowed them to gross the largest profits from cannabis sales of any entity while collecting taxes from private sales and revenue from expensive licensing. Taxes on cannabis companies are extremely high. The federal government collects $1 per gram or 10% of the sale price of the product, whichever is greater (Government of Canada 2018c). Then additional federal and provincial taxes are added.

The provincial governments maintain an almost complete control over what products are purchased and available for sale. They keep a provincial warehouse of products for retailers to purchase from. This all comes at an additional cost to retailers that persists even if they were to purchase directly from producers (British Columbia Liquor Distribution Branch 2018).

In BC, there is a provincial task force assigned to raid, seize and fine cannabis operations that are unlicensed. It has the Orwellian title of "Community Safety Unit". (British Columbia Ministry of Public Safety and Solicitor General 2019)

Since legalization, the VCBC has been raided 3 times by the British Columbia CSU despite its continued mandate of medical use only and history of setting legal precedents. Ted and the club were served 6.5 million dollars in fines; recently reduced to 3.2 million. The VCBC has had to move locations twice, recently adopting a beautiful, bright and spacious new home in downtown Victoria. The CSU has been granted powers by the provincial government that they believe supersede the Canadian Charter of Rights. This overstepping of authority is leading the VCBC into their next court battle with the legal support of Kirk Tousaw and Jack Lloyd Law Corporation.

First Nations

As enforcement continues, no social equity program has been proposed in Canada and no plan to grant amnesty to those punished for a crime that is no longer a crime. Bills were introduced to help cut down some of the red tape associated with the application process, but this was ineffective. In the first two years only about 500 pardons were granted while the government estimates that about 10,000 Canadians would be eligible for them.

The enforcement of cannabis prohibition does more than criminalize a medicinal plant: it enforces systemic racism and contributes to the ongoing project of colonialism. Discriminatory law enforcement practices have led to the disproportionate arrest and detention of Indigenous people, who suffered prohibitions' harshest consequences (Owusu-Bempah and Luscombe 2021). This mirrors broader patterns of colonial oppression, where Indigenous communities have historically been subjected to state violence and economic marginalization (Truth and Reconciliation Commission of Canada 2015). Prohibition is a tool used to control and punish marginalized groups, reinforcing deep socio-economic disparities that persist today.

Autonomously, First Nations communities across Canada have begun opening unlicensed cannabis dispensaries, challenging the state's monopoly over the cannabis market. This development reflects Indigenous self-governance, where First Nations exercise their rights to regulate commerce and medicine within their communities, despite the government's efforts to enforce compliance. These dispensaries are reminiscent of the grassroots cannabis dispensaries of the 2010s, serving both the adult-use market and supporting medical needs. Calls for enforcement by licensed cannabis retailers reveal the tension between the enforcement of regulations and Indigenous autonomy, as authorities apply the law unevenly, targeting unlicensed operations in a patchwork manner. This selective enforcement mirrors broader patterns of systemic inequality faced by First Nations.

BC Lawyer Robert Laurie breaks down Canada's legal market into a colour coded system. The White market is the legal market (dominated by white people); the black market is the hidden illegal activity (dominated by online sales); the Grey market operates illegally but in plain view, often challenging the law in court (groups like the VCBC), then you have the Red market, which is the indigenous sovereign market, and the Orange market, which are First Nations that have entered into preliminary agreements with the government to open legal cannabis businesses.

Some First Nations operate a hybrid model with both Red and Orange market businesses. The Williams Lake First Nation operates Sugar Cane Cannabis, a legal Farm Gate retail store and across the parking lot also operate Unity Cannabis, a retail store that sells edible cannabis products that are stronger than the legal limit, much like the VCBC. Williams Lake was the feature of the documentary *SugarCane*, nominated for best documentary at the 2025 Academy Awards.

First Nations in Canada have suffered colonial oppression, including forced assimilation through the residential school system, which aimed to eradicate their cultures and languages, resulting in intergenerational trauma and significant socio-economic challenges (TRC 2015). Recent findings of children buried in unmarked graves near residential schools have aggravated existing traumas and added significant weight to the conscience of Canadians (Schmidt 2021).

The Canadian government has a responsibility to acknowledge and address the historical injustices and ongoing impacts of colonialism on Indigenous peoples. Beyond legal reforms, there is a need for restorative justice, which includes a social equity program ensuring that Indigenous communities are not only given access to the cannabis market but are empowered to lead within it (First Nations Leadership Council 2018). Such a program would allow First Nations to rebuild their economies on their own terms, using a plant that has both economic and medicinal value. Economic empowerment through cannabis could offer a path toward healing the deep wounds of colonialism, providing a future where Indigenous autonomy is respected.

The conversation in the media around cannabis has degenerated since legalization, allowing politicians to become aloof to the subject. Media headlines about epileptic children and compassion clubs have been replaced by stories of taxation complaints and mass corporate layoffs. The 5 year Review of the Cannabis Act was delayed and when it was finally concluded, very few changes were suggested and none of them provided the relief the industry desired. The largest cannabis companies have spent billions of dollars only to continue to report losses each year.

Recently, the nations of Germany and Thailand rejected the Canadian approach to legalization. Germany chose social clubs with shared cultivation sites and Thailand is exploring a medical only program. These models are more closely related to how the VCBC operates than a legally licensed Canadian adult-use retail store.

On a global scale, reframing cannabis as a medicine, particularly for marginalized communities and those suffering from chronic illness, shifts the conversation from one of criminality, taxes or lay-offs to one of public health and compassion. As we focus on its medicinal value, we divert attention from the stigmatizing arguments of prohibitionists, presenting cannabis as an essential tool for healing rather than a societal harm. It is by beating this drum that we will expand the cannabis market and shrink the entrenched stigma.

Precedents

Since my court ruling others have used the precedent that we set to defend themselves against similar charges and ask questions of the law. In Alberta, Shaun Howell used it to defend his home processing of cannabis oil for his epileptic daughter. The Judge concluded that medical cannabis regulations "violate section 7 in relating to the prohibition on concentrations of THC in cannabis oil and extracts above 30 mg/ml, and in the manner of distribution of medical cannabis by LPs" (R. v. Howell 2019).

Medical cannabis regulations in Canada prohibit storefronts from distributing cannabis in person, creating significant barriers for individuals without a stable residence or credit card or with limited ability using technology. In Manitoba, a Métis man named Pat Warnecke used our precedent to successfully defend his dispensary that provided cannabis oil to people in his First Nations community, including those suffering from opiate addiction. The Judge's ruling was clear, "The evidence was overwhelming that the restriction to an online system of ordering undermined the health and safety of patients and was not rationally connected to the overarching goal of providing reasonable access in furtherance of the broader objective of public health and safety" (R. v. Warnecke 2019).

Cory Brewer, a member of the Okanagan Indian Band, is challenging cannabis regulations by arguing that government enforcement violates Indigenous rights protected under Section 35 of the Canadian Constitution (Constitution Act 1982) and the United Nations Declaration on the Rights of Indigenous Peoples (UNDRIP 2007). Brewer's challenge underscores the broader struggle for legal sovereignty, as Indigenous communities seek recognition of their right to control their own economic and medicinal resources. His dispensary, Timix'w Wellness, coincidentally filed legal action against the Community Safety Unit (CSU) on the same day as the VCBC, illustrating a growing legal movement where Indigenous cannabis entrepreneurs are pushing back against provincial overreach and asserting their constitutional rights.

Cannabis is not the first time First Nations have been passed over in the process of social reform.

When agriculture was introduced to the Canadian Prairies, many First Nations quickly adapted, becoming successful farmers despite severe constraints. Instead of being supported, they were met with punitive policies, such as the 1889 Peasant Farm Policy, which deliberately restricted their use of modern tools and access to markets. The intent was clear: to protect settler interests by preventing Indigenous competition.

In the early to mid-20th century, as Canada entered resource extraction booms in forestry, mining, and oil and gas, Indigenous communities were again left behind. Despite much of this development occurring on or near traditional territories, First Nations were not consulted and did not benefit economically. These industries were established on the assumption that the land belonged to the Crown. Even after court decisions recognized the duty to consult and accommodate, Indigenous nations remained peripheral to the profits extracted from their own lands.

The same exclusion happened on the water. For decades, Indigenous peoples were barred from participating in the commercial fishery. Their rights were limited to subsistence fishing while settler fishers dominated the industry and built generational wealth. It took the Supreme Court's R. v. Sparrow decision in 1990 to confirm that Indigenous fishing rights had constitutional protection. Even then, commercial access was only incrementally restored, and enforcement disputes remain unresolved today.

Legal victories in the 1990s, including Delgamuukw v. British Columbia and Haida Nation v. British Columbia, reaffirmed that Aboriginal title exists and that governments have a legal obligation to consult Indigenous peoples before approving resource development. These cases established that economic development could not proceed without addressing Indigenous rights.

Even when First Nations attempted to define new economies themselves, as with gambling in the 1990s, their autonomy was denied. In R. v. Pamajewon (1996), the Supreme Court ruled that high-stakes gambling was not an Aboriginal right protected by Section 35 of the Constitution. Yet First Nations did not retreat. They negotiated with provincial governments and secured the right to operate casinos, albeit under provincial oversight. Despite the constraints, these casinos became vital sources of income, employment, and community reinvestment.

As First Nations challenge cannabis laws today, they are continuing this legacy of advocating for their rights to control their economic futures. Indigenous communities are building their own dispensaries and production sites, often in legal grey zones, continuing the tradition of carving space for themselves in industries that originally shut them out.

As cannabis legalization unfolded in 2018, First Nations were again pushed to the margins. Provinces assumed authority over cannabis sales without acknowledging Indigenous jurisdiction. In response, some communities established their own cannabis laws and economies, asserting sovereignty over what grows on their land. Others are now challenging federal and provincial authorities, echoing the battles fought over fishing, gambling, and resource rights. Like those earlier struggles, the fight for cannabis sovereignty is not about special treatment: it is about correcting a long pattern of structural exclusion.

As First Nations challenge the cannabis laws, the VCBC will be by their side addressing the prohibition on medicine focused cannabis retail locations; the restriction on high-dose cannabis edibles and the lack of spaces for people to consume their cannabis medicines. We will be there to help publicize this development and restore to the spotlight the best qualities cannabis has to offer people and society

Ted envisions the VCBC opening community palliative care healing centers that give members the opportunity to garden their own cancer fighting cannabis plants, and enjoy a wide array of cannabis products with the support of an assortment of healing modalities.

Psychedelics

P silocybin experiences were an early source of inspiration for my work toward legalizing cannabis. Shortly after the announcement of our victory in the Supreme Court of Canada, we were visited by a local psychiatrist who had been experimenting with psilocybin in his practice. He had read our ruling and was interested in pursuing similar arguments for legal access to products extracted from psilocybin.

A few years later, Health Canada announced a special access program for psychedelic-assisted therapy (Health Canada 2020), following the long-standing tradition of Section 56 exemptions, as seen with cannabis in the case of Terry Parker in 2000 (R. v. Parker 2000). Thomas Hartle, who suffers from terminal cancer, successfully obtained legal access to psilocybin for therapeutic use (Friesen 2020). Like cannabis, the inadequacy of the special access programs is being challenged in court, where patients are using constitutional arguments rooted in Section 7 of the Canadian Charter of Rights and Freedoms—the same legal framework I used in my case (Canadian Charter 1982). Jody Lance, who suffers from debilitating cluster "suicide" headaches, successfully argued her case for the medicinal use of psilocybin, pointing to inadequacies in access. The emerging grey area in the legality of psilocybin reflects a larger societal shift, as legal challenges push the boundaries of acceptable medical use for previously prohibited substances.

Now, we are seeing mushroom dispensaries opening across Canada, and on First Nation territories, operating much like the cannabis dispensaries that preceded legalization. These establishments are emerging as *moral entrepreneurs* (Becker 1963), who work to shift public perceptions of formerly stigmatized substances by providing access to products in professional formats. "The Mushroom Dispensary" in Vancouver, run by cannabis pioneer Dana Larsen, represents a continuation of the precedent set by cannabis activists: challenging the status quo by normalizing access to these substances and advocating for their therapeutic potential. This emerging industry is walking the same path toward legitimacy that cannabis once took, demonstrating how social entrepreneurs push boundaries by occupying grey areas in the law.

Fortunately for the next generation of psychoactive drug legalizers, the cannabis movement has blazed a trail, revealing the strategic path forward for the "New Extra Regulatory Means" to legalization. As described by the crown prosecutor to the highest court of the land, "You produce the drug, distribute it, and if you're prosecuted, you call evidence in court to prove on an anecdotal basis that someone believes they need the drug and that it helps them" (R. v. Smith 2015).

The formula is clear: provide scientific evidence of relative safety, document personal testimonies, and build a public relations campaign that appeals to the good nature of the public. This multipronged approach reflects how social movements can work within the legal system while pushing its boundaries to force societal change.

These developments hint at the rise of the psychedelic movement in the wake of cannabis' success. Much like cannabis, many other psychoactive substances, psilocybin in particular, were wrongly demonized and classified based on outdated, moralistic fears rather than scientific evidence. Legal access to natural medicines such as cannabis and psilocybin is essential to harm reduction strategies and preventing undue suffering.

The years to come may see more groups like ours rise as moral entrepreneurs, clarifying the truth about which natural medicines should be made available in our society.

"Never doubt that a small group of thoughtful, committed citizens can change the world; indeed, it's the only thing that ever has."

~ Margaret Mead

Conclusion

While my battle has been won, the Drug War continues on. As of April 2025 more than 16000 people in British Columbia have died from Opiate related poisoning. Local efforts to provide cannabis as a substitute for dangerous opiates continue to face political pressure. The VCBC will continue to supply cannabis as a harm reduction measure and safer alternative to opiates for its many members who have successfully transitioned away from them.

The profiling of natural medicines such as cannabis and psilocybin as enemies in the war on drugs has misled generations of people. Confusing anti-drug messaging by falsely categorizing medicinal plants alongside deadly substances for political ends has compounded the drug problem, fueling the continued drug war. The failures of the war on drugs are visible in cities across the world, where 1 inch square baggies line the streets.

The VCBC has large churches on either side and is only 2 blocks from Victoria's open drug market. I often see people on the steps of the churches - asleep with a long stem glass pipe in their loosened grip - and sometimes I check if they are breathing. Seeing them makes me think back to my youth, as I held my own glass pipe and thought about what I might do with my life. The difference in what I had put into that pipe was the difference between a meaningful life and a silenced death.

As a child, I sang at the Church on Easter Sunday, exalting the mysterious stories of a healer from the ancient world. Learning of how some of the miracles performed by Jesus and his followers are attributable to cannabis lit up my imagination. If the Messiah was not a single person, but rather a role played by people challenging the establishment by sharing tightly controlled plant medicines, then there is historical, even mythical precedence for this work of legalization.

When my sister died of cancer, my families suffering began my journey. Knowing there are millions of other families who suffer the loss of their loved ones to cancer, I was determined to make a difference in their plight. Becoming part of the fellowship that is the cannabis community around the Victoria Cannabis Buyers Club led by Ted Smith allowed me to make that difference. Among other things, we have helped children with life threatening epilepsy live into adulthood and helped keep their parents from arrest for making them medicine. These are outcomes more rewarding than my wildest imaginings.

(Liam McKnight and Owen)

As I prepare to publish this book, it is from behind the counter at the VCBC where I work alongside Ted and a few others, to keep the medicine flowing to those who need it. We work and we prepare for another raid and for our next trip to the courthouse.

To my friends and colleagues at the VCBC, the members who became patient witnesses and the incredible Gayle Quin, Ted Smith and Kirk Tousaw: we have created a legacy of truth and compassion that lives on in our work and in the work of all those who are aligned with nature's helpful plant and fungal allies.

(The 2024 VCBC Crew: Owen, Julia, Ven, Clea, Ted and Nixon)

APPENDIXES

In this final section, I will outline many of the processes and methods of extracting cannabis and provide recipes from the Victoria Cannabis Buyers Club recipe book. With this knowledge in your hands, you can better prepare and consume your cannabis products at home.

Appendix A

Cannabis Extracts - Quick Reference

Solventless Extractions

Dry Sift Hash (Kief): This is a light, fluffy powder obtained by sifting cannabis through micron-sized screens, either using a grinder or tumbler. Also known as Kief or Pollen, it has a THC concentration of 20-60%.

Hand Rubbed Hash (Charas): A dark, sticky substance known as Finger Hash, produced through various methods of hand-rubbing cannabis flowers. It typically has a THC concentration of 20-60%.

Traditional Black Hashish: A dense, resinous block made by manually separating trichomes from cannabis plants, often through sieving or hand-pressing methods. It typically has a THC concentration of 40-60%.

Traditional Red/Blonde Hashish: Available in red and blonde varieties, this hashish is made by pressing trichomes from cannabis plants into firm, pliable slabs. Red Lebanese has a rich, earthy, and spicy profile, while blonde offers floral and herbal notes. It typically has a THC concentration of 40-60%.

Raw Leaf Juicing: A dark green liquid made from immature cannabis leaves. It's rich in THCa and lacks psychoactivity. This nutrient-dense juice is often consumed for its potential health benefits and therapeutic properties, such as anti-inflammatory effects, rather than for recreational use.

Rosin: A thick, sticky resin extracted from cannabis using heat and pressure. It retains a high terpene content and varies in concentration (50-70% from Flower, 60-90% from Hash).

Solvent Extractions

Ice Water (Bubble) Hash: Varies in color from light to dark grey/brown and is made using layers of micron-sized mesh bags. Requires drying and is known as Black Hash, with a concentration of 50-70% THC.

Honey Oil (RSO): A thick, dark, sticky liquid made using crude oil and flammable gasses. Named after Rick Simpson, it also has a THC concentration of 50-70%.

Shatter: Appears as an opaque or light orange, hard, brittle sheet. Created from crude oil and involves a process called winterization. Suitable for dabbing, it has a 60-90% THC concentration.

Live Resin / Sugar Wax: Characterized by its golden color, soft, moist, and crumbly texture. Made from fresh frozen or dried cannabis, it's flavorful and has a concentration of 60-70% THC.

Live Hash Rosin: A high-quality concentrate made by extracting resin from freshly frozen cannabis hash using heat and pressure. The term "live" refers to the use of live or freshly harvested plant material, which helps preserve the terpenes and cannabinoids. Live Hash Rosin typically has a THC concentration ranging from 60-90% and is prized for its potent effects and rich, complex flavor profile.

Diamonds: Produced under controlled pressure and temperature to form crystals and sauces. Known for their high potency with a 99% THC concentration.

HTFSE/HCFSE: Full Spectrum Extracts that include High Terpene (HTFSE) and High Cannabinoid (HCFSE) varieties, often featuring diamonds in sauce.

Carbon Dioxide (CO2): A dark, thick, sticky crude oil extracted without flammable gasses. Common in food and medical extracts, and used in vape cartridges. Its concentration ranges from 60-80% THC.

Distillate: A light yellow, thick, sticky oil made from crude oil or extract. It undergoes a secondary processing step and is odorless and flavorless, with a concentration above 90% THC.

Vape Liquid: A cannabis concentrate mixed with thinning agents for vaporization, typically containing 60-90% THC. It comes in clear or translucent form, often with reintroduced terpenes for flavor. Ideal for use in vape pens, it offers a discreet, fast-acting experience.

Isolate: A fine white powder, odorless and flavorless (no terpenes). Can be derived from hemp and made from distillate, with a 99% THC concentration.

Diluted Products

These include butter/veggie oils, tinctures, edibles, and topicals, which incorporate cannabis extracts in various dilutions for different uses and potencies.

Vegetable Oil: These oils, including hemp seed, MCT, sesame, and olive, act as carrier oils for cannabis extracts. They are used to dilute the potency of the extract, ensuring a controlled and consistent effect. Often chosen for their complementary health benefits, these oils make the cannabis extracts more versatile for cooking and consumption.

Tinctures: Tinctures are liquid cannabis extracts typically made using alcohol or glycerin as a solvent. They are designed for sublingual administration, where they are placed under the tongue for rapid absorption. An example of a commercial cannabis tincture is Sativex, used for therapeutic purposes.

Edibles/Topicals: Edibles and topicals represent a broad category of cannabis-infused products. Edibles come in various forms like chocolates, gummies, and cookies, incorporating cannabis oil or butter for ingestion. Topicals include a range of skincare products like creams and balms, using cannabis infusions for localized effects. These products allow for diverse and often discreet ways to consume cannabis, catering to different preferences and needs.

Cannabis Extracts - Long Reference
Solventless Extractions
Dry Sift

Separating the medicinal ingredients stored in the trichome heads from the remaining inert material might prove to be the single most important step in making clean cannabis medicines (Potter 2014). The bulbous glandular reservoirs dangle precariously, like the cap of a glass mushroom, waiting for the slightest agitation to leave their fibrous host, which may contain contaminants ranging from heavy metals and fertilizers to harmful molds and bacteria (Happyana et al. 2013). The cannabinoids held within the heads are intended by this mechanism to reach the receptor sites of mammals and perform their unique roles in their respective endocannabinoid systems (Pertwee 2008).

One simple approach to mechanically separating the resin-containing heads from the plant body is by sifting. Dry sifting for "kief" or "pollen" is an ancient technique involving the use of a screen or sieve upon which the raw material is worked or threshed to shake loose the trichome heads (Clarke 1998). Fabric screens with holes of varying sizes—typically in the range of 25–200 microns—allow the heads to fall through while much of the plant material remains on top (Clarke and Merlin 2013). Drier plant material will tend to make greener hash since more of the plant will powderize and pass through the screen. Using fresh material reduces the greening effect, and freezing makes the resin more brittle and even easier to separate (Rosenthal 2010).

The sifting process may be repeated to obtain multiple grades of purity. After separating much of the resin from the plant material through a wider screen (100–200 microns), a smaller mesh can be used until the required level of purity is obtained (Green 2017). The purest dry sift has a consistency much like taffy; it can be opaque or translucent and should be very sticky and malleable with a noticeable snap when cold. When exposed to heat, it will begin to bubble and release its vapors (Hash Marihuana & Hemp Museum n.d.). Modern takes on the dry sift method involve more advanced ways to agitate the material, such as vibratory sieves, ultrasonics, precise matching of resin head size to sieve hole size, as well as the use of dry ice (Green 2017).

Hand Rubbed

Although not as productive as dry sifting or making water hash, hand rubbing is one of the most basic methods of separating the medicinal trichome heads from the body of the plant. By separating the medicinal ingredients from the inert bulk of the plant, it is possible to produce a variety of edible and topical cannabis products.

When one approaches a mature cannabis plant, it appears to be covered by a fine layer of whitish fuzz; upon closer inspection, this fuzz resembles a dense mat of small mushroom-like structures. These "mushroom caps" (trichome heads) are glandular resin glands that contain cannabinoids and terpenes, designed to catch pollen from male cannabis plants in order to reproduce. While the female plant matures, she produces more resinous trichomes, which is believed to serve as protection against herbivores, pathogens, and ultraviolet radiation (Pate 1994). Skilled gardeners often separate male and female plants to prevent seed production, aiming for sinsemilla cultivation to maximize resin production (Small 2015).

The thickening layer of medicinal resin will stick to anything that touches it and can be separated with a little friction. As you handle the flower clusters and resin-covered foliage, the trichome heads can burst, releasing the encapsulated resin. The sticky gum will accumulate on your fingers until it becomes a dark, malleable tar-like substance.

This is an incidental form of extraction that occurs while the plant is being manicured. Often called "finger hash," the collected resin will soon coat a pair of scissor blades, gloves, or a tabletop with soft black tar, requiring a sharp edge to scrape it into shapes, commonly forming a ball.

This method has persisted in cannabis fields across mountainsides in India and Nepal, and under the African sun in Morocco and Malawi from ancient times up to the present day. In Nepal, where the cannabis plant has long been revered, hand rubbing is a primary method of resin collection. Hand rubbing can draw the resins from a living plant several times without significantly damaging it throughout the growing season, allowing the resin to regenerate. Interestingly, this gentle practice aligns with the concept of respecting all living beings that is inherent in Tibetan Buddhism (Dakpa 2005).

The resin provides the plant with protection from wind, low humidity, and ultraviolet radiation (Pate 1994). At higher altitudes, where cannabis produces more of this protective layer, hand-rubbed hash is known to offer a notable aroma and potency and is referred to as "cream" (Clarke 1998). Photo-journalist Laurence Cherniak, in his Great Books of Hashish, documents the production of Nepalese Temple Balls, which are sometimes said to include other medicinal plant resins (Cherniak 1982).

Black Hash

Traditional black hashish is a time-honored cannabis concentrate crafted using methods passed down through generations in regions like Afghanistan, Morocco, and Lebanon (UNODC 2009). Made by manually separating trichomes from the cannabis plant, often through hand-rubbing or sieving, it results in a dense, resinous product that varies in color, texture, and flavor depending on its origin and production process (Clarke and Merlin 2013).

The exterior is typically dark brown or black, with a lighter brown or greenish hue inside, indicating high resin content (Potter 2014). The texture ranges from soft and pliable to hard and brittle. Fresh hashish is more malleable, softening when warmed in the hand, while older or drier hash may crumble easily (Rosenthal 2010). Its quality is often judged by its balance of density and stickiness.

The aroma is earthy and aromatic, often with notes of pine, spice, or wood, sometimes accompanied by a hint of sweetness or floral undertones (Russo 2011). When smoked, it delivers a rich, deep flavor that mirrors the earthy and spicy notes of its scent, with subtle herbal or woody nuances depending on the strain and region (Clarke 1998).

High-quality hashish burns slowly and evenly, producing thick, aromatic smoke. When heated, it bubbles slightly—a sign of its high resin content and purity—and leaves minimal residue (Hash Marihuana & Hemp Museum n.d.). The slow burn and full-bodied smoke are hallmarks of premium traditional hashish.

Known for its potent and balanced effects, traditional hashish delivers a calming, euphoric high. Its effects are both cerebral and physical, promoting relaxation, introspection, and heightened sensory awareness (Atakan 2012). The long-lasting high makes it ideal for those seeking an extended, tranquil experience.

Traditional hashish embodies the rich history and craftsmanship of old-world cannabis culture, offering a luxurious and grounding experience that continues to captivate cannabis enthusiasts worldwide.

Red/Blonde Hash

Lebanese hashish is highly regarded for its historical significance and distinct qualities (Clarke 1998). It comes in two main varieties: red and blonde. The red variety is darker with a rich reddish-brown color, while the blonde has a golden or sandy-brown hue. Both are pressed into firm, slightly pliable slabs that soften when warmed by hand, making them easy to break apart and handle. The surface of Lebanese hashish is smooth, with a fine, powdery coating indicating high resin content.

The aroma is complex, with red Lebanese offering a rich, earthy scent mixed with spices, wood, and subtle fruity notes. The blonde variety has a more floral, herbal aroma with pine-like undertones. The flavor profiles mirror these aromas—red Lebanese hashish delivers deep, earthy, and spicy flavors with occasional sweet undertones, while the blonde version is lighter and more delicate, offering floral and piney tastes.

When lit, Lebanese hashish burns cleanly, producing thick, aromatic smoke and bubbling slightly when exposed to heat, a sign of its purity. It leaves minimal residue, a hallmark of its craftsmanship.

The effects of Lebanese hashish are balanced and long-lasting. Red Lebanese tends to offer a calming, body-focused high, while blonde Lebanese provides a more cerebral, uplifting experience. Both varieties deliver a smooth, sustained high without overwhelming intensity, making it a favorite among connoisseurs seeking a refined and nuanced experience.

Raw Juicing

When cannabis leaves are processed through a fruit and vegetable juicer, a thick, dark green liquid is separated from the plant pulp. If the leaves are picked before the plant matures, the majority of THC will still be in its acid form (THCA), producing little or no psychoactive "high" (McPartland and Russo 2001).

In their short film "Leaf", Dr. William Courtney and his wife, Kristen Courtney, suggest juicing 15 to 20 fresh leaves daily. To counteract the bitterness, they propose mixing one part cannabis juice with ten parts carrot juice. They recommend selecting leaves around 70–85 days after sowing and drinking the juice three times a day (Courtney and Courtney 2011).

With this cannabinoid-rich liquid, free of the psychoactive effects of THC, it is possible to increase the intake of cannabinoids significantly. The psychoactivity of THC makes it the dose-limiting factor in most cannabis products. Without the psychoactive effects, one can comfortably consume higher amounts of non-psychoactive cannabinoids like THCA and CBDA (McPartland and Russo 2001).

Rosin

The process of making rosin involves applying heat and pressure to cannabis flowers, kief, or hash to extract the resin (Rosenthal 2015). The result is a golden, sap-like substance rich in cannabinoids and terpenes, offering a clean, potent product without any residual solvents.

The simplicity of the rosin process is one of its greatest advantages. All it requires is a rosin press, which uses controlled heat and pressure to squeeze out the resin from the cannabis material. The key to a successful rosin extraction lies in finding the perfect balance between temperature and pressure. Too much heat can degrade the terpenes and cannabinoids, while too little pressure might result in lower yields. Most professionals use temperatures between 160°F and 220°F (71°C to 104°C), with pressure applied based on the specific material being processed.

One of the key benefits of rosin is that it retains the full terpene profile of the original plant. Since no solvents are used, none of the delicate aromatic compounds are lost, resulting in a flavorful and potent concentrate. Additionally, rosin can be made from both cured cannabis and fresh-frozen plants, the latter producing what is known as "live rosin." Live rosin, made from fresh-frozen flowers, retains even more of the plant's terpene profile, offering a more vibrant aroma and taste compared to traditional cured flower rosin (Backes 2017).

Rosin can be produced in small batches at home using simple tools like a hair straightener and parchment paper, though for higher yields and consistency, rosin presses are often preferred. The versatility of this method allows producers to create various textures of rosin, from a more solid "shatter" consistency to a softer, more pliable "budder" or "badder."

In addition to its clean extraction process, another reason for rosin's popularity is its accessibility and affordability. Unlike other concentrate-making techniques that require expensive equipment and solvents, rosin can be made with relatively low upfront investment, making it appealing to both small-scale home users and large-scale producers.

Rosin has become a favorite among cannabis connoisseurs due to its solvent-free purity, terpene retention, and robust cannabinoid profile. Whether used for dabbing, vaporizing, or as an ingredient in edibles and topicals, rosin offers a versatile and natural option for cannabis enthusiasts seeking high-potency, solventless concentrates.

SOLVENT EXTRACTIONS

Water/Bubble Hash

Water hash is another simple way to extract the trichome heads from the bulk of the cannabis plant. Similar to making dry sift hash, water or bubble hash is made using water to carry the medicinal trichome heads through a sieve or screen (Clarke 1998).

Before the dried cannabis is used, it should be thoroughly inspected for debris: stalks and fan leaves should be removed, leaving only the flowers and the small resinous leaves that surround them (Rosenthal 2010).

Bags with incrementally finer mesh sizes are placed one inside the other over a bucket. The water serves to carry the resin heads downwards in a cascade through the various mesh-sized "bubble bags" (Green 2017). Using very cold water or adding ice increases the brittleness of the trichomes, allowing them to separate more easily from the plant fiber. The ice also serves the mechanical function of knocking the heads off upon contact with the immersed plant material. Once the material is submerged, it must be stirred to encourage the further mechanical separation of the resin.

In ancient China and Afghanistan, water washes were performed once the resin had been dry sifted in order to purify it further. One of the drawbacks to using water to clean or aid extraction is that some of the terpenes (aromatic oils) produced in the trichomes are water-soluble and will be washed away. Terpenes don't only offer unique scents and flavors but work together to complement the effects of the cannabinoids.

You also must consider that once you get your resin wet, it must be dried properly or risk molding. One technique for drying is to freeze the hash before finely grating or "micro-planing" the hash evenly on the drying surface. It is important that the resin is spread thinly to facilitate drying. While keeping the maximum amount of surface area exposed is helpful for drying, it can cause your resin glands to degenerate. The THC in the resin will begin transforming into CBN while exposed to air, heat, or sunlight, offering fewer medicinal properties. The more it is exposed, the faster it will degrade. Using a cool, dark, dry room and employing a desiccant, such as thick cardboard, to absorb the moisture will prevent rapid degradation.

With the plant material and moisture out of the way, you are left with only the cannabinoids, some terpenes, and the plant wax shells that encapsulate them. By homogenizing the remaining medicine for laboratory testing, it is easier to standardize precise doses (Potter 2014).

Honey Oil, RSO or Phoenix Tears

For years, Rick Simpson and his website phoenixtears.ca have spread the message through the internet that cannabis oil can help people who have cancer. Although Simpson's work has been a recent revelation to many, the technique he uses to make his oil has been known for some time.

Rick taught people to reduce the plant matter in a solvent solution, typically using alcohol, to concentrate the cannabinoids and make "Rick Simpson Oil" (RSO), also known as "honey oil". When I was young, honey oil was commonly smoked in a pipe on a bed of ashes or smeared across a rolling paper, producing a powerful impact. However, Rick Simpson's revelation was that to treat serious medical conditions, you have to ingest this gooey extract or apply it directly to your skin.

Eating concentrated cannabis oil is intended to deliver a high dose of cannabinoids to assist with serious conditions like cancer. Rick Simpson decarboxylates his cannabis before reducing it with a solvent. He explains that it may take a person consuming the concentrated oil, referred to as "Phoenix Tears," up to five weeks before being able to reach a one-gram-a-day dose: "The daytime tiredness associated with this treatment fades away but the patient continues to sleep very well at night" (Simpson 2013).

While Rick Simpson affectionately calls his product "hemp oil," it is not made from hemp varieties but exclusively from high-quality female cannabis containing at least 20 percent THC or more. Industrial hemp is grown all around the world; in Canada, hemp is grown specifically to contain very little THC (Health Canada 2018).

Rick Simpson's film Run from the Cure became an internet phenomenon with over two million views on YouTube (Simpson 2008). While Rick's sentiment echoes that of many suffering from life-threatening conditions, some of his followers have taken his crusade to new levels of zeal. This fervor was exemplified during a Sensible BC campaign to decriminalize cannabis when a volunteer made a spectacle at a "Terry Fox Run" event.

"I ran the whole race screaming that marijuana cures cancer, because it does," Port Coquitlam organizer Christopher Skidmore told a news agency (Woodward 2013). He was shortly thereafter asked to stop canvassing. Campaign organizer Dana Larsen responded that cannabis derivatives have been shown in studies to kill cancer cells, but he believes that describing marijuana as a "cure" goes too far.

Dr. Donald Abrams, Chief of Hematology-Oncology at San Francisco General Hospital and an advocate for medical cannabis, agrees: "I do integrative oncology," he says. "So I hear about 'miracle cures' all the time. I hear about noni juice and graviola and many products. I think it does a disservice to the cannabis community to make claims that are not supportable. I may be seen as a naysayer but I'm not. I say 'Let's study it'" (Lee 2012).

Shatter

Shatter is a type of cannabis concentrate known for its brittle, glass-like texture that breaks apart easily (Small 2016). It is highly potent and often contains high levels of THC, making it one of the purest cannabis extracts available. Shatter is typically golden or amber in color, with a translucent appearance that sets it apart from other cannabis concentrates.

Shatter is commonly produced using butane hash oil (BHO) extraction methods. In this process, a solvent like butane is used to dissolve the trichomes—which contain cannabinoids like THC and CBD, as well as terpenes—from the cannabis plant material. After extraction, the mixture is purged of butane using a vacuum oven, leaving behind a concentrated extract.

One key factor in producing high-quality shatter is winterization, a process used to remove lipids, fats, and waxes from the extract (Hazekamp 2013). After the initial extraction, the mixture is dissolved in ethanol and cooled to sub-zero temperatures. This causes the undesirable fats and waxes to solidify and separate from the cannabinoids and terpenes. The mixture is then filtered, and the ethanol is evaporated, leaving behind a purer extract with fewer impurities.

Winterization improves the stability, clarity, and flavor of shatter by eliminating these unwanted compounds. The result is a cleaner, more potent product that is easier to work with and has a longer shelf life.

Shatter's glass-like structure is due to its molecular arrangement, making it a stable concentrate that can be stored for long periods. However, exposure to heat or humidity can cause shatter to become sticky or "sappy," so it should be stored in a cool, dry environment to preserve its texture.

Shatter is usually consumed through dabbing, a method that involves heating a small amount of the concentrate on a hot surface and inhaling the vapor (Atakan 2012). Dabbing provides a fast and efficient way to consume cannabinoids, making it popular for those seeking strong, immediate effects.

Live Resin

Live resin is a highly sought-after cannabis concentrate known for its vibrant flavor, soft, moist texture, and golden color (Thompson et al. 2020). It is typically made from fresh-frozen cannabis plants, preserving a full spectrum of cannabinoids and terpenes that are often lost during traditional drying and curing processes. This results in a concentrate with a more robust terpene profile, making it especially appealing to those who value the aromatic and flavorful aspects of cannabis.

The extraction process for live resin begins by freezing cannabis plants immediately after harvest. This preserves the delicate compounds within the plant, especially the terpenes, which can degrade with exposure to heat, light, or air. The fresh-frozen material is then extracted using methods like butane hash oil (BHO) extraction, helping to maintain the plant's original terpene and cannabinoid content (Dryburgh et al. 2018).

Live resin typically contains 60–70% THC, making it potent while also offering a richer flavor profile compared to other concentrates. Its moist, crumbly texture distinguishes it from concentrates like shatter or rosin, and it is often referred to as "sugar wax" due to its granular appearance.

This concentrate is commonly consumed via dabbing, where a small amount is vaporized on a hot surface and inhaled. Dabbing allows for rapid onset and provides an intense, flavorful experience, which is one of the reasons live resin has become a favorite among cannabis connoisseurs. The preservation of terpenes enhances the overall entourage effect, offering a fuller, more balanced experience that many users prefer over isolates or less flavorful extracts.

Live resin's appeal lies in its ability to deliver not only high potency but also a rich sensory experience, making it a top choice for those seeking both strength and flavor in their cannabis consumption.

Live Hash Rosin

Live hash rosin is a relatively new and increasingly popular method of extracting the full spectrum of cannabinoids and terpenes from fresh cannabis plants (Smart et al. 2017). Unlike traditional hash or bubble hash, which typically use dried plant material, live hash rosin is made from fresh-frozen plants that are processed immediately after harvest. This approach preserves volatile terpenes and other delicate compounds that are often lost during drying and curing.

The process begins with selecting premium cannabis flowers that are frozen immediately after being harvested, preserving the plant's cannabinoid and terpene profile at its peak. The frozen material is then used to make ice water hash (bubble hash) by agitating the frozen buds in ice water to separate the trichome heads from the plant matter. This step isolates the medicinal trichomes without the need for solvents, making it a cleaner and more natural method of extraction.

Once the trichome heads have been separated and collected through a series of sieves, they are dried thoroughly to prevent mold and degradation. The dried hash is then placed in a rosin press—a device that uses heat and pressure to extract the valuable resin from the hash. The resulting product is a sticky, sap-like substance that retains the full range of cannabinoids and terpenes from the original plant, offering a more potent and flavorful experience compared to other hash types.

One of the main attractions of live hash rosin is that it is a solventless concentrate. Traditional extraction methods often use chemical solvents like butane or ethanol, which can leave behind trace amounts of chemicals in the final product. By contrast, live hash rosin is considered a purer and more natural option, appealing to those who prioritize clean cannabis products. The use of fresh-frozen plant material also ensures that more terpenes—responsible for the flavor and aroma of cannabis—are retained, offering a robust and flavorful experience that many users find superior to other concentrates.

This method of extraction is labor-intensive and requires significant technical expertise, making live hash rosin one of the most premium and sought-after cannabis products available. However, its growing popularity and widespread acclaim suggest that live hash rosin represents the future of high-quality cannabis concentrates.

While live hash rosin is primarily used in vaporizers or dab rigs for inhalation, it can also be added to edibles or topicals to provide a potent effect. Many enthusiasts prefer live hash rosin for its "entourage effect," where the cannabinoids and terpenes work synergistically to produce a more complete and balanced experience than isolates or other concentrates.

Diamonds

Diamonds are a highly potent form of cannabis concentrate, prized for their crystalline structure and extreme THCA (tetrahydrocannabinolic acid) purity. These concentrates, often referred to as THCA diamonds, are produced by allowing cannabinoids to crystallize under controlled pressure and temperature conditions (Stahl and Miller 2019). The resulting diamonds are typically combined with a terpene-rich "sauce," which adds flavor and enhances the overall effects of the product.

The extraction process begins with creating a cannabis extract using solvents like butane or CO_2. The extract is then subjected to a process called "diamond mining," where it is placed in a sealed container to allow the cannabinoids to slowly crystallize over several weeks. This slow process allows the formation of nearly pure THCA crystals, which can reach up to 99% purity (Deahl 2019).

Diamonds are typically consumed through dabbing, providing an intense and fast-acting experience due to their high potency. While the diamonds themselves are mostly flavorless, when paired with the terpene-rich sauce, the combination offers a robust, flavorful, and balanced experience.

Their unmatched potency makes diamonds a popular choice for experienced consumers seeking powerful effects. The presence of terpenes in the sauce contributes to the entourage effect, enhancing the overall experience by synergistically interacting with the THC. This combination of purity and flavor has solidified diamonds as a premium cannabis concentrate in the market.

HTFSE/HCFSE (Full Spectrum Extracts)

Full Spectrum Extracts, such as HTFSE (High Terpene Full Spectrum Extract) and HCFSE (High Cannabinoid Full Spectrum Extract), represent cannabis concentrates that aim to preserve the complete range of cannabinoids, terpenes, flavonoids, and other beneficial compounds found in the plant (Lewis et al. 2018). These extracts are sought after for their balance between potency and flavor, offering a more authentic cannabis experience compared to isolates or refined extracts.

HTFSE is characterized by its rich terpene content, providing a highly aromatic and flavorful experience. Terpenes are responsible for the distinct flavors and aromas of cannabis, and in HTFSE, they are preserved in high concentrations to maintain the essence of the plant (Booth and Bohlmann 2019). This makes HTFSE an ideal choice for those who prioritize the sensory aspects of cannabis.

HCFSE focuses on delivering high cannabinoid content, particularly THC or CBD, in concentrations often reaching 80–90% (Raber et al. 2015). This version of full-spectrum extract prioritizes potency, delivering powerful effects while still preserving some of the terpenes and other plant compounds that contribute to the entourage effect.

Often, these two varieties are combined in a form known as "diamonds in sauce." In this product, the HCFSE diamonds (crystallized THCA or CBDA) are suspended in the terpene-rich HTFSE sauce, creating a potent and flavorful concentrate (Baron

2018). This blend allows users to enjoy the high potency of the cannabinoid diamonds and the full flavor profile provided by the terpene sauce.

HTFSE and HCFSE are typically consumed through dabbing, allowing users to experience the immediate effects and intense flavors these concentrates provide. Their balanced composition, combining cannabinoids and terpenes in their natural ratios, is ideal for those seeking a full-spectrum experience that preserves the plant's integrity.

Carbon Dioxide (CO2) Extract

CO_2 extract is a dark, thick, and sticky cannabis concentrate produced using carbon dioxide as the solvent. This method of extraction is popular for its safety and versatility, as it does not involve the use of flammable gasses like butane or propane (Raber et al. 2015). CO_2 extraction is commonly used in food and medical cannabis products and is a preferred choice for vape cartridges due to its clean extraction process.

In the CO_2 extraction process, carbon dioxide is pressurized until it reaches a supercritical state, where it behaves as both a liquid and a gas. In this state, CO_2 efficiently extracts cannabinoids, terpenes, and other valuable compounds from the cannabis plant, resulting in a crude oil concentrate (Rademacher et al. 2019). This oil can then be further refined or used as-is, depending on the desired end product.

CO_2 extracts typically contain a THC concentration ranging from 60–80%, making them potent yet versatile (Hazekamp 2018). The extract retains much of the plant's terpene profile, allowing for flavorful and aromatic vape cartridges and other products. One advantage of CO_2 extraction is that it allows for precise targeting of specific compounds, making it useful for creating full-spectrum products or isolating particular cannabinoids.

This concentrate is often used in vape cartridges because it can be adjusted to a consistency suitable for vaporization while maintaining high potency and retaining the natural flavors of the plant. Additionally, CO_2 extraction is widely regarded as a clean and safe method, as it does not leave behind harmful solvent residues, making it ideal for both recreational and medicinal applications (Raber et al. 2015).

Distillate

Distillate is a highly refined cannabis concentrate that is typically clear or light yellow in color, with a thick, sticky texture and a THC concentration that can exceed 90% (Hazekamp 2018). It is produced through a process that involves taking crude cannabis oil and subjecting it to a secondary distillation step. This process isolates and purifies cannabinoids, removing impurities such as plant material, terpenes, chlorophyll, and other compounds, resulting in an odorless and flavorless final product.

Because distillate is neutral in taste and aroma, it is highly versatile and commonly used as a base ingredient in edibles, vape cartridges, tinctures, and topicals. The distillation process works by heating the crude oil under reduced pressure to separate the cannabinoids from other compounds, allowing for precise control over the final potency. The result is an extract that is both potent and pure.

Though distillate lacks natural flavor or smell, terpenes or flavorings can be added back to create a more enjoyable experience, particularly in vape cartridges (Peace et al. 2016). Adding terpenes can enhance the aroma and flavor and contribute to the entourage effect, where cannabinoids and terpenes work synergistically to enhance the overall experience.

Vape Liquid

Vape liquid, also known as vape juice or e-liquid, is a cannabis concentrate used in vaporizers and vape pens. It is typically a blend of cannabis distillate or CO_2 oil mixed with thinning agents like propylene glycol (PG) or vegetable glycerin (VG) to create the right consistency for vaporization (Giroud et al. 2015). However, due to health concerns associated with some thinning agents, many manufacturers now use terpenes or other diluents instead (Blount et al. 2020).

Vape liquid comes in a range of THC concentrations, usually from 60% to 90%, depending on the base extract. The distillation process removes most plant compounds, leaving a clean, potent liquid. Terpenes are often reintroduced to enhance flavor and aroma, mimicking the natural taste of cannabis strains or offering alternative profiles such as fruity or minty.

The liquid is typically clear or slightly translucent, with a smooth, thick consistency ideal for vaporization. The heating element inside a vape pen turns the liquid into vapor, which is inhaled for quick and efficient cannabinoid absorption.

Vape liquids are appreciated for their convenience and discretion, offering a smoke-free option with minimal odor. The effects depend on the strain used and the concentration of cannabinoids and terpenes. High-THC vape juice provides a potent, fast-acting effect, while CBD or balanced blends offer milder, therapeutic effects (MacCallum and Russo 2018).

The versatility and ease of use of vape liquids make them a popular choice for both recreational and medicinal users, offering a controlled and convenient way to consume cannabis.

Isolate

Isolate is the purest form of cannabis concentrate, appearing as a fine white powder that is both odorless and flavorless due to the absence of terpenes and other plant compounds (Hazekamp 2018). It is typically made from distillate through an additional refinement process that removes all compounds except the targeted cannabinoid—most often CBD or THC—resulting in a product that is up to 99% pure (Hazekamp 2018).

Isolate can be derived from either hemp or cannabis and is commonly used by those seeking the effects of cannabinoids without any flavors, aromas, or the influence of other compounds found in full-spectrum or broad-spectrum extracts (Bonn-Miller et al. 2017). Since it contains no terpenes, isolate is a completely neutral product, making it ideal for edibles, tinctures, or topicals where flavor is not desired (Hazekamp 2018).

Due to its purity, isolate is highly versatile. It can be consumed on its own, mixed into various products, or added to other concentrates to increase potency (MacCallum and Russo 2018). Its fine powder form also allows for precise dosing, making it a popular choice for both recreational and medical users who need to control their intake carefully (MacCallum and Russo 2018). The high concentration, reaching up to 99% THC or CBD, ensures a consistent effect, making it one of the most potent and targeted cannabis products available (Hazekamp 2018).

Diluted Products

Vegetable Oils

Decarboxylation transforms cannabinoid acids into their active forms. Once this process is completed, the starting material can be immersed into a medium of your choosing to facilitate ingestion. Diluting cannabinoids in vegetable oil makes it easier to measure doses; the compounds fuse with the carrier, dispersing their properties into the solution.

When making edible products, a measured amount of extracted cannabinoids can be incorporated into recipes, providing consistent and long-lasting effects. Monitoring one's response to dosage takes time, and the mantra "start low, go slow" is advised when becoming familiar with edible products, as individual tolerance can vary widely.

Dispensaries like the VCBC provide diluted extract products of varying strengths that are suited to their members' needs. Dutch researcher Arno Hazekamp conducted research to understand cannabis extraction into various mediums. He compared several commonly used preparation methods based on the content of cannabinoids, terpenes, and residual solvent components, using solvents including ethanol, naphtha, petroleum ether, and olive oil (Hazekamp 2016).

Hazekamp found that olive oil was the most beneficial medium "based on the fact that it extracted higher amounts of terpenes than the other solvents/methods, especially when using an extended heating time" (Hazekamp 2016, 135). Olive oil extraction involves heating the oil to the boiling point of water by placing a glass container with the product in a pan of boiling water. Olive oil extracts cannot be concentrated by evaporation, meaning that consumers may need to ingest a larger volume to achieve the same effects.

Olive oil is cheap, non-toxic and doesn't produce flammable gasses. It can enhance the bioavailability of cannabinoids, as they are fat-soluble and the additional oil aids in their absorption (Grotenhermen 2003). Extra virgin olive oil is preferable and should be stored away from light, air, and heat to preserve its quality. For those making edible or topical preparations, olive oil is considered a top choice.

Tinctures

In the late nineteenth century, cannabis tinctures were widely prescribed for analgesic, sedative, and narcotic purposes, and by some accounts, they were used as primary pain relievers until the invention of aspirin (Mikuriya 1973). Sativex is a modern version of this approach—a sublingual cannabis tincture spray (nabiximols) produced by GW Pharmaceuticals in the United Kingdom and licensed to Bayer Pharmaceuticals. It is now available by prescription in Canada for conditions such as multiple sclerosis (MS), neuropathic pain, and as an adjunctive treatment for cancer patients (Health Canada 2015).

Solvents are used to extract compounds from plants. Non-polar solvents like butane and olive oil are widely used to extract oils in the food and health industry. Alcohol is a polar solvent, meaning it can extract a broader spectrum of compounds from the plant, including cannabinoids, terpenes, chlorophyll, and waxes (Hazekamp 2013). Separating the trichome heads from the plant material before extraction can help reduce the number of non-cannabinoid compounds and potential contaminants in the final product.

Cannabis tinctures can vary in potency based on factors such as the ratio of plant material to solvent, the concentration of the solvent, and the duration of the extraction process (Hazekamp 2013).

Longer extraction times and higher-proof alcohols may result in stronger tinctures. 4-6 weeks is recommended but 2 weeks may suffice in an emergency. Shaking the jar once a day may aid the infusion process. When you're satisfied with the potency, the plant material can be filtered out and the solution stirred before being poured into bottles for administration.

A spray or drop of tincture under the tongue will absorb quickly into the bloodstream through the mucosal membrane of the mouth, potentially leading to faster onset of effects compared to oral ingestion (Huestis 2007). This method allows for more precise dosing, as individuals can monitor their intake drop by drop.

With the aid of laboratory analysis, distinct cannabis tinctures have emerged offering various ratios of cannabinoids, such as high CBD and low THC (e.g., 20:1 ratio), equal THC and CBD (1:1 ratio), and high THC and low CBD (e.g., 4:1 ratio) (MacCallum and Russo 2018). These different formulations allow individuals to choose products that best suit their specific needs and preferences.

Appendix B

This is an amended copy of the recipe book that I was arrested using in 2009 and that featured as evidence in the Trial. The recipes are continuously being updated and improved upon by our excellent bakers. This basic, albeit simplified guide, can help serve as a basis for your own explorations into edible cannabis. The VCBC plan to release an updated version in the near future.

The VCBC Recipe Book

By Gayle Quin and Ted Smith

Our Recipe Book is a guide to preparing and using cannabis medicines. We recognize that every individual has their own preference, medical needs, and experience. This will provide many of the procedures to prepare and utilize edible or skin cannabis products they may require. These recipes and techniques are the result of 29 years of making cannabis-based products with many people contributing information and advice. A huge thanks goes out to all who helped in the development of these medicines.

These medicines can be made in any kitchen using tools and products found in most grocery stores. We provide standard procedures for making oils of varying potency. All of our Edible and Topical recipes are exactly as we make them at the VCBC.

Methods

Eating cannabis differs greatly from smoking in a few major ways. Eating can induce heavy drowsiness in a short period of time, therefore we advise against driving or operating machinery after eating cannabis. The onset can be short, as quick as 10 minutes, or take up to a few hours, so have patience before redosing (beware the munchies). The 'body-stone' effect lasts many hours, providing relief through a long night's sleep. It's advisable to start with a low dose (1/4 or ½ a cookie) and increase in moderation to meet your needs.

Raw materials – All of the cannabis plant can be used to make medicine, people often discard large quantities of leaf and stalk into dumpsters or compost it. Our edible and topical products rely on the supply of different grades of leaf donated to us.

Different grades – Leaf is divided into 3 grades. The Highest Grade is used for edible products, then Ryanol and the lowest grade for Skin Products. If mold is found the bag should be discarded.

At least 3 strains – Scientists have uncovered a vast spectrum of trace chemical components in the cannabis plant called Cannabinoids. Each has its own effects in interaction with the Cannabinoid receptors throughout our entire body. Only a limited portion of the known Cannabinoids are present in each strain. By combining 3 strains or more we can increase the number of Cannabinoids present in our products, increasing their spectrum of efficacy.

About Cannabis product testing and research – It is an exciting prospect to work with analytical testing and you may seek out a lab that will test any materials that were grown or processed at home. We found that regular product testing helped fill some blindspots.

Decarboxylation – Cannabis is extremely interesting in that 2/3 of its chemical makeup is inactive until heated. This is why the main way of ingesting cannabis continues to be smoking. Various cannabinoids like THC, CBD and CBN appear as acids in the raw plant. Over time these acids turn into THC, CBD and CBN but it is much more common to make the conversion using heat.

Heating cannabis increases its potency and without it you don't get very high if you make a cannabis salad (unless you toast your buds first). However, you don't want to expose it to too high or prolonged a temperature or you start to destroy its active chemicals.

Spread the ground bud/leaf evenly (up to 1 inch thick) on a baking sheet and heat it to approx. 300'F for 30 minutes. Switch the tray levels half way and stir the herb.

We do this before adding the plant material to the oil, effectively converting the dormant THC-acids and CBD-acids into active THC and CBD. This process releases vapor in a similar way to a vaporizer. We advise using a fan and/or sealing the room and making the most of your experience.

Buying Ingredients

A tasty brownie or chocolate chip cannabis cookie will not necessarily suit the particular diets of people with medical needs. The VCBC makes a variety of edible products to suit the general needs of the membership that include Sugar, Dairy and Gluten Free. Some recipes call for flax water as a vegan alternative to eggs. When buying ingredients, we choose whole, raw, organic, locally produced products where possible.

Hemp seeds are the most balanced source of omega-3 and omega-6 essential fatty acids. The body cannot produce these EFA's so they have to be taken in with the foods we eat. Hemp seed oil, olive oil, grape seed oil and coconut oil are popularly used as a base for the medicinal infusion and also contain EFAs.

Honey provides a natural preservative base rich in nutrients and minerals. Similarly to the vegetable oils, honey can be infused in a double boiler on low heat by allowing the honey to melt and re-heat, repeating this process for up to 3 days before straining out the plant material. Other natural preservative sweeteners like agave and maple syrup can also be infused with dry kief hash, and used in medicinal teas or soft drinks.

Lecithin comes in liquid or granule form for baking or in capsules as a supplement. Lecithin is found in all living cells of the human body. It aids the body's use of fats and oil-soluble vitamins by emulsifying them to a form we can use. This is why we add it to our cannabis baking, to help our bodies use all the Cannabis oil. Lecithin breaks up cholesterol to help prevent Arteriosclerosis. Lecithin is essential to a healthy nervous system as it is found in higher concentrations in the Myelin sheath, (the fatty protective coating of the nerves).

Resource Checklist

3 Kinds – Leaf or Bud
Grinder
Digital Scale
Toaster Oven – Baking trays
Double Boiler and an Element
Colander/Strainer and Cheesecloth
Resealable bags
Jars (Clear Glass)
Hand Grinder – for making Oat flour
Blender – for grinding Goji berries and blending Salve
A Capping Tray & large syringe – For making Ryanol
Bottles /Jars – for Salves and Massage oil

Making Ghee: In a heavy stainless steel pan (or double boiler), melt butter on medium heat. Scoop the white foam from the surface and discard it. This is clarifying the butter of moisture and nonfat milk solids. The whole process will take 30 - 45 minutes.

Decarboxylation

Decarboxylation is the act of heating the plant material carefully to activate the THC from its dormant acid form. Chemically, this process removes CO_2 from the THC molecule, making THC available to bind with the cannabinoid receptors. This process happens naturally as the plant matter dries. Through a series of tests, we determined that heating at approximately 300 degrees fahrenheit for 30 minutes can transform close to 98 percent of the inactive cannabinoids.

Infusing Cannabis

View our Decarboxylation and Infusion video tutorial here

www.youtube.com/watch?v=riYj9lg08H8

1. Divide leaf and Bud by quality: the highest quality leaf is used for edibles; the least quality for skin products.

2. Grind to a fine consistency (but not powder) and store in sealed bags in a cool dark place labeled with the date, quality and # of strains in the bag.

3. Combine three or more different strains in a large bowl.

4. Weigh out the amount indicated for the desired potency on the "Preparing Oils and Butter" chart.

5. Heat Oil to medium or prepare Ghee.

6. Decarboxylate and add leaf and cook at medium heat on a double boiler for 6 hours.

7. Strain leaf through cheesecloth and squeeze to get maximum oil.

8. Add 250g (½ jar) liquid lecithin (for edibles) and stir well.

9. Cool slightly and pour into jars.

10. Label contents and date.

11. Put in refrigerator.

12. Infused oil will last in the refrigerator for a long time.

Edibles

Cookies are made of leaf infused butter, 60% whole-wheat / 40% unbleached stone ground flour, raw sugar, organic eggs, baking soda, sea salt and powdered kelp. They come in 5 flavors; Peanut butter (least amount of sugar and high in protein), Peanut butter and chocolate chip, Double chocolate chip with cocoa powder and chocolate chips, Ginger (good for soothing the digestive system) and Chocolate chip with white and dark chocolate.

Cookies

We bake all of our cookies at 250°F for 25 minutes

Rotating halfway through baking time

To make about 44 cookies

We've found that ¼ of a cookie this size is a good starting dose

Preparing Oils and Butter

Cannoil
43 Grams Bud – 1 Litre Olive Oil
Add 11 tbsp. lecithin after straining

Green Butter
2 Oz. leaf – 1 lb. Butter
Add 5 tbsp. lecithin after straining

Buddha Ball Oil
4 2/3 Oz. Leaf – 1 Litre Olive Oil
Add 11 tbsp lecithin after straining

Extra Strength
1 Oz. Bud – 1 Litre Olive Oil
Add ½ bottle lecithin after straining

Massage Oil
14 Oz. bunk leaf – 1 Litre Olive Oil
Add ½ bottle vitamin E oil

Ryanol
4 2/3 oz. leaf – 1 Litre Grape seed Oil
Add 11 tbsp. lecithin after straining

With oils and/or butter stored in the fridge you can begin to make the medicines.

(This is the chart we used to proportion our different oils.)

Ginger

- 8 cups flour
- 4 tsp. baking soda
- 2 tsp. salt/kelp

- 4 tbsp. powdered ginger

Mix well

- 4 eggs
- 320g – 1½ cups molasses
- 1 ½ cups Cannabutter
- 2 cups raw sugar

Regular Chocolate Chip

- 8 cups flour
- 4 tsp. baking soda
- 2 tsp. salt/kelp mix

Mix

Begin to melt 1 ½ cups white chocolate chips
Stir on low heat

- 5 eggs
- 1 ½ cups Cannabutter
- 2 cups raw sugar

Mix

- Add white chocolate
- And 1 ½ cups chocolate chips

Mix lightly

Peanut Butter

- 7 cups flour
- 4 tsp. baking soda
- 2 tsp. salt/kelp

Mix

- 4 eggs
- 1 1/2 cups Cannabutter
- 2 cups raw sugar
- 1/2 kg peanut butter

Mix well

Make 4 plain (if you like plain)

- add 1 ½ cups of chocolate chips

Mix lightly

Double Chocolate

- 7 cups flour
- 4 tsp. baking soda
- 2 tsp. salt/kelp mix
- 1 cup cocoa powder

Mix

- 7 eggs
- 1 ½ cups Cannabutter
- 2 cups raw sugar

Mix

- Add 1½ cups chocolate chips

Mix lightly

Oatmeal

- 4 ½ cups oats
- 4 ½ cups flour
- 4 tsp. baking soda
- 2 tsp. salt/kelp mix
- 4 tsp. clove powder
- 6 tsp. cinnamon powder

Mix

- 5 eggs
- 1 ½ cups Cannabutter
- 1 cup raw sugar
- 1 cup honey

Mix

- 1 cup chopped Apricots

Mix lightly

Capsules

During my trial in 2012, the federal government made the argument that the only difference between chewing the dried flowers (buds) and making an edible is that cookies are tastier. Tastiness doesn't serve a medical purpose and certainly isn't protected as a constitutional right. The Judge rightly saw through this argument particularly because one of the products the club makes, which all the patient witnesses use, is a flavourless cannabis oil infused gel capsule.

The capsule, named Ryanol after a former baker, is filled with a cannabis infused hemp oil. Olive, hemp, and coconut oil are used as a base for capsules, each helping to facilitate the bodies' absorption of the fat soluble cannabinoids. Capsules are small and easy to swallow. The similarity of capsules to pills makes them more accessible to patients and doctors familiar with conventional medical approaches: people who understandably don't consider a cookie to be a medicinal tool.

Ryanol is one of the the lowest dose capsule available at the V-CBC, offering a way for patients unfamiliar with eating cannabis to ease their way into it. Ryanol fits with the axiom of "Dose low, Go Slow." By starting out with a small amount, a patient can more carefully titrate their dose to their desired level. The V-CBC's cannabis capsules contain 0.75mL of organic oil infused with the specific active ingredients needed to achieve the desired effects.

Patients may come with a variety of dietary requirements including sugar-free, gluten-free and dairy-free that prevent them from indulging in common cannabis edibles. The simplicity of the infused oil capsules make them the most widely accessible product at the club. Each capsule has been infused with 100mg of the active ingredients from a selection of cultivars including Sativa, Indica and CBD dominant plants.

The VCBC now makes a long list of capsules that are designed to occupy the spectrum of strengths and effects their members seek. Patients report that by eating just 1 or 2 of these capsules, 1 to 3 times a day, they can achieve relief from pain, nausea, anxiety (including anxiety exacerbated by THC) and muscle-spasms without feeling high or having undesired side effects. The club receives donations of leaf from their long-term growers and collects the stems that are removed when the dried buds are sold: reusing these to make affordable low strength infused oil capsules.

With a capping tray and a bag of gel caps, it can take under ten minutes to make 100 capsules. It is important that your capping tray is completely dry, any moisture will cause the gel capsule to melt, which can get messy. After removing the cap and placing it into a hole, use a syringe, (or a squeeze bottle with a narrow spout) to fill the capsule with infused oil. It takes a steady hand to avoid making a mess before carefully putting the little caps back on.

Ingredients

- Organic vegetable oil infused with a variety of cannabis cultivars.
- Capsules made from 100% vegetable cellulose
- Sunflower Lecithin

Buddha Balls

One popular edible is the Budda Ball (named after one of Ted's former bakers). Patients report Budda Balls useful for compromised digestive systems, severe weight loss, and blood-sugar disorders. Buddha balls are intended as a meal supplement for those with wasting disorders associated with HIV/Aids and Chemotherapy while having the added benefit of pain management and nausea suppression. They are simple and easy to make.

Buddha Balls Recipe

In a large mixing bowl add:
- 4 cups rolled oats

3 cups shredded coconut
1 cup raw unsalted sunflower seeds
1 1/2 cups pumpkin seed protein
1/2 cup hemp or whey protein
1/2 cup hemp hearts
Mix
- add 1 cup Budda Ball oil

Mix
- add 400g honey

Mix thoroughly
Put 1 cup Almond powder in a small bowl
Form the balls and roll in almond powder
Add 1/2 cup chocolate chips (optional)
Makes 24
Package, label, refrigerate

Topical Cannabis Massage Oils

Regular Cannabis Oil is an excellent pain reliever because it stimulates localized THC and Cannabinoid receptors throughout our bodies to help the cannabis we smoke go directly to the site most in need. It also acts as an anti-inflammatory by stimulating circulation. Cannabis is also used for almost every condition of the skin from eczema to fungus, as well as atopic dermatitis. It may also be used topically for stopping migraines and headaches. All other massage oils are mixed 50/50 with Cannabis oil and herbal infusions wild-crafted by volunteers.

Regular
Heat: 2 cups Massage Oil

- Add 25 mls. of Vitamin E oil

Stir

Cool slightly and bottle

Combinations

For Arnica, St. Johns Wort, Wild Yam or Comfrey massage oils, mix 2 cups melted herbal infusion with 2 cups regular massage oil.

- Add 25 mls. of Vitamin E oil

Stir

Cool slightly and bottle

- Comfrey Oil add 2/3 cup Hemp Seed Oil

Arnica makes an excellent treatment for inflammations caused by things like arthritis and sprains. It will reduce swellings and relieve pain associated with these conditions. Arnica works by stimulating blood circulation and intercellular fluid exchange and is an accepted ingredient for many arthritic and athletic preparations. We have had 2 surgeries cancelled from its regular use. It also soothes minor burns, ulcers, eczema, and acne. This oil is not to be used on broken skin or open wounds, as arnica can act as an anti-coagulant (stops blood from clotting).

Comfrey is our newest skin product and the first to have the added benefits of hemp seed oil. Most useful for acceleration of wound healing, fractures, gastric, varicose and duodenal ulcers, hiatus hernia, ulcerative colitis, and hemorrhages wherever they occur, improve circulation, lung complaints such as bronchitis, irritable cough, and pleurisy muscular rheumatism and swollen joints, gout, painof stumps from amputation, paralyzed joints and limbs caused by over exertion,dislocation, sprain or shock, bone infections, slipped and herniated discs, alltypes of injuries, contusions. ecchymosis and bruises.

Peppermint, Eucalyptus is wonderful to rub on your chest for chronic bronchitis, asthma, influenza (flu), and whooping cough.

It can also be used for fever headaches, sore throats, rashes, stomach bloating, and neuralgic and rheumatic pains. It may also be used as a rub for your pets to help repel fleas and mites. Chinese Mint, Camphor will help all lung complaints, local rheumatisms, sprains and strains, bruises and neuralgia. It's also used as a rub for stomach and bowel complaints such as spasmodic cholera, flatulent colic and diarrhea.

Salve

Making a basic salve is just one step beyond preparing a topical massage oil. By stirring melted beeswax into an infused vegetable oil you can produce a semi-solid medicinal salve to rub into your skin. Combining the active ingredients in the infused oil with beeswax allows the preparation to remain on the surface of the skin longer, reducing the mess sometimes associated with massage oils. Salves are often used to localize medicinal effects to the area of need, such as skin lesions or joint pain.

Cannabinoids bind to CB1 and CB2 receptor sites in the nerve fibres, sweat glands and a number of cells present in our skin. Topical application provides a way for the cannabinoids to activate these receptors without entering the bloodstream and travelling to the brain, important if you don't want to feel 'high'. Topical application may provide sufficient relief in itself, or act in addition to eating or inhaling cannabis.

Dispensaries often offer cannabis massage oils and salves extolling their anti-inflammatory, analgesic, and localized health benefits. They are most commonly used by patients with arthritis who find that applying topical cannabis to their joints allows them to loosen up enough to perform daily tasks. Other members have found cannabis salve helps other skin conditions including eczema, psoriasis, and atopic dermatitis.

Elaborations on the basic recipe can be made by adding essential oils or using vegetable oils infused with other herbs. The VCBC have created several different salves to combine the effects of cannabis with other herbs suited for specific conditions. A combination with arnica infusion is commonly used for circulation and stiff joints. Essential oils are combined to create a 'tiger balm' style preparation for deep muscle pain. Using a very similar technique, the V-CBC make a lip balm using regular massage oil, organic shea butter, organic beeswax, and crystalized vitamin C.

Different herbs come with their own warnings such as Arnica, which should not be used on open skin or by women who are pregnant or breastfeeding. Some dispensaries have started using DMSO in their topical medications. DMSO is predominantly used as a vehicle for anti-fungal medications, enabling them to penetrate, not just skin, but also toe and fingernails. Extra caution is required when using DMSO, infections may occur where special care isn't paid to ensure sanitary conditions.

Ingredients
- Cannabis leaf infused olive oil
- Vitamin E (to help with absorption)
- Organic beeswax

If possible use a double boiler to keep a low heat, if not, you can use a spare 1L. glass peanut butter jar in a pot of water.
Melt 1 1/3 cups of organic beeswax (shaved if possible)
Warm 2 cups of infused massage oil
Add 25 ml. vitamin E. oil to the massage oil
Stir well
Add melted beeswax
Stir very well
Allow to cool slightly
Carefully pour into jars
We make approx. 16 4 oz. jars
Label and refrigerate.

Suppositories

Suppositories are particularly helpful for people with gastrointestinal difficulties, lower back pain, prostate, rectal and vaginal cancer, an impaired jaw or throat or whose nausea and vomiting prevent effective oral application. This route may also be suitable where restrictions on oral ingestion before and after surgery apply. But it needn't be an option of last resort. Due to the large surface area available for absorption, rectal administration provides the most effective way for your body to take in the medicinal compounds.

Inhalation is the least efficient method offering 10 – 25% bioavailability; Oral around 20%; In a study involving THC-HS* Rectal application delivered around 50% – 70% efficiency with more predictable effects between different individuals. Suppositories avoid the gastrointestinal system where metabolites separate and break down the constituent compounds. One of these metabolites is 11-Hydroxy-?9-THC, which is a psychoactive compound similar to ?9-THC.

Oral doses can take up to 2 hours before their medicinal effects are noticed by the patient. There is the potential that your previous meal will effect the rate at which the medicine will take effect. Most people begin to notice initial effects of a suppository within the first 10 – 15 minutes after insertion. Impedances to absorption could include dehydration; the presence of fecal matter and cysts or tumours inside the rectal wall. While this may slow or prevent the compounds entering the bloodstream, the application of cannabinoids directly to those sites of concern may help to activate local endocannabinoid receptors.

Similarly to edible cannabis, the effects of a suppository are long lasting, often ranging between 4-8 hours depending on the individual's physiology and tolerance to cannabis. The VCBC provides three different strengths to suit their many members needs: a low strength dose for general maintenance; a high strength dose for breakthrough pain and a low psycho-activity dose made with 1:1 CBD cultivars. On the Cannabis Digest website you can find an article outlining in detailed instructions how to insert a cannabis suppository.

Suppositories are quick and easy to make. An infusion of cannabis in coconut butter is portioned into small rounded shapes. These can be individually weighed to help ensure consistent doses; then wrapped in wax paper, bagged, labelled appropriately and refrigerated out of the reach of children and pets.

Ingredients:

Organic cocoa butter

Organic coconut butter infused with the inflorescences (flowers) of different cultivars of cannabis including CBD+.

*Delta9 THC-HS (hemisuccinate) is not exactly the same as Delta9 THC. It has undergone chemical stabilization through processing aids such as polyethylene glycol (PEG)-400 and vitamin E succinate (VES) to reduce degradation during hot-melt production at lower temperatures.

APPENDIX C

Timeline References

This reference list is a companion to the digital timeline resource that contains all of the events, media, video and blog articles that accompany this book. You can peruse the timeline by going to the timeline link. Some entries were taken from The Canadian Press and are referred to as R. v. Smith Timeline.

Digital Timeline

www.tiki-toki.com/timeline/entry/196941/R.-v.-Smith-Timeline

Digest Articles

1. Smith, Ted. "Bake-Op." Cannabis Digest, January 5, 2010.

2. Smith, Owen. "Bites from the Bakery." Cannabis Digest, April 26, 2010.

3. Smith, Ted. "CBC Bakery Raided." Cannabis Digest, April 27, 2010.

4. Smith, Owen. "CBC of C Product Testing." Cannabis Digest, August 30, 2010.

5. Smith, Ted. "Examining the Parker Decision...Ten Years Later." Cannabis Digest, November 1, 2010.

6. Smith, Owen. "Product Development." Cannabis Digest, November 2, 2010.

7. Smith, Owen. "Melanoma and Cannabis." Cannabis Digest, January 15, 2011.

8. Smith, Owen. "Advanced Product Development." Cannabis Digest, April 20, 2011.

9. Smith, Ted. "Cookie Trial to Commence." Cannabis Digest, April 21, 2011.

10. Smith, Owen. "Eating Cannabis as Medicine." Cannabis Digest, July 14, 2011.

11. "Health Canada Pulls the Plug on Growing." Cannabis Digest, July 14, 2011.

12. Smith, Owen. "Synchronicity in Whole Plant Medicine." Cannabis Digest, October 16, 2011.

13. Smith, Ted. "Dispensaries Deserve Exemptions." Cannabis Digest, October 16, 2011.

14. Smith, Ted. "Will the Pot Laws Fall Again?" Cannabis Digest, January 15, 2012.

15. Smith, Owen. "Phytocannabinoid Therapeutics." Cannabis Digest, January 15, 2012.

16. "Criminal Trials or Clinical Trials." Cannabis Digest, April 24, 2012.

17. Smith, Ted. "Cookie Trial Chips Away at MMAR." Cannabis Digest, April 24, 2012.

18. Smith, Owen. "Concentrating on Cannabinoids." Cannabis Digest, July 10, 2012.

19. Smith, Ted. "Here Comes the Tax Man." Cannabis Digest, July 10, 2012.

20. Fink, Ryan. "Trial by Fire." Cannabis Digest, July 10, 2012.

21. Smith, Ted. "Sometimes, Dreams Come True." Cannabis Digest, November 4, 2012.

22. Smith, Owen. "Baker's Journey Through Court." Cannabis Digest, January 31, 2013.

23. Smith, Owen. "Docs, Stocks and Two Legal States." Cannabis Digest, April 13, 2013.

24. Fink, Ryan. "Game Changer." Cannabis Digest, April 13, 2013.

25. Smith, Owen. "Access to Extracts." Cannabis Digest, July 27, 2013.

26. Smith, Ted. "Medical Marijuana Patient Revolt." Cannabis Digest, October 27, 2013.

27. Smith, Owen. "Dilemmas of Mainstream Cannabis." Cannabis Digest, October 27, 2013.

28. "Medical Marijuana in Tea or Baking Faces Another B.C. Court Challenge." Cannabis Digest, December 4, 2013.

29. Smith, Owen. "Appeal Court Grills Defence in Extract Trial." Cannabis Digest, January 26, 2014.

30. Smith, Owen. "Cannabis Extracts 2 – Health Canada 1: A Win for Patients!" Cannabis Digest, August 14, 2014.

31. Smith, Ted. "Appeal Takes Smith to Ottawa." Cannabis Digest, September 11, 2014.

32. Smith, Ted. "High Court Calls for Extract Interveners." Cannabis Digest, November 19, 2014.

33. Smith, Ted. "Supreme Court Extract Case Set for March." Cannabis Digest, November 26, 2014.

34. Smith, Owen. "GoFundMe: Cannabis Oil to the Supreme Court of Canada." Cannabis Digest, November 27, 2014.

35. Smith, Ted. "R. v. Smith." Cannabis Digest, January 14, 2015.

36. Smith, Owen. "Deciphering R v Smith." Cannabis Digest, July 24, 2015.

Media Articles

1. "Cannabis Buyers' Club Raided." Times Colonist, December 4, 2009.

2. "VicPD Report." Victoria Police, December 8, 2009.

3. "Alleged Marijuana Bake Shop Busted." The Canadian Press, December 9, 2009.

4. Hatherly, Joanne. "Marijuana 'Baker' Hoping for a Day in Court." Times Colonist, December 6, 2009.

5. "Pot Gossip." Monday Magazine, May 5, 2010.

6. Dickson, Louise. "Court Urged to Snuff Out Medical Pot Access Rules." Times Colonist, January 17, 2012.

7. Dickson, Louise. "Mayor's Letter to Minister Becomes Evidence in Pot Trial." Times Colonist, January 18, 2012.

8. Dickson, Louise. "Nothing Unique About Dried Pot, Court Told." Times Colonist, January 24, 2012.

9. Dickson, Louise. "Trust a Key Ingredient of Cannabis Cookies, Court Told." Times Colonist, January 25, 2012.

10. Dickson, Louise. "Cannabis Cookies and Lozenges Ease My Chronic Pain, Woman Tells Court." Times Colonist, January 26, 2012.

11. "Justice System Is Broken." Monday magazine, February 1, 2012.

12. Spalding, Derek. "Pot-trial Lawyer Given Time to Prepare Questioning." Times Colonist, February 2, 2012.

13. Dickson, Louise. "Court Mulls Challenge to Pot Laws." Times Colonist, March 11, 2012.

14. "BC Supreme Court Gives Health Canada Time to Rewrite Dried Pot Rules." The Canadian Press, April 27, 2012.

15. Pope, Danielle. "Weed: Now Legally Edible." Monday Magazine, April 20, 2012.

16. Mulgrew, Ian. "Ottawa Drags Out Medical Pot Reform." Vancouver Sun, June 12, 2012.

17. "Medical Marijuana Club in Victoria Hit with $150K HST Bill." The Canadian Press, September 7, 2012.

18. "Editorial: Tax on Medical Pot No Joke for Users." The Canadian Press, September 11, 2012.

19. "Pot-club Operator Is Happy to Pay Taxes." The Canadian Press, September 18, 2012.

20. "Pot Baker in Clear, but More Battles May Loom." The Canadian Press, December 29, 2012.

21. "Kirk Tousaw on CFAX." CFAX news, January 8, 2013.

22. "Cannabis Baker Acquitted on Drug Charges." The Canadian Press, January 11, 2013.

23. "One Win for All Cannabis-kind." The Canadian Press, January 16, 2013.

24. "Judge Dismisses Bid for Extension on Medical Marijuana Changes." R. v. Smith Timeline, June 1, 2013.

25. "Medical Marijuana in Tea or Baking Faces Another B.C. Court Challenge." R. v. Smith Timeline, December 4, 2013.

26. Mulgrew, Ian. "Judges Mull Legality of Hash Brownies for Medical Users." Vancouver Sun, December 6, 2013.

27. "BC Court Says Restrictions on Medical Marijuana Are Unconstitutional." Vancouver Sun, August 14, 2014.

28. "Medical Pot Cookie Prohibition Ruled Unconstitutional." R. v. Smith Timeline, August 14, 2014.

29. "Pot-laced Products Ruled Constitutional for Medical Purposes in Canada." RT News, August 15, 2014.

30. "We Can Relax Now: Ottawa-area Licensed Pot User Reacts to B.C. Ruling." Vancouver Metro, August 16, 2014.

31. "Medical Pot User Pleased with Court Ruling." The Canadian Press, August 16, 2014.

32. "BC Court Ruling on Edible Marijuana Opens the Door to Expanding Medicinal Uses." The Canadian Press, August 16, 2014.

33. Soupcoff, Marni. "The War on Pot Brownies." National Post, October 16, 2014.

34. "Ottawa Appealing Medical Marijuana Ruling." Times Colonist, October 1, 2014.

35. "Medical Marijuana Cookie Case Hits Supreme Court." National Post, March 22, 2015.

36. "Parents Treating Epileptic Girl with Cannabis Oil Want Treatment Legalized." National Post, May 10, 2015.

37. "Georgia Straight: Supreme Court of Canada Upholds Acquittal of B.C. Man Who Baked Marijuana Cookies for Compassion Club." Georgia Straight, June 11, 2015.

38. "Supreme Court of Canada Redefines Medical Pot." National Post, June 11, 2015.

39. "Supreme Court of Canada Okays Medicinal Pot Cookies, Other Cannabis Products." National Post, June 11, 2015.

40. "Medical Marijuana Activist Owen Smith 'Vindicated on the Highest Level'." CBC News, June 11, 2015.

41. "Victoria Man Wins Major Court Battle Over Medical Marijuana." Times Colonist, June 12, 2015.

42. Rice, Clayton Q.C. "Supreme Court Rules Medical Marihuana Law Is Arbitrary." National Post, June 11, 2015.

43. "R. v. Smith: Removing the Arbitrariness in the Regulation of Medical Marihuana." The Court, November 10, 2015.

44. Sherrin, Christopher. "R v Smith and Judicially Reviewing the Scope of Criminal Law under the Charter." The Court, April 20, 2016.

Video Entries:

1. "Bakery Raid Press Conference." Cannabis Digest Youtube, December 6, 2009.

2. "Bake Op Press Conference." Cannabis Digest Youtube, January 15, 2010.

3. "A Channel News Covers the Arrest." A Channel News, January 15, 2010.

4. "Shaw TV News - The Daily." ShawTV, January 9, 2010.

5. "Return of the Charges and the Cannabis Digest Announced." Cannabis Digest Youtube, April 21, 2010.

6. "CHEK 6 News, Bakery Trial." Chek 6 News, January 17, 2012.

7. "Face to Face with Ted Smith." Victoria Community TV, January 21, 2012.

8. "Press Conference at the Victoria Courthouse." Cannabis Digest Youtube, January 16, 2012.

9. "Press Conference at the Victoria Courthouse." Cannabis Digest Youtube, April 13, 2012.

10. "CTV News - Landmark Decision." CTV News, April 14, 2012.

11. "Ted and the Taxman Press Conference." Cannabis Digest Youtube, September 13, 2012.

12. "Owen's History of the VCBC Lecture." Cannabis Digest Youtube, November 29, 2012.

13. "Charges Dropped Press Conference." Cannabis Digest Youtube, December 27, 2012.

14. "CHEK News - Charges Dropped." CHEK News, December 28, 2012.

15. "Bubbleman Interviews Ted." Bubbleman's World Youtube, December 7, 2013.

16. "R. v. Smith Press Conference." Cannabis Digest Youtube, August 14, 2014.

17. "Kirk Tousaw on Bubbleman's World." Bubbleman's World Youtube, August 24, 2014.

18. "My QP: Why Does My Child Have to Smoke His Medical Marijuana?" CBC News My QP, November 14, 2014.

19. "The Question of Extracts in Canada (Part 1)." Cannabis in Canada, November 17, 2014.

20. "The Question of Extracts in Canada (Part 2)." Cannabis in Canada, November 23, 2014.

21. "The Ted Smith Chronicles." Cannabis in Canada, December 29, 2014.

22. "Supreme Court of Canada." Cannabis Digest Youtube, March 20, 2015.

23. "Rona Ambrose Outrage." Cannabis Digest Youtube, June 11, 2015.

24. "Owen Smith CTV on The Supreme Court of Canada Marijuana Ruling." CBC News/Pot TV, June 11, 2015.

Bibliography

Owen Edward Smith

Baum, Dan. 2016. "Legalize It All: How to Win the War on Drugs." Harper's Magazine, April 2016.

Becker, Howard S. 1963. Outsiders: Studies in the Sociology of Deviance. New York: Free Press.

Bukovsky, Vladimir. 1978. To Build a Castle: My Life as a Dissenter. New York: Viking Press.

Hall, Wayne, and Michael Lynskey. "Is Cannabis a Gateway Drug? Testing Hypotheses About the Relationship Between Cannabis Use and the Use of Other Illicit Drugs." Drug and Alcohol Review 24, no. 1 (2005): 39-48. https://doi.org/10.1080/09595230500126698.

Cohen, Stanley. 1972. Folk Devils and Moral Panics: The Creation of the Mods and Rockers. London: MacGibbon & Kee.

Gasnier, Louis J., dir. 1936. Reefer Madness. Motion Picture Ventures.

Le Dain, Gerald, Heinz Lehmann, Ian Campbell, Peter Stein, and Marie-Andrée Bertrand. 1972. Cannabis: A Report of the Commission of Inquiry into the Non-Medical Use of Drugs. Ottawa: Information Canada.

Leary v. United States. 1969. 395 U.S. 6.

Hari, Johann. 2015. Chasing the Scream: The First and Last Days of the War on Drugs. New York: Bloomsbury.

Mallea, Paula. 2014. The War on Drugs: A Failed Experiment. Toronto: Dundurn Press.

Mann, Ron, dir. 1999. Grass. Lions Gate Films.

United Nations. 1961. Single Convention on Narcotic Drugs, 1961. New York: United Nations.

United States. 1970. Comprehensive Drug Abuse Prevention and Control Act of 1970. Public Law 91-513. U.S. Statutes at Large 84:1236.

Leon (Ted) Edward Smith

Bennett, Chris. 1995. Green Gold the Tree of Life: Marijuana in Magic and Religion. Vancouver: Access Unlimited.

Boyd, Susan C. 2004. From Witches to Crack Moms: Women, Drug Law, and Policy. Durham, NC: Carolina Academic Press.

Herer, Jack. 1985. The Emperor Wears No Clothes. Van Nuys, CA: Ah Ha Publishing.

Oxford English Dictionary. n.d. "Ted, v.¹." Accessed [22/09/2024].

Smith, Ted. 2012. Hempology 101: The History and Uses of Cannabis Sativa. 4th ed. Victoria, BC: International Hempology 101 Society.

Chris Bennett

Bennett, Chris. 2001. Sex, Drugs, Violence and the Bible. Vancouver: Forbidden Fruit Publishing.

Consroe, Paul F., and George C. Wood. 1975. "Anticonvulsant Nature of Marihuana Smoking." Journal of the American Medical Association 234 (3): 306–07.

Cunha, J. M., E. A. Carlini, A. E. Pereira, O. L. Ramos, C. Pimentel, R. Gagliardi, W. Lander, R. N. Mechoulam, and S. E. Sanvito. 1980. "Chronic Administration of Cannabidiol to Healthy Volunteers and Epileptic Patients." Pharmacology 21 (3): 175–85.

Davis, James P., and H. H. Ramsey. 1949. "Antiepileptic Action of Marihuana-Active Substances." Federation Proceedings 8: 284.

Grinspoon, Lester, and James B. Bakalar. 1993. Marihuana, the Forbidden Medicine. New Haven, CT: Yale University Press.

Holy Bible. 1611. King James Version.

R. v. Parker. 2000. 49 O.R. (3d) 481 (Ontario Court of Appeal).

R v. Smith & Budda

Heath, Robert G., A. T. Fitzjarrell, C. J. Fontana, and R. E. Garey. 1980. "Cannabis Sativa: Effects on Brain Function and Ultrastructure in Rhesus Monkeys." Biological Psychiatry 15 (5): 657–90.

Herer, Jack. 1985. The Emperor Wears No Clothes: The Authoritative Historical Record of Cannabis and the Conspiracy Against Marijuana. Van Nuys, CA: Ah Ha Publishing.

Institute of Medicine. 1999. Marijuana and Medicine: Assessing the Science Base. Washington, D.C.: National Academy Press.

National Research Council. 1982. Marijuana and Health. Washington, D.C.: National Academy Press.

Mushrooms

Leary, Timothy, Ralph Metzner, and Richard Alpert. 1964. The Psychedelic Experience: A Manual Based on the Tibetan Book of the Dead. New York: University Books.

McKenna, Terence. 1993. True Hallucinations: Being an Account of the Author's Extraordinary Adventures in the Devil's Paradise. New York: HarperCollins.

Spirituality

Ownby, David. 2008. Falun Gong and the Future of China. New York: Oxford University Press.

Tong, James W. 2009. Revenge of the Forbidden City: The Suppression of the Falungong in China, 1999–2005. New York: Oxford University Press.

Festivals

Campbell, Joseph. 1949. The Hero with a Thousand Faces. Princeton, NJ: Princeton University Press.

Pollan, Michael. 2018. How to Change Your Mind: What the New Science of Psychedelics Teaches Us About Consciousness, Dying, Addiction, Depression, and Transcendence. New York: Penguin Press

Nichols, David E. 2016. Psychedelics. London: Routledge.

Dana Larsen

Sensible BC. 2013. "About Sensible BC." http://www.sensiblebc.ca/about

Stop the Violence BC. 2011. Breaking the Silence: Cannabis Prohibition, Organized Crime, and Gang Violence in BC. Vancouver, BC: Stop the Violence BC Coalition. https://stoptheviolencebc.org

Potheadbooks. 2020. Green Buds and Hash, The Pie-Eyed Piper, Hairy Pothead. Accessed September 20, 2023. https://www.potheadbooks.com/.

PotTV. 2021. PotTV Online Community Archives. Accessed September 20, 2023. https://www.pottv.com/.

Washington Referendum 2012. 2012. Initiative 502: Legalization of Marijuana. November 6, 2012. https://results.vote.wa.gov/results/current/Initiative-502-legalization-of-marijuana.html.

Colorado Amendment 64. 2012. Amendment 64: Marijuana Legalization. November 6, 2012. https://leg.colorado.gov/sites/default/files/images/olls/legalization/Amendment%2064.pdf.

Werb, Dan, Greg Rowell, Gordon Guyatt, Thomas Kerr, Julio Montaner, and Evan Wood. 2011. "Effect of Drug Law Enforcement on Drug Market Violence: A Systematic Review." International Journal of Drug Policy 22 (2): 87–94. https://doi.org/10.1016/j.drugpo.2011.02.002

A Dream

Binswanger, Ingrid A., Patrick M. Krueger, and John F. Steiner. 2009. "Prevalence of Chronic Medical Conditions Among Jail and Prison Inmates in the USA Compared with the General Population." Journal of Epidemiology & Community Health 63 (11): 912–919. https://doi.org/10.1136/jech.2009.090662

My Sister, Ceri

Australian Cancer Council. 2020. Skin Cancer Statistics and Issues. Accessed September 20, 2023. https://www.cancer.org.au/about-us/policy-and-advocacy/prevention/uv-radiation/related-resources/skin-cancer-incidence-and-mortality

Canadian Cancer Society. 2021. Melanoma Statistics. Accessed September 20, 2023. https://cancer.ca/en/cancer-information/cancer-types/melanoma-skin/statistics

Leary, Timothy, Ralph Metzner, and Richard Alpert. 1964. The Psychedelic Experience: A Manual Based on the Tibetan Book of the Dead. New York: University Books.

World Health Organization. 2021. Melanoma Statistics by Country. Accessed September 20, 2023. https://www.who.int/news-room/fact-sheets/detail/cancer.

Arrested

Bains, Camille. 2007. "Edibles and the Law: The Wreck Beach Case." Vancouver Sun, June 25

Charges

King, Martin Luther Jr. 1963. Letter from Birmingham Jail. April 16.

Kirk Tousaw

R. v. Malmo-Levine. 2003. 3 S.C.R. 571.

R. v. Beren. 2009. BCSC 429.

The Harper Conservative Government

Bill C-26. 2007. An Act to Amend the Controlled Drugs and Substances Act and to Make Related and Consequential Amendments to Other Acts. 2nd Session, 39th Parliament, 2007. Ottawa: Parliament of Canada.

Bill C-15. 2009. An Act to Amend the Controlled Drugs and Substances Act and to Make Related and Consequential Amendments to Other Acts. 2nd Session, 40th Parliament, 2009. Ottawa: Parliament of Canada.

Bill S-10. 2010. An Act to Amend the Controlled Drugs and Substances Act and to Make Related and Consequential Amendments to Other Acts. 3rd Session, 40th Parliament, 2010. Ottawa: Parliament of Canada.

Doob, Anthony N., Cheryl Marie Webster, and Rosemary Gartner. 2009. Issues Related to Harms Caused by Mandatory Minimum Sentences. Toronto: Centre for Criminology, University of Toronto.

Standing

Hogg, Peter W. 2007. Constitutional Law of Canada. 5th ed. Toronto: Thomson Carswell.

Lord's Day Act. 1906. S.C. 1906, c. 27.

R. v. Big M Drug Mart Ltd. 1985. 1 S.C.R. 295.

Recorded History of Cannabis Extracts

Elphick, Maurice R., and Michaela Egertová. 2001. "The Neurobiology and Evolution of Cannabinoid Signalling." Philosophical Transactions of the Royal Society B: Biological Sciences 356 (1407): 381–408. Accessed September 30, 2024. https://doi.org/10.1098/rstb.2000.0787

Adamson, Peter. Al-Kind?. New York: Oxford University Press, 2007.

Stanford Encyclopedia of Philosophy. "Al-Kindi." Last modified May 18, 2016. https://plato.stanford.edu/entries/al-kindi/.

Whitney, William Dwight. Atharva-Veda Sa?hit?. Cambridge, MA: Harvard University, 1905.

Encyclopædia Britannica Online. "Atharvaveda." Accessed [Date of Access]. https://www.britannica.com/topic/Atharvaveda.

Bennett, Chris. Cannabis and the Soma Solution. Walterville, OR: Trine Day, 2010.

Inner Traditions. "Author: Chris Bennett." Accessed [Date of Access]. https://www.innertraditions.com/author/chris-bennett.

Atalay, Serdar, Izabela Jarocka-Karpowicz, and Elzbieta Skrzydlewska. "Antioxidative and Anti-Inflammatory Properties of Cannabidiol." Antioxidants 9, no. 1 (2019): 21. https://doi.org/10.3390/antiox9010021.

Clarke, Robert C. Hashish!. Los Angeles: Red Eye Press, 1998.

Lu, Hua, and Ken Mackie. "An Introduction to the Endogenous Cannabinoid System." Biological Psychiatry 79, no. 7 (2016): 516–525. https://doi.org/10.1016/j.biopsych.2015.07.028.

Guzmán, Manuel. "Cannabinoids: Potential Anticancer Agents." Nature Reviews Cancer 3, no. 10 (2003): 745–755. https://doi.org/10.1038/nrc1188.

Galve-Roperh, Ignacio, Cristina Sánchez, Maria L. Cortes, Tamara del Pulgar, Marta Izquierdo, and Manuel Guzmán. "Anti-Tumoral Action of Cannabinoids: Involvement of Sustained Ceramide Accumulation and Extracellular Signal-Regulated Kinase Activation." Nature Medicine 6, no. 3 (2000): 313–319. https://doi.org/10.1038/73171.

Health Canada. Information for Health Care Professionals: Cannabis (Marihuana, Marijuana) and the Cannabinoids. Ottawa: Health Canada, 2013. https://www.canada.ca/en/health-canada/services/drugs-medication/cannabis/medical-use-cannabis.html.

"Cannabis Research and Data." Last modified October 30, 2018. https://www.canada.ca/en/health-canada/services/drugs-medication/cannabis/research-data.html.

Herodotus. The Histories. Translated by Aubrey de Sélincourt. Revised by John Marincola. London: Penguin Books, 1996.

Encyclopædia Britannica Online. "Herodotus." Accessed [Date of Access]. https://www.britannica.com/biography/Herodotus-Greek-historian.

Encyclopædia Britannica Online. "Hua Tuo." Accessed [Date of Access]. https://www.britannica.com/biography/Hua-Tuo.

Jiang, Hong-En, Xiao Li, Yue-Xia Zhao, David K. Ferguson, Friederike Hueber, Subir Bera, Torsten Denk, and Cheng-Sen Li. "A New Insight into Cannabis sativa (Cannabaceae) Utilization from 2500-Year-Old Yanghai Tombs, Xinjiang, China." Journal of Ethnopharmacology 108, no. 3 (2006): 414–422. https://doi.org/10.1016/j.jep.2006.05.034.

Li, Hui-Lin. "An Archaeological and Historical Account of Cannabis in China." Economic Botany 28, no. 4 (1974): 437–448. https://www.jstor.org/stable/4253423.

Needham, Joseph. Science and Civilisation in China. Vol. 5, Part 5: Chemistry and Chemical Technology. Cambridge: Cambridge University Press, 1986.

O'Shaughnessy, William B. "On the Preparations of the Indian Hemp, or Gunjah." Provincial Medical Journal and Retrospect of the Medical Sciences 5, no. 123 (1843): 343–347. https://www.ncbi.nlm.nih.gov/pmc/articles/PMC2490264/.

Parkinson, John. Theatrum Botanicum: The Theater of Plants. London: Thomas Cotes, 1640.

Reynolds, J. Russell. "Therapeutic Uses and Toxic Effects of Cannabis Indica." The Lancet 135, no. 3479 (1890): 637–638. https://doi.org/10.1016/S0140-6736(01)92414-8.

Russo, Ethan B. "History of Cannabis and Its Preparations in Saga, Science, and Sobriquet." Chemistry & Biodiversity 4, no. 8 (2007): 1614–1648. https://doi.org/10.1002/cbdv.200790144.

Unschuld, Paul U. Medicine in China: A History of Pharmaceutics. Berkeley: University of California Press, 1986.

Young, Francis L. In the Matter of Marijuana Rescheduling Petition, Docket No. 86–22. DEA Administrative Law Judge Opinion and Recommended Ruling, Findings of Fact, Conclusions of Law and Decision, 1988. https://www.ccguide.org/young88.php.

Canadian Medical Association (CMA). "Cannabis." Accessed [October 1, 2024]. https://www.cma.ca/cannabis.

Cannabidiol (CBD): Critical Review Report. Geneva: World Health Organization, 2018. https://www.who.int/medicines/access/controlled-substances/CannabidiolCriticalReview.pdf.

State Medical Marijuana Laws. National Conference of State Legislatures. Last modified February 3, 2021. https://www.ncsl.org/research/health/state-medical-marijuana-laws.aspx.

U.S. Food and Drug Administration. "FDA Approves First Drug Comprised of an Active Ingredient Derived from Marijuana to Treat Rare, Severe Forms of Epilepsy." News release, June 25, 2018. https://www.fda.gov/news-events/press-announcements/fda-approves-first-drug-comprised-active-ingredient-derived-marijuana-treat-rare-severe-forms.

The Road to Legalization

City of Vancouver. 2015. "Medical Marijuana-Related Uses Licensing Program." Accessed September 30, 2024. https://vancouver.ca/doing-business/medical-marijuana-related-business.aspx.

Haidt, Jonathan. 2012. The Righteous Mind: Why Good People Are Divided by Politics and Religion. New York: Pantheon Books.

Hashim, Asad. 2016. "Toronto Blocks Dispensary Entrance with Concrete Slabs." Global News, June 23, 2016. Accessed September 30, 2024. https://globalnews.ca/news/2782727/toronto-blocks-dispensary-entrance-with-concrete-slabs/.

Lucas, Philippe. 2008. "Regulating Compassion: An Overview of Canada's Federal Medical Cannabis Policy and Practice." Harm Reduction Journal 5 (5): 1–13.

R. v. Beren. 2009. BCSC 429.

R. v. Parker. 2000. 49 O.R. (3d) 481 (Ontario Court of Appeal).

R. v. Smith. 2012. BCCA 407.

R. v. Smith. 2015. 2 S.C.R. 602.

Legalization

Becker, Howard S. 1963. Outsiders: Studies in the Sociology of Deviance. New York: Free Press.

British Columbia Liquor Distribution Branch. 2018. "Cannabis Wholesale Operations." Accessed September 30, 2024. https://www.bcldb.com/cannabis-wholesale.

British Columbia Ministry of Public Safety and Solicitor General. 2019. "Community Safety Unit." Accessed September 30, 2024. https://www2.gov.bc.ca/gov/content/safety/public-safety/community-safety-unit.

First Nations Leadership Council. 2018.BC-FNLC Working Group on the Legalization and Regulation of Non-medical Cannabis [Accessed September 30, 2024.] https://www.bcafn.ca/priority-areas/economic-development/cannabis/fnlc-working-group-cannabis.

Government of Canada. 2016. "Access to Cannabis for Medical Purposes Regulations (SOR/2016-230)." Canada Gazette Part II 150, no. 17 (August 24): 1690–1762. Accessed September 30, 2024. https://gazette.gc.ca/rp-pr/p2/2016/2016-08-24/html/sor-dors230-eng.html.

Government of Canada. 2018a. "Cannabis Regulations (SOR/2018-144)." Canada Gazette Part II 152, no. 14 (July 11): 2966–3128. Accessed September 30, 2024. https://gazette.gc.ca/rp-pr/p2/2018/2018-07-11/html/sor-dors144-eng.html.

Government of Canada. 2018b. "Roles and Responsibilities under the Cannabis Act." Health Canada. Accessed September 30, 2024. https://www.canada.ca/en/health-canada/services/drugs-medication/cannabis/resources/roles-responsibilities-under-cannabis-act.html.

Government of Canada. 2018c. "Excise Duty Framework for Cannabis Products." Canada Revenue Agency. Accessed September 30, 2024. https://laws-lois.justice.gc.ca/eng/regulations/SOR-2019-78/FullText.html.

Government of Canada. 2019a. "Regulations Amending the Cannabis Regulations (New Classes of Cannabis) (SOR/2019-202)." Canada Gazette Part II 153, no. 12 (June 26): 2966–3056. Accessed September 30, 2024. https://gazette.gc.ca/rp-pr/p2/2019/2019-06-26/html/sor-dors202-eng.html.

Owusu-Bempah, Akwasi, and Alex Luscombe. 2021. "Race, Cannabis and the Canadian War on Drugs: An Examination of Cannabis Arrest Data by Race in Five Cities." International Journal of Drug Policy 91: 102937.

Schmidt, Sarah. 2021. "Discovery of Unmarked Graves at Former Residential Schools Prompts Calls for Action." CBC News, June 25, 2021. Accessed September 30, 2024. https://www.cbc.ca/news/politics/residential-schools-graves-politics-1.6078385.

Truth and Reconciliation Commission of Canada. 2015. Honouring the Truth, Reconciling for the Future: Summary of the Final Report of the Truth and Reconciliation Commission of Canada. Winnipeg: Truth and Reconciliation Commission of Canada. Accessed September 30, 2024. https://publications.gc.ca/site/eng/9.800288/publication.html

Precedents

Constitution Act, 1982. Section 35. Government of Canada.

R. v. Howell, 2019 ABPC

R. v. Pamajewon, [1996] 2 S.C.R. 821.

R. v. Wernecke, 2019 MBPC

United Nations. United Nations Declaration on the Rights of Indigenous Peoples. 2007. https://www.un.org/development/desa/indigenouspeoples/declaration-on-the-rights-of-indigenous-peoples.html.

Psychedelics

Becker, Howard S. 1963. Outsiders: Studies in the Sociology of Deviance. New York: Free Press.

Canadian Charter of Rights and Freedoms. 1982. Part I of the Constitution Act, 1982, being Schedule B to the Canada Act 1982 (UK), c 11.

Canadian Centre on Substance Use and Addiction (CCSA). 2020. "Opioids." Accessed [Date]. https://www.ccsa.ca/opioids.

Friesen, Joe. 2020. "Terminal Cancer Patient Becomes First Canadian to Legally Use Magic Mushrooms for Therapy." The Globe and Mail, August 4, 2020. https://www.theglobeandmail.com/canada/article-terminal-cancer-patient-becomes-first-canadian-to-legally-use-magic/.

Health Canada. 2020. "Health Canada Grants Exemptions to Allow the Use of Magic Mushrooms for Anxiety Therapy." News release, August 4, 2020. https://www.canada.ca/en/health-canada/news/2020/08/health-canada-grants-exemptions-to-allow-the-use-of-magic-mushrooms-for-anxiety-therapy.html.

Larsen, Dana. 2020. "The Mushroom Dispensary." Accessed [Date]. https://www.themushroomdispensary.com.

Mead, Margaret. n.d. Quote. https://www.goodreads.com/quotes/24578-never-doubt-that-a-small-group-of-thoughtful-committed-citizens.

R. v. Parker, [2000] O.J. No. 2787 (Ontario Court of Appeal).

R. v. Smith, [2015] 2 S.C.R. 602.

Cannabis Extraction

Atakan, Zerrin. 2012. "Cannabis, a Complex Plant: Different Compounds and Different Effects on Individuals." Therapeutic Advances in Psychopharmacology 2 (6): 241–254.

Backes, Michael. 2017. Cannabis Pharmacy: The Practical Guide to Medical Marijuana—Revised and Updated. New York: Black Dog & Leventhal Publishers.

Bonn-Miller, Marcel O., Mallory E. Loflin, Brian F. Thomas, et al. 2017. "Labeling Accuracy of Cannabidiol Extracts Sold Online." JAMA 318 (17): 1708–1709.

Cherniak, Laurence. 1982. The Great Books of Hashish: Book I. Toronto: Access Unlimited.

Clarke, Robert Connell. 1998. Hashish!. Los Angeles: Red Eye Press.

Clarke, Robert Connell, and Mark D. Merlin. 2013. Cannabis: Evolution and Ethnobotany. Berkeley: University of California Press.

Courtney, William L., and Kristen Courtney. 2011. Leaf [Documentary film]. Accessed [Month Day, Year].

CTV News. 2013. "Pot Petitioner Blows Smoke About Medicinal Effects." CTV News, September 16. https://bc.ctvnews.ca/pot-petitioner-blows-smoke-about-medicinal-effects-1.1457832.

Dakpa, Tsering. 2005. "The Buddhist View of Nature and the Environment." In Encyclopedia of Religion and Nature, edited by Bron Taylor, 239–242. London: Continuum.

Deahl, Dani. 2019. "How Cannabis 'Diamond Mining' Became More Than a Trend." The Verge, July 19. https://www.theverge.com/2019/7/19/18718133/cannabis-diamonds-thca-marijuana-concentrates.

Dryburgh, Laura M., Scott P. Bolan, Jan G. Grobbelaar, et al. 2018. "Cannabis Contaminants: Sources, Distribution, Human Toxicity and Pharmacologic Effects." British Journal of Clinical Pharmacology 84 (11): 2468–2476.

Giroud, Céline, Sara de Cesare, Pascal Berthet, et al. 2015. "E-Cigarettes: A Review of New Trends in Cannabis Use." International Journal of Environmental Research and Public Health 12 (8): 9988–10008.

Green, Greg. 2017. The Cannabis Grow Bible: The Definitive Guide to Growing Marijuana for Recreational and Medical Use. 4th ed. San Francisco: Green Candy Press.

Grotenhermen, Franjo. 2003. "Pharmacokinetics and Pharmacodynamics of Cannabinoids." Clinical Pharmacokinetics 42 (4): 327–360.

Happyana, Nina, Yoshiaki Agnolet, Gian Carlo Muntendam, David van Dam, Ben J. J. van der Klift, and Robert Verpoorte. 2013. "Analysis of Cannabinoids in Laser-Microdissected Trichomes of Cannabis sativa Using LC–MS and Cryogenic NMR." Phytochemistry 87: 51–59.

Hazekamp, Arno. 2016. "Cannabis Oil: Chemical Evaluation of an Upcoming Cannabis-Based Medicine." Cannabis and Cannabinoid Research 1 (1): 139–154.

Hazekamp, Arno. 2018. "Cannabis Extraction Methods." In Handbook of Cannabis and Related Pathologies, edited by Victor R. Preedy, 19–27. San Diego: Academic Press.

Hash Marihuana & Hemp Museum. n.d. "Hashish: The Art of Making and Smoking." Accessed [Month Day, Year]. https://hashmuseum.com/en/hashish.

Health Canada. 2018. "Industrial Hemp Licensing Application Guide." Government of Canada. https://www.canada.ca/en/health-canada/services/publications/drugs-health-products/industrial-hemp-licensing-application-guide.html.

Huestis, Marilyn A. 2007. "Human Cannabinoid Pharmacokinetics." Chemistry & Biodiversity 4 (8): 1770–1804.

Lee, Martin A. 2012. Smoke Signals: A Social History of Marijuana—Medical, Recreational, and Scientific. New York: Scribner.

Lewis, Margaret M., Kimberley Yang, Yasmin E. Wasilewski, et al. 2018. "Chemical Profiling of Medical Cannabis Extracts." ACS Omega 3 (10): 11001–11013.

MacCallum, Cheryl A., and Ethan B. Russo. 2018. "Practical Considerations in Medical Cannabis Administration and Dosing." European Journal of Internal Medicine 49: 12–19.

McPartland, John M., and Ethan B. Russo. 2001. "Cannabis and Cannabis Extracts: Greater Than the Sum of Their Parts?" Journal of Cannabis Therapeutics 1 (3–4): 103–132.

Mikuriya, Tod H. 1973. Marijuana: Medical Papers 1839–1972. Oakland, CA: Medi-Comp Press.

Pate, David W. 1994. "Chemical Ecology of Cannabis." Journal of the International Hemp Association 1 (1): 29–32.

Peace, Michelle R., Madeline Butler, Lindsay Wolf, and Hannelore B. Poklis. 2016. "Evaluation of Two Commercially Available Cannabidiol Formulations for Use in Electronic Cigarettes." Frontiers in Pharmacology 7: 279.

Pertwee, Roger G. 2008. "The Diverse CB1 and CB2 Receptor Pharmacology of Three Plant Cannabinoids: D9-Tetrahydrocannabinol, Cannabidiol, and Tetrahydrocannabivarin." British Journal of Pharmacology 153 (2): 199–215.

Potter, Derek J. 2014. "A Review of the Cultivation and Processing of Cannabis sativa for Production of Prescription Medicines in the UK." Drug Testing and Analysis 6 (1–2): 31–38.

Rademacher, Matthias, Thomas Sauer, and Gerhard Sadowski. 2019. "Selective Extraction of Cannabinoids from Cannabis sativa L. Using Supercritical CO_2: Experiments and Modeling." The Journal of Supercritical Fluids 146: 208–216.

Raber, Jeffrey C., Svetlana Elzinga, and Charles Kaplan. 2015. "Understanding Dabs: Contamination Concerns of Cannabis Concentrates and Cannabinoid Transfer During Dabbing." Journal of Toxicological Sciences 40 (6): 797–803.

Rosenthal, Ed. 2015. Beyond Buds: Marijuana Extracts—Hash, Vaping, Dabbing, Edibles, and Medicines. Oakland, CA: Quick American Publishing.

Russo, Ethan B. 2011. "Taming THC: Potential Cannabis Synergy and Phytocannabinoid–Terpenoid Entourage Effects." British Journal of Pharmacology 163 (7): 1344–1364.

Simpson, Rick. 2008. Run from the Cure: The Rick Simpson Story [Documentary film]. Accessed [Month Day, Year].

Simpson, Rick. 2013. Phoenix Tears: The Rick Simpson Story. Self-published.

Small, Ernest. 2016. Cannabis: A Complete Guide. Boca Raton, FL: CRC Press.

Smart, Robert, Daniel K. Price, Rosanna Smart, and Rosalie Liccardo Pacula. 2017. "Variation in Cannabis Potency and Prices in a Newly Legal Market: Evidence from 30 Million Cannabis Sales in Washington State." Addiction 112 (12): 2167–2177.

Stahl, Vasyl, and John Miller. 2019. "Crystallization of Cannabinoids Using Advanced Techniques." Journal of Cannabis Science and Technology 2 (3): 45–53.

Thompson, Gary R., Bonni Goldstein, and Joseph T. Malone. 2020. "Cannabis and the Nervous System: Clinical Implications for Neurologists and Patients." Neurotherapeutics 17 (1): 31–34.

United Nations Office on Drugs and Crime (UNODC). 2009. Recommended Methods for the Identification and Analysis of Cannabis and Cannabis Products. Vienna: United Nations.

R. v. Smith Digital Timeline Reference

QR Code
Scan with your camera.
Best results in landscape view.

Web Link
www.tiki-toki.com/timeline/entry/196941/R.-v.-Smith-Timeline

www.ingramcontent.com/pod-product-compliance
Lightning Source LLC
Chambersburg PA
CBHW020513080526
44583CB00013B/588